Strategic Transf

Strategic Transformation

Changing While Winning

Manuel Hensmans
Professor of Strategic Management, Solvay Brussels School of Economics and Management, ULB, Brussels, Belgium

Gerry Johnson
Emeritus Professor of Strategic Management, Lancaster University Management School, Lancaster, UK

George Yip
Professor of Management, China Europe International Business School, Shanghai, China

palgrave macmillan

Softcover reprint of the hardcover 1st edition 2013 978-1-137-26845-7
MyCopy version of the orginal edition 2013

First published 2013 by
PALGRAVE MACMILLAN

Palgrave Macmillan in the UK is an imprint of Macmillan Publishers Limited, registered in England, company number 785998, of Houndmills, Basingstoke, Hampshire RG21 6XS.

Palgrave Macmillan in the US is a division of St Martin's Press LLC, 175 Fifth Avenue, New York, NY 10010.

Palgrave Macmillan is the global academic imprint of the above companies and has companies and representatives throughout the world.

Palgrave® and Macmillan® are registered trademarks in the United States, the United Kingdom, Europe and other countries

DOI 10.1057/9781137268464

This book is printed on paper suitable for recycling and made from fully managed and sustained forest sources. Logging, pulping and manufacturing processes are expected to conform to the environmental regulations of the country of origin.

A catalogue record for this book is available from the British Library.

A catalog record for this book is available from the Library of Congress.

Springer.com/mycopy

Paz y René
Phyl
Moira, Andrew and Sarah

Contents

Acknowledgements

There are many people whom we have to thank for their support and encouragement over the last 9 years. We would like to address a special acknowledgment to the Advanced Institute of Management Research (AIM) directors, Robin Wensley and Andy Neely, as well as the AIM team, in particular Claire Fitzpatrick and Esmé Foster, for their precious help during this project. Robin Wensley has been particularly supportive and patient. Tim Devinney was a close and essential collaborator during stage 1 of the project. Pierre Richard also contributed to that first stage. For stage 2, we had the help of Shameen Prashantham as well as several MBA students at Strathclyde University Business School. Many AIM colleagues provided us with valuable feedback and support throughout: Richard Adams, Tina Ambos, Elena Antonacopoulos, Julian Birkinshaw, Ian Clarke, Rick Delbridge, Modestas Gelbuda, Mark Healey, Susan Hill, Gerard Hodgkinson, Michael Mol, Janine Nahapiet, Ellen Pruyne, Jonathan Sapsed, and many others. In stage 3, Jochem Kroezen conducted the important confirmatory analysis of the transcripts.

Completing the story of Cadbury Schweppes would not have been possible without Sir Adrian Cadbury's close involvement. Thanks to you and your wife, Sir Adrian, for allowing a visit to your private archives, along with the encouragement of a fresh bowl of soup and delightful lunch conversation.

A large part of our empirical work consisted in scouring the public and private archives of our three pairs of companies. In this regard, we would like to thank Jeannette Strickland, Leslie Owen, and the entire Unilever Archives & Records Management group at Port Sunlight for their wonderful collaboration in granting us access to Unilever's archives. We are also grateful to Rowena Austin, Mike Clark, and Steve Williams for liaising contacts with potential interviewees and organizing access to private archives at, respectively, Smith & Nephew, Cadbury Schweppes, and Unilever.

It is fair to say that this book would not have been possible without the passionate involvement of our interviewees. We thank all of them. We experienced many memorable moments during our interviews.

We also thank the members of our Corporate Advisory Panel and other advisors we consulted: John Morgan of BP, Don Argus of BHP, Shumeet Banerji of Booz Allen & Hamilton, Mark Bezant of Deloitte, Antonio

Borges of Goldman Sachs, Clive Butler of Unilever, Michael Goold of Ashridge, Donald Hepburn of Unilever, Andrew Likierman of London Business School, Paul March of London Business School, Chris Masters, John Ormerod of Deloitte, Nick Owen of Deloitte, Andrew Pettigrew of Said Business School at Oxford University, and Donald MacLean at Glasgow University.

Simon Caulkin did a great job of making our work more readable and accessible before we submitted it to publishers, and Chris Taylor helped to rewrite an early draft of this book. Vickey Young at Lancaster University Management School also liaised with interviewees on our behalf. We are also grateful to Stephen Rutt and Eleanor Davey-Corrigan of Palgrave Macmillan for agreeing to publish this book, to Hannah Fox for her assistance, to Carrie Walker for her editorial work, and to the team at Aardvark Editorial.

Finally, all of this would not have been possible without the unrelenting support of our families and friends.

About the Authors

Manuel Hensmans is a Professor of Strategic Management at Solvay Brussels School of Economics and Management, ULB. Before joining Solvay, he was a research associate at London Business School and Strathclyde Business School. Manuel is a research fellow at the Advanced Institute of Management Research, UK, and was a Marie Curie fellow at Manchester School of Management. Manuel's research focuses on how firms can grow sustainably – without experiencing or causing major stakeholder crises. He has conducted projects at board of directors level with multiple organizations in the UK, the Netherlands, and Belgium to study this question. Manuel has also prepared the business plan and collected the funding for an e-government company. Within the same scope of research, Manuel studies the historical relation between entrepreneurship and democratization processes in the Dutch and English retail banking sectors. His research has been selected among the best papers of the journal *Long Range Planning* and the Strategic Management Society Conference. Manuel teaches MSc, MBA, and Executive courses in (international) strategy and innovation. He has acted as an executive lecturer at Rotterdam School of Management and an executive tutor at London Business School. Manuel holds a PhD from Rotterdam School of Management, Erasmus University, and MSc degrees in applied economics and applied computer sciences from the Catholic University of Leuven, Universidad Autónoma de Madrid, and Free University of Brussels. (mhensman@ulb.ac.be or mhensmans@telenet.be)

Gerry Johnson is Emeritus Professor of Strategic Management at Lancaster University School of Management and a senior fellow of the UK Advanced Institute of Management Research. He has a BA in social and physical anthropology from University College London and a PhD from Aston University. He is co-author of Europe's best selling strategic management text *Exploring Strategy* (Prentice Hall, 9th edn, 2011), author of *Strategic Change and the Management Process*, co-author of *The Exceptional Manager*, and editor of *Business Strategy and Retailing*, the *Challenge of Strategic Management*, and *Strategic Thinking*. Professor Johnson's research interests are in the field of strategic management practice, in particular with processes of strategy development and change in organizations. He has published in the *Academy of Management Review*, the *Academy of Management Journal*, the *Journal of Management Studies*, the *Strategic Management Journal*, *Organization Studies*, the *British Journal of Management* and *Human Relations*. As a consultant, he is a partner in Strategy Explorers (www.strategyexplorers.com) and works at a senior level with management teams on issues of strategy development and strategic change.

George Yip is Professor of Management and Co-director of the Centre on China Innovation at China Europe International Business School. He lives in London, Shanghai, and Maine, USA. Professor Yip is also a senior fellow of the Advanced Institute of Management Research, and a fellow of the Academy of International Business. His latest book is *Managing Global Customers* (Oxford University Press, 2007). An earlier book, *Total Global Strategy: Managing for Worldwide Competitive Advantage* (Prentice Hall, 1992, 1995) was selected as one of the 30 best business books of 1992 and has been published in 10 languages, with a third edition in 2011. His extensive full-time business experience includes vice-president and director of research & innovation at Capgemini Consulting, product and account management with Unilever companies, and senior manager of Price Waterhouse's strategic management consulting services in the eastern USA. Previous academic positions include dean of Rotterdam School of Management, Erasmus University, and professor at UCLA, University of Cambridge, and London Business School. As a consultant, board director, and speaker, he works with companies on issues of international strategy, strategic transformation, and innovation. He holds BA and MA degrees in economics from Cambridge University, and MBAs from Cranfield School of Management and Harvard Business School, along with a doctorate from Harvard. (gyip@ceibs.edu or gyip33@gmail.com)

ADVANCED INSTITUTE OF MANAGEMENT RESEARCH

This study was funded primarily by AIM Research. AIM is the UK's research initiative on management, set up by the national government to improve management research and practice in the UK. AIM comprises an active network of UK and international academics that also engages extensively with business practitioners. AIM is funded by the Economic and Social Research Council and the Engineering and Physical Sciences Research Council. See www.aimresearch.org.

PART I

What's the Problem?

CHAPTER 1

The Challenge of Change

Every decade has at least one: IBM in the 1980s, General Motors and Marks & Spencer in the 1990s, Dell, Nissan, Sony, BP, Toyota, and Nokia in the new millennium. The pattern is so familiar that it has come to seem inevitable. A company that is admired and respected as a paragon of its industry falters and runs into financial crisis. Hero becomes zero. Shareholders rebel, managers are sacked, and ultimately major change ensues. What is going on here? Why don't organizations see what's coming, or if they do, why don't they react until the 11th hour? Why does it take a crisis to induce change?

Success is a paradox. Naturally, success is ardently desired and pursued, then feted and envied when achieved. But along with the applause come invisible dangers. Not surprisingly, successful businesses, usually to the approval of shareholders, seek to build on their success; the impulse is to go on doing what they are good at, only more so. But over time their very success seems to blind them to the changing reality of their business environment. Imperceptibly, their picture of what is happening diverges from real events. They "drift;" indeed, in this book, borrowing from other studies, we refer to the phenomenon as "strategic drift." Performance declines, sometimes gently, sometimes less so, until the inevitable eventually has to be faced and radical change takes place.

This is of course a hugely inefficient and wasteful pattern of change. For customers, managers, suppliers, and workers alike, the damage is immense. Jobs, shareholder value, the supply chain, and the economy as a whole all suffer. Sometimes the business itself disappears, either being swallowed up by another or going out of business altogether. Gary Hamel calls this a third-world dictatorship model of change and adds: "A turnaround is a transformation tragically delayed – an expensive substitute for well-timed adaptation." If the pattern is indeed inescapable, it is also highly regrettable. So, is it inevitable? Some argue it is, that it is the natural evolution of businesses. Or is it avoidable? Can businesses both build on their success and also transform the basis of their success? Before going any further, we need to dig a little deeper into these issues.

THE PROBLEM OF STRATEGIC DRIFT

Why is our research important? We believe that it raises major questions about the received wisdom that managers use to guide responses to one of their most significant challenges: managing strategic change.

Not surprisingly, most company strategies are based on what has been done in the past – especially if it was successful – and change only gradually. For example, for decades until the early 1990s, Sainsbury's formula of selling superior-quality food at reasonable prices made it consistently one of the top-ranking retailers in the world. Under the patriarchal guidance of a succession of Sainsbury family chief executives, it steadily extended its product lines, enlarged its stores, and widened its geographical coverage, without ever deviating from its tried-and-tested methods – refusing to branch out into clothes or other non-food items, for example. Most successful businesses resemble Sainsbury's. They go through long periods of relative *continuity* during which established strategy changes, but only *incrementally*, building on what has been successful in the past.

Without necessarily being conscious of it, firms develop a "dominant logic," a way of doing business, unique to each, around which all the different aspects of the business tend to cohere. It is "a way of doing things around here" that is at the same time a major asset and a major potential liability. The benefit is that those who work in it, or indeed deal with the organization, know where it is coming from and how it operates. The approach may have been the foundation of success in the past. The disbenefit is that it can be so dominant that it not only crowds out any other way of doing things, but also denies or smoothes out contrary evidence, with the result that the dominant logic remains unchallenged. What was previously a source of strength becomes the opposite – the invisible bars of a prison from which it is very hard to escape.

There are good reasons why this should be so. It does not make sense for strategy to change faster than the markets in which a company operates. Why should managers change a winning formula, especially if it is built on capabilities that have yielded advantage or innovation in the past? Clever managers may have learned how to spin variations around their successful formula, in effect experimenting without moving too far from their comfort zone or capability base. So they will argue with some justification that their organization is in fact changing.

The tendency, then, is for strategies to develop incrementally on the basis of the dominant logic of businesses, but to fail to keep pace with a changing environment, a tendency that has been described as "strategic drift."[1] Problems do not arise because organizations fail to change *at all*, but because the rate or nature of change of strategy lags behind the rate of change in their environment. Thus, while Sainsbury's continued on its well-trodden way, rival Tesco, starting from a much less successful base, was developing much larger stores with a wider range of goods, including non-food. It was also modifying its distribution logistics and supply chain. There was no single point in time when Tesco "changed." The modifications took place over many years – and Sainsbury's managers were well aware of them.

So changes in the market do not need to be dramatic or invisible for drift to occur. The problem was that, as with many organizations, Sainsbury's strategy failed to address the changes. Why not? There are several contributory reasons.

A common management mantra is that managers should "stick to the knitting," that is, focus on their core competences and stick to doing what they know best. It sounds plausible (remember that "sticking to the knitting" was one of the attributes of Peters' and Waterman's excellent companies in *In Search of Excellence*). The snag is that sticking to the knitting can easily develop into corporate sclerosis or what Dorothy Leonard Barton[2] calls "core rigidities." If managers do only what they know best, there comes a time when core competences become so taken for granted, so ingrained, that they are impossible to shift even when they become redundant.

As an example, consider how Sainsbury's decades of postwar success came to be identified with CEO John (now Lord) Sainsbury, whose empathy with customer needs and intuitive understanding of the details of retailing were legendary. Not only were these skills tacit, but managers, staff, and even retail analysts took for granted that they would be enough to sustain the fortunes of the business into the future. Imperceptibly, taken-for-granted ways of seeing and doing things take root in an organization's culture. Core assumptions, organizational routines and structures, even the stories people tell each other, all cohere to reinforce "the way we do things around here." So the Sainsbury way was not just a matter of the formalized buying and distribution systems, or even the undoubted centralized power wielded by John Sainsbury. It was also enacted in his legendary retail "feel," his attention to detail, his ritualized store visits, the stories staff told about them, and the expectations that they read into them.

In these ways, an organization's historical legacy comes to weigh heavily on the present. This is encapsulated in the idea of *path dependency*, where formative early events and decisions establish "policy paths" that effectively condition the future,[3] sometimes trumping apparently superior present alternatives. Cadbury was profoundly influenced by its Quaker origins. The founding ethos of Sainsbury's to provide value for money and good quality endures to this day. Early decisions about how the Dutch and the British would work together in Unilever, not least in the top executive team, indelibly marked the company's character over decades. Not surprisingly, whether consciously or not, firms develop strategy – which markets and segments to enter, how to build their infrastructure, where to diversify – around path-dependent capabilities that gradually become second nature. Strategies themselves become so deeply grooved that there seems no more possibility of an alternative than there is for a needle on a gramophone track. Thus, in sum, do businesses, not least successful ones, come to be captured by, and victims of, their own dominant logic[4] – a tendency graphically described by Danny Miller as the Icarus Paradox?[5]

The way in which individual managers perceive the world can also contribute to an imperceptible drift of strategy away from reality. We are all "boundedly rational" – that is, we can only operate within the limits of our knowledge and experience. More formally, we make sense of the world by applying that knowledge and experience in the shape of mental models, beliefs about the way the world works that function as a kind of pattern recognition system allowing us to relate present problems to past events and interpret one in the light of the other. This has major advantages – indeed, we couldn't function without such models. But there are downsides too. By definition, models are simplifications of reality, rules of thumb that enable us to use partial knowledge to interpret complex situations. The danger of "selective attention," as it is called,[6] is that managers use the wrong simplification, or alternatively that they apply the same one to every situation (to a man with a hammer every problem is a nail ...), in effect editing out information that does not fit the model. Unfortunately, this sometimes leads to severe errors as managers fail to pick up crucial indicators because they are scanning the environment for known issues rather than unknown ones.[7] All this will lead to a bias toward continued incremental strategic change.

To continue the Sainsbury story, as Tesco prospered, Sainsbury managers clung to the conviction of their own superiority on the grounds that they were doing better in terms of sales per retail square foot – their traditional yardstick of success. Tesco was by then changing the nature of the game by building much bigger stores. But Sainsbury's chosen measure gave it no cause to alter its tried-and-tested strategy, or the unshakeable conviction that it was in little danger from what it saw as a downmarket rival offering inferior products.

Office politics and power games can also play a part in entrenching individual positions and fostering compromise around existing strategy. Together, these are powerful forces. Just how powerful is shown by well-documented cases in which managers have been aware of market shifts, well positioned to take advantage of them, even intellectually conscious of the need to alter strategic direction, but still unable to do so. Take, for example, the story of Motorola.[8] Motorola's success was built on innovation bubbling up from a wellspring of technological expertise. In the mid-1980s it was the world leader in analogue cell phones, a logical progression from the military walkie-talkie systems it had developed after the war. By 1994 it had a whopping 60 percent share of the US cell phone market. However, that decade saw the arrival of mobile digital technology, which offered clear advantages over analogue including better reception and security, clearly setting the scene for the development of a mass market. Sure enough, consumer demand for digital phones exploded; Motorola, claimed CEO Robert Galvin, "was at the forefront of the development of digital technology." Yet it chose to stick with analogue for years, lucratively licensing its digital technology to Nokia and Ericsson instead. Incredibly, even when increasing royalties were telling it in the most direct fashion that digital was taking off, and wireless carriers were pleading with it to develop digital devices, Motorola launched and aggressively promoted a new analogue phone. From a once-dominant position, by 2008 the company's share of the global handset market had sunk to 23 percent, and it continued to shrink.

To make matters worse, the significance of shifts in the marketplace may be easier to spot *in hindsight* than at the time. Managers will understandably hesitate to alter a winning strategy on account of what seem initially like blips or fads, or a temporary downturn. Then, by becoming more efficient, cutting costs, or making acquisitions, the company may ironically for a time hide the reality of strategic drift from itself, as well as from investors and observers. At Sainsbury's, shareholder returns continued to grow year on year well into the 1990s. Only subsequently did it become apparent that growth was latterly in effect an overdraft drawn against the future, only achieved at the expense of reinvestment in the business infrastructure.

MANAGING CHANGE

Airport bookshops are full of tomes that assume that strategic change is rare and radical, interspersed between long periods of inactivity. In these accounts, change management is all about overcoming core rigidities and crafting quite new ways of seeing business realities, often in the face of actual or impending financial crisis. Such narratives almost always privilege stories of heroic change leaders who step in to rescue the business and single-handedly reshape it for a new era of prosperity. All too rarely do they focus on what might be called the real challenge of managing strategic change, which is to ensure that transformation occurs while the business is still ahead.

Whether in academia or the business press, a kind of fatalism rules. Firms are born, and some will prosper; those that prosper will eventually be subsumed into their own overdominant logic and succumb to drift; shock treatment will bring some round, but others will fail and go under, eventually spawning new businesses, and so the cycle goes on. But is this cycle really inevitable? Can there be major strategic change without financial crisis? Are there examples of firms that have remained successful by continuously transforming themselves at the same time? If so, what is different about them, and how have they done it? Could their lessons help companies to avoid the perils of strategic drift and the value-destruction of lurching, crisis-induced change? The stakes are high. This book sets out to provide some answers.

MANAGEMENT CONSEQUENCES AND IMPLICATIONS: RECEIVED WISDOM AND SOME QUALIFICATIONS

If left to themselves, the tendency for companies to drift away from strategic "true north" is unavoidable, and managers should presumably be taking action to counteract it. However, some of the assumptions they use to guide them in this search may be questionable – and the questioning in turn points to some of the findings and arguments we develop in subsequent chapters of the book. To put those findings in context, we need to understand the main lines of conventional thought, which we outline below.

Managing strategy is about the future ... or is it?

Fundamental to the concept of strategy is that it looks toward the *future*. Popular management writers Robert Heller and Edward de Bono head their web page with the strap line: "Forget the past and aim your future strategy toward a clear end result." A common critique of managers is that they are hidebound by a past that prevents them from exploiting opportunities that may arise in the future. Consider the two main tools used by managers in thinking about strategy.[9] By far the most common is SWOT – assessing a company's strengths, weaknesses, opportunities, and threats. In so far as the past plays a role here, it is in the identification of, perhaps, strengths but certainly weaknesses. It is the future where the opportunities and maybe the threats come from. The second most popular tool is scenario-planning, which is at bottom a means of opening managers' eyes to the possibilities of different futures. The dominant view is clear: it is here, in the future, that opportunities for strategic breakthroughs lie, and it is on here that managers should learn to focus.

Yet this future-facing orientation ignores powerful grounds for thinking both that the past matters and that history is far from being an exclusively negative influence. "Anyone who wants to design for the future has to leaf through the past,"[10] reads a caption in the BMW Design Museum in Munich. The museum may be about the history of BMW, but one of its lessons is that the past is a fertile source of new ideas and innovation. As if to emphasize it, the firm has sited its innovation and technology division adjacent to the museum and the company archives. Research evidence, too, tends to support the common-sense idea that innovation often stems from capabilities inherited and nurtured from the past. As technologies change, firms possessing accumulated relevant experience and skills tend to innovate more than those that are not so equipped.[11] Alternatively, capabilities built up in related technologies may yield new combinations of knowledge as they are adapted in innovative ways to new technological opportunities. For example, the development of lighting systems was derived from the way in which gas was distributed.[12] In the same way, the TV industry was developed by radio manufacturers, not by firms starting with a technological blank slate.[13]

Implicit in the influential resource-based view of strategy is also that the past matters. In this view, competitive advantage lies in an organization's competences – sometimes referred to as "intangible assets" – that have accumulated over time and become embedded in an organization's culture. Managers should deliberately seek out opportunities that fit and build on those competences. But how easy is it for managers to take an objective, dispassionate view of these invisible resources? What we know about core rigidities, cognitive bias and organizational politics – indeed, strategic drift in general – suggests that such objectivity is problematic. Indeed, as enthusiasts of the resource-based view themselves acknowledge, there is an even knottier problem. A firm's historical culture can only be a source of competitive advantage if it is valuable, rare, and difficult to imitate. If it is easy to assess and manage, anyone can do it and it confers no lasting advantage. But the logical extension of this is that the most difficult competences for competitors to obtain or imitate are those that managers themselves do not explicitly manage, that are taken for granted – and this takes us back to the argument that it is these which are likely to become "core rigidities."

The overall lesson seems to be that managers need to be able to see the past in relation to the future and challenge one against the other – to ask what is relevant from the past that can help with the future, but also what the future demands but does *not* require from the past. At the same time, they must constantly be posing the question of how far environment and market changes are playing into the hand of their path-dependent capabilities – or not, as the case may be. In other words, managers need to develop a sensitivity not only to the historical capabilities that matter, but also to their relationship to an evolving environment. Less clear is how they can do this.

Build dynamic capabilities ... based on what?

Another idea put forward is that a business's competences or intangible assets should not be thought of as static, as the resource-based view tends to assume. In a turbulent environment, or one in which the pace of change is accelerating, it is *dynamic capabilities*, or the capacity to *renew and recreate strategic capabilities* to meet the needs of a changing environments, that are key to success.[14] Dynamic capabilities can range from the relatively formal, such as systems for new product development or procedures for agreement on capital expenditure, to the informal ability, say, to speed up decision-making when a quick response is needed. Capabilities might include strategic moves, such as acquisitions or alliances as a means of learning new skills, or "organizational knowledge" embedded in the culture of the organization about how to adapt to moving circumstances, or how to innovate. So here again we meet the idea that capabilities that endow competitive advantage are lodged in the collective, accreted experience of people in the firm over time.

Some believers in "hypercompetition" go further, arguing that change is now happening so fast that the pursuit of sustainable competitive advantage is a chimera, and a dangerous one at that, diverting attention as it does from the reality that the only advantage is the ability to change more quickly than one's rivals – in other words, dynamic capabilities on steroids.[15] Less clear in both cases, however, is where the origins of such dynamic capabilities lie and how the latter might account for their positive impact, as opposed to the harmful influence exercised by other legacies of the past. This is perhaps not surprising: very few studies have attempted to uncover and explain such origins and their influence, and those that do have concentrated on the present rather than the past, and do not look at the promising but difficult-to-research informal and behavioral aspects of organizational life. So we end up with an interesting concept, but one that is not very useful in answering the question, "OK, so what do we do now?"

Organizational learning and the "learning organization"

The same objection applies to the related concept of the "learning organization": the idea that organizations should regenerate themselves from within by continuously adding to and exploiting the knowledge, experience, and skills of their members around a shared purpose or vision.

The learning organization is a conscious challenge to the traditional conception of organizations as hierarchies and bureaucracies set up to achieve order and maintain control, for stability rather than change. Advocates of the learning organization[16] argue that the collective knowledge of all the individuals in an organization far exceeds what the organization itself "knows" and is capable of doing ("If only IBM knew what IBM knows"). One reason is the formal organizational structures that prevent the exchange of such knowledge and stifle creative responses to change. To loosen these constraints and improve responsiveness to opportunities and threats, it is preferable to think of organizations as social networks[17] rather than hierarchies, where different interest groups cooperate and potentially learn from each other, lessening the common risk of ideas arising in one part of the business fizzling out as they meet indifference or hostility elsewhere. In this process, managers would play a less directive and more facilitative role. The learning organization, then, is one inherently capable of change as it exploits a capacity for continual *organizational learning*.

Central to the idea of organizational learning is the need to recognize the value of multiple sources of strategy development within a context that is sensitive to them. Such a context is likely to be:

- *pluralistic*, surfacing and welcoming different, even conflicting, ideas, and making them the basis of debate. There is an emphasis on the importance of questioning and challenging received wisdom and custom.
- *experimental*, so that ideas are tried out in action and in turn become part of the learning process.

- *tolerant* not only of new and perhaps contradictory ideas, but also of the inevitable blind alleys and errors that following them leads to.

There are, however, at least two problems with organizational learning as advanced in the literature. The first is, does it actually exist? The logic seems to arise more from disquiet with traditional concepts and workings of organizations than from firm studies of what might work better. Given this, the second problem, unsurprisingly, is that it is unclear what organizations actually do to become learning organizations. In other words, organization learning looks more like a "wish list" than a practical guide to management action.

There have been a few management scholars whose research points toward the benefits of organizational learning and suggests ways in which this might occur – but they are few. For example, in the 1980s James Brian Quinn acknowledged that managers mostly manage strategy incrementally. They typically change by building on and amending what has gone before. However, he pointed to the potential benefits of this, arguing that in successful firms this took the form of what he described as *logical incrementalism.*[18] Managers in such firms have a general rather than a specific view of where they want their business to be in the future. Faced with the futility of attempting to reduce the uncertainty of the future by making accurate predictions, they try to stay attuned to environmental signals by testing changes in strategy in small-scale steps – building on acquired experience but also experimenting with "side-bet" ventures. This, then, is a positive view of incremental change – "a conscious, purposeful, proactive, executive practice," in the words of James Quinn.

In many respects, both the idea of dynamic capabilities and the learning organization also correspond to the call by Gary Hamel for "resilient" organizations that continually reinvent themselves by refusing to take their success for granted and building the capability to imagine new business model.[19]

It's down to good leadership

What emerges from all this is that the succesful management of strategy is indeed demanding. It is not enough for managers to be acutely aware of the – often hidden – legacy competences their organization might use to build competitive advantage in the present. They must also create or nurture dynamic capabilities – that is, the ability consciously to modify these organizational competences and thus construct new bases of competitive advantage for the future. So managing strategy so as to avoid strategic drift surely requires exceptional *strategic leaders*.

But what does this actually mean? Leaders are often categorized in two ways. On one side are *instrumental or transactional leaders*,[20] who focus on control and order. Their emphasis is on continuity and improving the current situation, probably by instrumental means. On the other side are *charismatic or transformational leaders* who search for future opportunities, build a vision to match, and energize people to achieve it. These are change agents. The assumption is that transformational leaders can dramatically lift performance by giving people a guiding star and inspiration through times of turbulence and uncertainty.[21]

Both of these roles may be needed. But in the literature, the emphasis is split between the two. Given a general acceptance of the likelihood of strategic drift, it might be thought that charismatic leaders would have the best chance of making bold and radical decisions that would allow the company to break the bonds of the past. There are plenty of popular books about what it takes to be a charismatic leader, especially by executives who see themselves as such or academics who have studied them.[22] But this is not a uniform view. Other influential writers assert that charismatic leadership is unnecessary, even dangerous. According to Jim Collins, some of the most successful leaders are characterized by what he calls their "ordinariness,"[23] their success in his view being more to do with persistence and clarity of purpose than personal charisma.

Still others point to the need for leadership to fit the context. That is, there is no one right leadership style; what is required is the ability to tailor strategic leadership style to context.[24] Truly successful leaders have to be acutely aware of the circumstances in which they are operating and adopt the style suited to those circumstances. More generally and in the perspective of the theme developing here, strategic leaders will both comprehend and be able to manage the delicate balancing act of maintaining the competences that sustain continuity while fostering or generating the dynamic capabilities that can keep the organization abreast of changes in its environment.

The value of alignment ... or of difference

The notion that strong leaders direct strategy goes hand in hand with the received wisdom that they are also responsible for aligning the business and its culture around a core ideology or vision – hence the notion of the importance of core values, vision statements, mission statements, strong cultures all helping to ensure that an organization is pulling in the same direction. Thus, Jim Collins and Jerry Porras have argued that the long-run success of many US companies – such as Disney, General Electric, or 3M – can be attributed at least in part to strong core values.[25] This seems plausible. After all, the opposite of such internal coherence is fragmentation, disharmony, and potential chaos. Again, however, there are dissenting voices.

If there is unity around a common direction, how is change to take place? This takes us straight back to our starting point and some of the underlying causes of strategic drift, not least the danger of being wedded to tried-and-tested bases of success that, over time, calcify into the organizational structure. As you might expect, there is extensive research on the value of consensus or conflict in organizations. However, the results need some unpacking. Most of the research has sought to establish whether there is a relationship between consensus and performance, to which the answer is that sometimes there is, sometimes there isn't, and sometimes researchers can't decide.[26]

More insightful perhaps is research that has tried to unravel what type of consensus or conflict is more or less helpful. For example, Allen Amason's studies[27] make an important distinction between "cognitive conflict" – substantive, lively debate about real strategic issues – and "affective" or emotional conflict, which is damaging. In the view of Steve Floyd, who also researches these issues:

> it depends largely on where one is in the strategy development process. At earlier stages, where there is considerable uncertainty about what to do, the important thing is to get input and withhold judgment. This favors conflict, at least of the cognitive or constructive type. At later stages, however, alignment becomes important and more consensus is necessary.[28]

This does, of course, assume that the cognitive and affective (or emotional) aspects can coexist or be somehow separated – no easy matter.

Stanford Business School's Robert Burgelman has worked for many years with Intel, in particular its then CEO, Andrew Grove. He argues that all organizations face "strategic inflection points," shifts in fundamental business dynamics that they must recognize and act on. But how can they do this when they are striving might and main to maximize their competitive advantage and returns in the prevailing industry structure? Burgelman's argument, based on his observations at Intel, is that managers need to keep their ears open for hints of what he calls "strategic dissonance" in their organizations. Somewhere, probably close to the market and perhaps therefore among the junior ranks, there will be malcontents who champ at the prevailing strategy, perceiving it to be lagging behind the industry curve. The temptation is to marginalize such voices, blot them out, or at the extreme eliminate them as disruptive forces. No, say Burgelman and Grove.[29] Senior executives need urgently to teach themselves to distinguish dissonant "noise" in the organization from the "strategic signaling" of a potential strategic inflection point.

The need is therefore to value dissent rather than suppress it. This can be painful and difficult. But top managers must get past knee-jerk reactions, whether personal affront, disrespect for past success, or outrage at the undermining of agreed current strategy, to channel dissent, wherever it comes from, into a "searing intellectual debate" until a clearer pattern emerges. This may well mean running with new ideas and experiments to establish just what makes sense and what does not – including having the discipline to intervene to halt the experiments when it becomes clear that they are not going anywhere.

There are thus two key elements here. Tolerating, even encouraging, dissent – what Intel calls "constructive confrontation" – is the first thing. But second is the necessity for management to possess the authority and legitimacy to make decisions about the direction to be followed that, once taken, are taken as binding by everyone in the organization – including previous dissenters. Despite the dissent, therefore, in the end it comes back to top management, with the rest of the organization figuring as something of a "black box." And once again, practical advice on how to establish and maintain a dissent-friendly "culture" is conspicuously lacking.

Organizational ambidexterity

Many of the ideas raised so far come together under the umbrella concept of *organizational ambidexterity*. Managing incrementally assumes that managers *exploit* the capabilities that have been built up over time and give rise to the success of their organization. But managing incrementally runs the risk of degenerating into drift. The danger of an *exploitation*-only focus is that managers neglect the *exploration* of new sources of capability and strategic innovation. The obvious conclusion is that managers need to do both – they must develop what has come to be known as "organizational ambidexterity." Saying it is one thing, delivering it quite another, however, the problem being that each is generally acknowledged to require a quite different management style, organizational systems, and cultural context.

Several means have been put forward for overcoming this difficulty. Burgelman and Grove think it is the job of leadership and the top management team to reconcile the opposites, valuing divergent views and integrating potential contradictory behaviors. Others stress the need to break up conformity and group-think through *diversity*, whether ethnic, gender, personality type, or employment history.[30] Like the constructive confrontation it is supposed to favor, diversity is not necessarily easy to handle, requiring managers who are not only comfortable with experimentation, mavericks, even eccentrics,[31] but also have ability to get the most out of them.

Some early studies suggested that another way forward was the creation of separate units for exploration and exploitation.[32] For example, while the main core of the business might be managed to drive ahead with existing strategy, separate intrapreneurial units could be set up to explore fresh options, ring-fenced from the tight controls appropriate for exploitation.[33] Or, in the absence of separate business units, temporary project-based teams serve the same purpose. Others have proposed that organizations might switch periodically between exploiting and exploring phases. In their study of hi-tech industries in Silicon Valley, for example, Shona Brown and Kathy Eisenhardt[34] described this as "time pacing." In some companies, individuals do this too. At Google and 3M, for example, and at other companies even in manufacturing, people are encouraged to intersperse the "day job" (exploitation) with time spent on developing a pet innovation project of their own (exploration).

The difficulty, though, is that we have no way of knowing which of these explanations, or combination of them, really matters. Furthermore, although the studies purport to explain how organizations build ambidexterity (and therefore avoid strategic drift), most of them are not historical in nature. They tend to focus on organizations that are *currently* successful and innovative and explain why this might be so. Not elaborated, on the other hand, is whether they have successfully avoided drift over time: and since the whole issue of drift is to do with the weight of the past, this leaves the explanations looking tantalizing but inadequate. So for example, the original hypotheses about structural ambidexterity came out of studies of what looked like highly innovatory organizations in the 1980s – Hewlett Packard, ABB, and Johnson & Johnson. With the possible exception of Johnson & Johnson, these are not examples that have stood the test of time, which is the whole point of the exercise. Other studies are based on surveys of managers in apparently innovative organizations, asking them to account for their innovations – essentially opinion surveys. And others again are essentially theoretical. The bottom line is that we actually know little about how and if organizational ambidexterity comes about in an historical context.

Complexity theory

Conventional thinking about strategy starts from two central assumptions:

- Firms are *hierarchies* with managers at the apex to make decisions sitting over people below them to carry out what they decide. Strategies travel down the organization from top to bottom.
- Although the world in which organizations operate is complex and uncertain, rational analysis can do much to reduce that. Organizations, like economies, are *rational systems* striving toward an equilibrium of performance.

But what happens to strategy and change if these assumptions are false? This is the starting point for complexity theory, a set of ideas that offers a strikingly different view of the world that has of late become much more accessible and attractive to managers. Complexity theory begins with the assumption that the world, whether physical or economic, is precisely *not* a linear system where the challenge is to find platforms of predictability and equilibrium, but rather a complex, unstable system with multiple, interdependent influences on outcomes. To complicate matters further, apparently insignificant initial influences can have enormous later consequences, without the linkages between them being either clear or even visible (the famous storm from a butterfly's wing). From our point of view, the interest of such a system is that it contains within it seeds of innovation and novelty that managers might potentially nurture to their advantage. Shona Brown and Kathy Eisenhardt[35] drew on these ideas to explain the success of high-tech firms in Silicon Valley. To the notions of complexity theory they added some lessons from evolutionary theory that further reinforced their case. This very different way of conceiving of organizations suggests the following.

Whether the concern is with species, as in the natural world, society, or indeed ideas in organizations, novelty proceeds from diversity and difference; at the extreme, uniformity leads to stasis and death. For managers, the implications are clear, if not always comforting. They should be chary of assuming they can control or plan the generation of new ideas. Rather, they should seek to encourage them by nurturing the natural variety occurring in all organizations, often unrecognized, particularly at lower levels, and in embryonic form – what Bill McKelvey calls the "distributed intelligence" of an organization.[36]

How can managers create the context and conditions most conducive for ideas to emerge?:

- Since high levels of control and strict hierarchy are likely to encourage conformity and reduce variety, establishing *appropriate* levels of control becomes crucial. Some complexity theorists argue that innovation and creativity emerge when there is just enough order to prevent complete anarchy, but not so much that it chokes innovation. This is the idea of 'the "edge of chaos"[37]: innovation occurs most readily when the organization never quite settles down into equilibrium, and volatility arising from variation is given sufficient rein, although of course not to the extent that it stops the organization from functioning.
- *Order-generating rules.* There is no need for elaborate control – complexity theory suggests that ordered patterns of behavior come about through just a few order-generating rules[38] or, as Eisenhardt calls them, "simple rules,"[39] the very few but absolute requirements within which latitude and improvisation can occur.
- *Pattern recognition.* Organizational ideas are more likely to emerge from an ability to recognize promising patterns than from formal analysis and planning. Managers should concentrate on honing their sensitivity to emerging patterns and wean themselves off a reliance on formal tools and techniques.

Complexity theory draws attention to the way ideas in organizations bubble up from below. The implication is that strategy development, too, is not attached to just one part of the hierarchy. Instead, it emerges from the working out of organic processes within the system. Top managers become the architects of the context, shapers of ideas that arise rather than designers of solutions.

OUR STUDY

What should be clear from the discussion so far is two key messages. First, it is not at all clear how it is possible for firms to both achieve high performance and make significant changes. There are strong arguments to suggest it is unlikely, and a lack of hard evidence on how it might be achieved. Second, the views about how it might be achieved are based, very largely, on mainly ahistorical research – regrettable since it is clear that history plays a crucial role, for good or bad, in the strategy development of firms. We began thinking seriously about these issues in 2003. The research on which the book is based, a story in its own right, is described in more detail in Chapter 2, but in summary it consisted of two stages.

The first was to establish whether we had a book to write at all. Were there were any major UK firms that had not only been financially successful over long periods, but had also radically changed their strategies at the same time? Was strategic transformation without financial collapse a chimera, a beast that existed only in myth, or were there real examples? To find out, we trawled published data, using a number of different measures, to compare 215 of the largest publicly listed UK firms with thousands of their international peers in different industry sectors over a 20-year period from 1984 to 2003. We chose a relatively long period of time and triangulated performance by taking multiple measures because we wanted to avoid the methodological criticisms leveled at some other studies of high-performing companies. We used peer benchmarking as a basis for our judgments. Equally, we factored in changes in industry cycles of performance. If an industry sector was in overall decline or ascension, we took that into account. So, to qualify, firms had to perform at the frontier of the performance in their sector consistently over two decades. With such strict criteria, we did not expect a large number of outstanding qualifiers. And indeed, of the 215 UK candidates, just 28 came through the first round. These are explained more fully in Chapter 2.

We then went on to consider which of these 28 had not only attained consistently high levels of performance, but had also effected major strategic transformation while doing so. We examined the published data on these firms over the same 20-year period, by charting changes in their products, their markets, their governance, organizational structures, and business models. Again, we did not expect to find a large number of qualifiers, and we were right: it is interesting to note that of the 28 consistently high achievers, most had *not* made major strategic changes. In fact, many seemed to inhabit secure industry niches or work in relatively protected industry environments. Of the 28 firms, just six might be described as "successful strategic transformers" (SSTs). On closer examination this came down to four, again explained in Chapter 2.

The second stage of our project was to focus on three of these firms to understand the management processes at work within them, again over an extended period. In particular, we were interested in establishing if common patterns of management might explain how they combined strategic transformation with continuous financial success. Had they developed the dynamic capabilities to stay ahead of change, and if so, what were their origins? We were aware of the pitfalls that can waylay attempts to pinpoint the causes of managerial success, in particular "recency bias," the tendency to explain success in terms of current management and recent phenomena. The firms we were studying had long histories, certainly more than the 20 years we had studied in the figures in stage 1. So our historical studies spanned a period of up to half a century. If these firms had long histories, those histories were likely to be relevant. If history can be trawled for the roots of failure, we should not ignore it when looking for the sources of success.

This stage of our work was hugely time-consuming. For each of the three firms we studied, we identified a comparator. The comparators were not failed firms. We thought of them as "bronze medal" winners to our three "gold medalists." They were companies that had followed the classic cycle of success and drift. We then negotiated entry into all six organizations – it took 2 years to gain access at the level we needed – to discuss the historical management processes at work in each. In the end, we were able to interview almost 50 current and past executives who had been intimately involved in plotting the strategic course of their organizations. They included present chief executives, chairmen, and directors as well as past employees and retired executives, from whom we were able to gain insights about management practices and processes from up to half a century before. We were also fortunate to be allowed to consult the archives of some of our firms, enabling us check the oral accounts of events against the recorded data.

What we found

Managers are faced with a perhaps bewildering array of different suggestions on how, in general terms, to manage long-term strategy development and, more specifically how to avoid the problem of the firm's historical capabilities for success becoming rigidities that can lead to strategic drift and eventual crisis. Pulling the discussion of these approaches to strategy and change together, what does it tell us? Given the many factors militating in its favor, some observers would argue that this pathology of firms is inevitable. In so far as it can be avoided or overcome, existing research seems to suggest some agreement on two overarching findings:

- *The need for duality*. Managers must find a way of balancing the benefits of the past, not least the organizational capabilities that may historically have been the source of competitive advantage and success, with a keen awareness of what is changing around them and the opportunities and threats that result. Putting this another way, organizations need the ability to manage both the exploitation of existing capabilities and the exploration of new ones. They must develop what have become known as dynamic capabilities.

- *Organizational capabilities.* No one individual, however exceptional his or her leadership skills, can single-handedly assure the future, especially of large, complex organizations. The ability to adapt and learn has to be embedded in the fabric of the organization itself. As to how managers are to do this, there is no clear answer. But it is likely to entail a willingness to encourage internal questioning and challenge of the status quo, as regards both core assumptions and taken-for-granted ways of doing things. Traditional approaches to the organization, with their emphasis on hierarchical lines of control and planned uniformity of purpose and delivery, seem unlikely vehicles for achieving it.

So much we learn from existing research and current literature. But the same literature tells us that the tug of the past is so strong that it takes an exceptional company to escape it. Are there any such exceptions? If so, how have they done it? Was it through the sorts of mechanisms reviewed in this chapter? Or by other means? What does it take for a company to become master of its past and thus also of its present and future? It is impossible to answer such questions without looking at its history. A common concern about the research reviewed in this chapter is the paucity of empirical and especially historical evidence to support its conclusions. It treats organizational structures and systems, the behavior of managers and others within organizations, and the culture and context in which they work, as givens. Without an explanation of how such systems and behaviors come about, how are managers to decide how to manage their history? Although many of the writers claim to be addressing the challenges we identify here, they typically base their arguments on studies of organizations as they currently exist. But this is like trying to assess the importance of a fossil find without examining the geological record. The only way to reach firm conclusions about practical action today is to study corporate success over the long term: to set the corporation in its historical record. Our study therefore emphasized longitudinal and historical perspectives.

Stage 1 of our study confirmed that strategic drift and value destruction do indeed form a common pattern. Yet this makes it all the more striking that a few firms – the exceptions – bucked the trend and did manage to make major strategic change without being forced into it by crisis. Their performance is thus especially worth studying. Note that we do not promise that our champion firms – the SSTs – will always avoid strategic drift. What we do claim, however, is that there are lessons to be learned from their performance over one, lengthy period of time – 20 years.

The overriding lesson of our study is how much history matters. In ways that companies sometimes are not even conscious of, the past weighs heavily on the present. This runs counter to the prevailing and pervasive tendency to account for corporate success in the present tense – attributing it to this current executive or that recent decision. We come to a markedly different conclusion: that the performance of the "strategic transformers" we studied is rooted in, and cannot be separated from, their history. By studying them over time, we identified a number of "traditions" that ran through the history of the SSTs but were absent from those of other firms. Traditions are patterns of belief or models of conduct that are transferred from the past into the present across generations. We suggest that these traditions made it possible for executives to reconcile the difficulties of managing continuity and change at the same time. Each of the firms we studied had developed mechanisms for doing this. The traditions we identified – and which we demonstrate and explain in the rest of the book – are these:

A tradition of continuity. A company has a tradition of continuity when successive generations of a company's dominant coalition are able to reinvent a timely variation on their company's historical success theme. By dominant coalition we mean a company's established leadership, typically a grouping organized around the CEO, chief executive, chairman, or, in UK companies, sometimes the chief financial officer. Within the tradition of continuity, such leaders have as their primary focus the reinvention of the company's historically distinctive business model in terms befitting contemporary industry conditions.

A tradition of anticipation. A company has a tradition of anticipation when it institutionalizes a space for alternative leaders to anticipate a timely variation on the old success theme and prepare a "behind the scenes" platform for change. These alternative leaders form an "alternative dominant coalition" or shadow leadership for change. These alternative leaders are able to accelerate the pace of transformation, not by forcing the issue, but by using *"happy accidents"* to gain a broad platform of support. Happy accidents are serendipitous dynamics or events that allow for an acceleration of the pace of transformation in the direction anticipated by alternative leaders.

A tradition of contestation. Contestation may be thought of as a culture of challenge, a management style that places emphasis on internal competition, debate, discussion, and a self-critical scrutiny of decisions, performance, and improvement. Our three SSTs demonstrated such contestation, whereas the comparator companies manifested cultures of conservatism, characterized by conformity or obedience to hierarchy, an emphasis on continuity, resistance to ideas from outside the firm and a "not invented here" mentality, defensiveness around decision-making, and the promotion of people likely to "toe the line" rather than challenge the status quo.

A tradition of mobility. A company has a tradition of mobility if it has institutionalized routines of recruitment, promotion, and exit that are informal tests of ability rather than formal human resources procedures. These are distinctive informal rules or norms that not only appeal to the most skilled candidates – equally crucially, they also do not filter out a leavening of "skilled mavericks." They link the promotion and exit of employees to their ability to participate in a continuous process of internally generated or home-grown company transformation.

Let's be clear. Each of these traditions had historical roots. These were not characteristics that had been deliberately formulated at a particular point in time. They had developed incrementally over generations of managers – to the point where we wondered how conscious managers were of the value of such a historical legacy. And herein lies our question mark over the future: unless their managers are aware of the benefits of the traditions they have inherited, and can cherish and nurture them, there is no guarantee that they will avoid strategic drift down the line.

Somewhat paradoxically, it may be managers from other companies who can more easily learn from the lessons we draw and relate them to their own organizations. These are conclusions we draw toward the end of the book.

STRUCTURE OF THE BOOK

The book proceeds as follows. Part I contains Chapters 1 and 2, which set up why and how we conducted this study. In Chapter 2, we explain in more detail how this study was undertaken. We do this in part because it is an interesting story in its own right. Perhaps more importantly, though, we are well aware that much of the "success literature" is tainted by criticism of its research design or failure adequately to explain the basis its claims. We tackle these issues in Chapter 2, which also sets out the main findings from the first stage of the research.

Part II of this book provides the detailed histories of the six companies. Readers with limited time may want to skip to Part III, which provides our interpretation, frameworks, and recommendations for action. In Part II,

Chapters 3 and 4 lay out the findings of stage 2, the historical stage, of our research. In Chapter 3, we provide an account of the historical development of the management processes at work in our three SSTs. In Chapters 4 and 5, we describe further developments and breakthroughs during the 20-year period of exceptional financial performance (1984–2003) of the strategic transformers. In Chapter 6, we describe both the history and the developments at the three comparators.

In Part III, Chapter 7 then considers the differences in the three pairs of firms and explains the four traditions of transformation we identify. Drawing on archive data and our interviews, we show how the historical traditions worked to foster or block strategic transformation in the paired firms. The final chapter, Chapter, 8, then considers these findings as they relate to management more generally. What are the lessons and are they applicable to others? How can managers manage better in the present by learning from their past? For good or ill, history is one of their most powerful and underused resources.[40]

CHAPTER 2

The Study

Everything told us that the past was more important in understanding the corporate present than is generally acknowledged. But did we have a story to tell beyond the purely anecdotal? To find out was a voyage of discovery in its own right. Were there companies that had managed to carry out real strategic transformation without the urgent pressure of financial crisis? If so, how had their history prepared them for such change? To answer those questions, we had to devise a research method that would allow us not only reliably to identify companies that had financially outperformed the pursuing pack over a long period of time – by a creative use of both primary and secondary sources, we also had to get behind the financial statistics to establish which companies had transformed themselves and develop a theory that would account for such apparently exceptional behavior.

In short, we needed to design a research methodology that was both highly rigorous and exhaustive. It would eventually consist of three main stages. First, we needed to identify long-term superior financial performance in order to generate a preliminary list of corporate high achievers. Second, we had to whittle down this "long list" to those (if any) that had also undergone successful strategic transformation. Only then could we apply our third methodology to investigate *how* some of these companies had managed to reinvent themselves. As a further final precaution, we checked our research findings against a textual analysis of our interview transcripts to ensure against personal bias and to pick up any undetected historical patterns.

STAGE 1: IDENTIFYING LONG-TERM PERFORMERS

Each of these stages presented its own issues and problems. For example, even the business of establishing long-term success is fraught with pitfalls.

Many popular books purporting to explain corporate success have been undermined by what has come to be known eponymously as the "In Search of Excellence effect," in which companies presented as corporate stars suddenly turn into dogs after publication.

There are a number of traps here. For a start, any one-dimensional measure of performance, particularly over the short term, is highly dependent on the start and end points, making it an inherently poor predictor of future performance. Second, the measure usually used as the sole performance criterion, total return to shareholders (TRS),[1] hides a number of potential distortions and differences between companies that make it a treacherous guide at best.[2] It is affected by many intermediate outcomes, including levels and growth rates of profits and return on investment, and many other nonfinancial variables such as competitive advantages and company reputation – and the effect of these intermediate outcomes accumulates over time. Market movements can wildly inflate (or deflate) notional shareholder returns, as in the dot.com bubble of 2000, independent of the actions of top management. Even TRS devotees are now questioning the primacy of shareholder value.[3] Again, companies and their top managers have different objectives, both from other firms and at different times – a growing, younger company may choose to place much more emphasis on revenue or market share growth than on profits, for example. For all these reasons, TRS on its own can be an unreliable barometer of *past* performance, let alone the future.

The frontier approach to measuring performance

To avoid these drawbacks, we decided to use an approach known as "frontier analysis." Frontier analysis has the benefit of allowing the application of multiple measures, over a long period of time, combined with a comparison with peers.[4]

For those requiring more detail, we provide a technical description in a Methodology Appendix at the end of the chapter. But it will help to give a simple graphic example here. Figure 2.1 shows a hypothetical industry performance frontier for 1 year, plotting the performance of five companies, A, B, C, E, and F, on two dimensions of performance, x_1 and x_2. A, B, and C are all at the industry performance frontier for that year, *even though each has achieved a different combination of performance on the two measures*. A scores highest on x_1 and C on x_2, while B does not score most highly on either measure. None of the three firms clearly outperforms the other two. Nor can we say that any one underperforms the others.[5] They are "frontier" firms – in contrast to companies E and F, which are clearly outperformed directly or indirectly by their rivals. F, using the same performance measures in the same ratio, can be directly compared with B: it does less well on both measures. Company E has a unique scoring combination and therefore cannot be compared directly with any other; but it is well behind the frontier at point d, which is a combination of the positions of A and B.

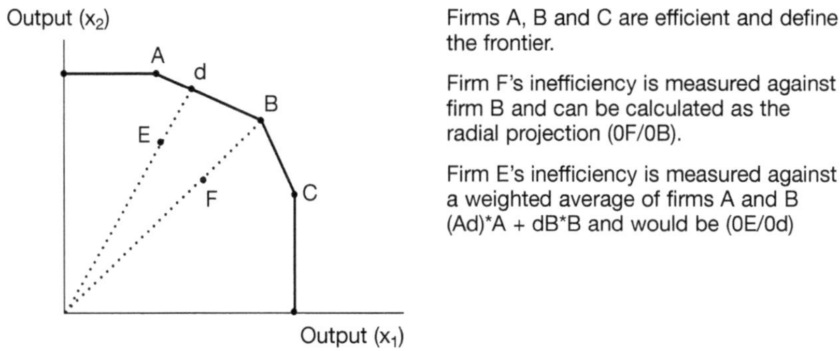

FIGURE 2.1 | A frontier with two dimensions of performance

For our purposes, frontier analysis had a number of advantages. Since the technique builds a performance pattern from a series of independent annual measures rather than from measuring change from year to year, it is not sensitive to the start-and-end-date issue that notoriously skews so many performance comparison exercises. It is also extremely flexible: it can accommodate a mix of performance measures – reflecting, for example, the expectations of a range of different stakeholders – and still produce a company ranking. What is more, companies can excel on different criteria and still be ranked against each other – in effect, it can compare apples with oranges. (Pursuing that analogy, frontier analysis can rank an apple as being closer to apple perfection than an orange is to orange perfection. Dog-show judges do the same when they select a "best in show" animal from a number of "best in breeds".)

For effective frontier analysis, the important thing is that there should be a broad, diverse collection of measures relating to the underlying issue(s) of interest. Adding more measures provides more information, allowing the investigator to differentiate exactly where a single firm is out- or underperforming its peers. Sensitivity analysis permitted us not only to examine the diversity of the measures needed, but also to establish whether different weightings and grouping affected the form and substance of the frontier.

Examining performance over multiple years

We decided to take UK public companies as our starting sample. Obviously, since we are based in the UK, access to companies in stage 3 would be far easier. Also, along with the US, companies in the UK have very well-reported financial data. Lastly, UK public companies are disproportionately important in the global economy. A recent study found that British firms account for 8.8 percent of the revenues of all publicly listed companies in the world, nearly double the 4.8 percent share of global gross domestic product held by the UK economy as a whole.[6]

Our starting data were provided by the Bureau van Dijk's Osiris database. Osiris contains annual report data on 30,000 public companies (as well as 8,000 unlisted and delisted companies) from around the globe for up to 20 years and covers more than 125 countries. To identify *some* British companies exhibiting long-term superior performance, we began by choosing 38 industry sectors in the database that had significant numbers of large UK companies (that is, ranking in the top global 50 or 100 by size in the industry) and for which good data were available (Table 2.1). The two criteria of a significant presence of UK companies and good data meant that we excluded 43 industries.[7] Nearly all of the excluded industries have few British companies in their global top 100, with the notable exceptions of pharmaceuticals and various financial service industries, all of which suffered severe data problems as a result of prolific merger and acquisition activity over the period. We were also looking for comparators – industry peers of the kind that managers in our companies would be likely to benchmark themselves against. The comparators were all publicly listed firms, both British and non-British to give an element of international comparison, and likewise in the global top 50 or 100 in each industry.

TABLE 2.1 | Industries analyzed and not analyzed

Industries analyzed	Industries not analyzed
Advertising	Advanced industrial equipment
Aerospace	Agriculture
Airlines	Aluminum
Apparel	Automobile
Broadcasting	Auto parts
Building materials	Banks, excluding savings and loans
Casinos and gaming	Biotechnology
Chemicals, specialty	Chemicals, commodity

Industries analyzed	Industries not analyzed
Communications	Clothing and fabrics
Department stores	Computers
Distillers and brewers	Consumer electronics
Diversified manufacturing	Consumer services
Drug stores	Cosmetics
Entertainment	Diversified financial
Food	Diversified technology
Furnishings and applications	Electric components
Grocery stores	Factory equipment
Heavy construction	Financial advisors
Household nondurables	Fixed-line communications
Leisure	Footwear
Lodging	Forest products
Medical devices	Healthcare providers
Medical supplies	Heavy machinery
Mining	Home construction
Office equipment	Household products, durable
Oil	Industrial services
Packaging	Insurance, full line
Precious metals	Insurance, life
Publishing	Insurance, property
Restaurants and pubs	Internet services
Retailers, specialty	Investment services
Ship-building	Nonferrous metals
Shipping	Oil drilling, equipment
Soft drinks	Pharmaceuticals
Steel	Pipelines
Telecoms	Pollution control
Transport services	Real estate
Utilities	Savings and loans
	Semiconductors
	Software
	Tires
	Tobacco
	Toys

Selection of the time period

How long is long enough to measure sustainable superior performance? The 3–5-year period chosen by most researchers has the advantage of ease of management. Unfortunately, it bears little relation to the longevity of the factors that underlie it. There are now many schools of thought on what drives superior performance. Among strategists, the two dominant paradigms of competitive positioning[8] and superior resources[9] both emphasize the long-lived nature of such foundations. A study by Morgan Stanley concluded that, depending on the industry, it would take a well-financed and aggressive competitor between 2 and 23 years to establish a business able to take on leading incumbents on equal terms.[10] In addition, companies need to see off challenges from new competitors or new challenges from old ones. Such challenges tend to be episodic, sometimes occurring many years apart.

Any performance measure should also take in at least one complete business cycle, which may last 10 years or more from peak to peak, not to mention less predictable periodic marketplace or other upheavals, such as the rise of the Internet or the banking crisis. In all, there are strong grounds for studying performance over decades rather than years, as a number of previous efforts have done[11] – and this is what we chose to do too, basing our study on the 20 years from 1984 to 2003. We chose these dates partly because the latter year was the most current one in the database, but also because the period is also a good test for British companies in that it coincides with the moment that the pro-market reforms undertaken by Prime Minister Margaret Thatcher began to bite, substantially affecting the economic climate in which those companies operated. In addition, this period saw at least one economic cycle including the boom and bust of the Internet bubble, as well as the stock market meltdown in 1987, providing a stern extra test for sustained performance.

Selection of measures

We chose five ratios to measure our companies on: profit margin (percent), return on shareholders' funds (percent), return on total assets (percent), return on capital employed (percent), and cash flow to operating revenues (percent). To ensure robustness, we checked our results against alternate sets of measures, some of which included shareholder returns (TRS and Tobin's q). These criteria threw up a few other high performers but raised no question marks against our original qualifiers.

Selection of performance criteria

To qualify as a long-term superior performer, a company had to satisfy stringent criteria. It had to have:

- existed for 20 years;
- ranked in the top one-third of the industry performance distribution for the entire 20-year period;
- suffered no more than 2 years of consecutive decline in performance, for only one of which it had fallen below the one-third cut-off. In other words, a firm could, on average, have been in the top one-third over the 20-year period but have had 2 years of declining performance, with 1 year in which its performance was only in the top half of all firms. This would have disqualified the firm based on the consistency of performance criterion.

The qualifying British industries and companies

In the end, of 215 firms examined, just 28, or 13 percent, passed our performance test (Table 2.2). The list threw up some surprises. While we might have guessed the names of some our qualifiers – BP, Cadbury Schweppes, and Tesco would have figured on most lists, for example – others, such as Unilever and Whitbread, were less expected. It is safe to say that A.G. Barr and Bespak, two other exemplars, would have been on few observers' radar screens. And here we have to insert the usual buyers' warning. As with all performance rankings, ours applies only to the period under study. It is not and cannot be a predictor of future performance. As our study has taught us, the longer a company sustains superior performance, the greater the possibility of creeping obsolescence in its business models and strategies, as well as increasing competitive envy, imitation, or challenge on the part of its rivals.

Apart from superior performance, what did our qualifiers have in common? At this stage, we started to think of them (although not exclusively) in three broad preliminary categories. A number, typified by Unilever and Shell, were already both large and successful in 1984. They operated in competitive industries, but not punishingly so. Clearly, their established assets and strategic position, combined with some evolutionary changes in strategy, went a considerable way toward explaining their consistent superior performance over the period. For obvious reasons, we called them "large survivors."

"Protected nichers," on the other hand, were companies like A.G. Barr, a Scottish manufacturer of specialized beverages such as Irn-Bru, and Bespak, which produces drug delivery and similar medical devices; these, although excelling within their niches, rarely ventured outside them. As with the first group, their history mattered, but it had exposed them to less competition than some other groups.

TABLE 2.2 | UK companies qualifying as long-term superior performers (1984–2003)

Industry	Companies
Advertising	Taylor Nelson Sofres
Aerospace	Cobham, Meggitt, Smiths Group
Alcoholic beverages	Allied Domecq, Scottish & Newcastle
Apparel	Next
Casinos and gaming	Hilton Group, Stanley Leisure
Construction	Balfour
Drug stores	Boots Group
Entertainment	EMI Group
Food	Cadbury Schweppes, Unilever
Grocery stores	Tesco
Household nondurables	Reckitt Benckiser
Medical devices	Smith & Nephew
Medical supplies	Bespak, Huntleigh Technology
Office equipment	Domino Printing
Oil	BG Group, BP, Shell
Packaging	Bunzl
Restaurants and pubs	Greene King, Whitbread
Soft drinks	A.G. Barr
Telecom	Vodafone

Using the same reasoning in reverse, there were a number of companies that seemed more promising from a historical point of view. These were the ones we termed "successful challengers": firms such as BP, Cadbury Schweppes, Smith & Nephew, and Tesco, which started the period as medium-sized companies up against much larger, formidable competitors, and over the 20 years had clearly transformed not only their mix of businesses, but also their business and management models.

In the end, however, it was not the identity of the companies that mattered, nor could we prejudge them. What mattered was that we had a robust sample of companies that had performed sufficiently well relative to their international peers over a long enough period to ensure that success was most unlikely be accidental. The next step was to find out which, if any, had managed to transform themselves strategically while doing so.

STAGE 2: DIAGNOSING STRATEGIC TRANSFORMATION

What does strategic transformation mean in practice? We looked for major changes in *strategy content*, *organization*, and *complementarities between them*. Changes in strategy and structure are usually well signalled and relatively easy to identify, comprising alterations to business models, geographical and product markets, portfolios, management systems, and governance. Slightly less obviously, effective strategic transformation involves more than making a few strategic or structural changes, even important ones. By definition, transformation is all or nothing: a halfway house, comprising some of the bundle of complementary activities that made up the old archetype and some of the new, is a perilous place to be. There is no choice, then, but for a transforming firm to go the whole hog and shift bodily from one organizational bundle to another. Hence the firm needs to look for complementarities.

How we identified strategic transformation

Our second stage consisted of searching secondary data to build a 20-year historical timeline for each of the 28 companies that had survived the first-round cut. These event histories became the basis for deciding which firms met our three (strategy, organization, complementarity) criteria to qualify as strategic transformers. To eliminate any unconscious bias, we compared and debated our judgments with those of a class of MBA students, small groups of whom took responsibility for separately analyzing the performance of two or three of the 28 candidates. From this process emerged a short list, which we discussed in similar fashion with an advisory group of academics and senior executives before arriving at a final choice.

What were the results? In brief, the first two stages of our enquiry had confirmed that our initial instinct was correct: successful strategic transformation without a financial crisis was extremely rare. Frontier analysis and historical research had whittled down our initial sample of 215 corporate high fliers to just six left standing. But the six showed that the second part of the hypothesis was also still intact: successful strategic transformers, or SSTs, as we came to call them, did seem to exist. BP, Cadbury Schweppes, EMI, Smith & Nephew, Tesco, and Vodafone were there to prove it.

On closer examination, we narrowed the list down still further. The strategic changes EMI had made were very largely to do with portfolio rationalization, and this was not what our study was concerned with. And Vodafone was only just born as a business in 1983, which ruled out any attempt to study strategic transformation in relation to its history. That left just four.

To delve into the reasons why one firm transformed itself while another did not, our research design required us to measure each SST against a comparator company – a firm in a similar industry that had achieved a respectable but not quite as good a performance, and comparable but not as extensive strategic transformation. In other words, we wanted to see how and why "gold medalists" differed from "bronze medalists."[12] Table 2.3 shows the four pairs of SSTs and their challengers.

TABLE 2.3 | The SSTs and their comparators

SSTs	Comparators
BP	Shell
Cadbury Schweppes	Unilever
Smith & Nephew	SSL International
Tesco	J Sainsbury

The pairs selected

Based partly on our likely ability to get access to top current and retired executives, the final choice came down to three pairs of companies operating in three different industries, all with long and distinguished pasts.

We shall have much more to say about each of these companies in Chapters 4, 5, and 6. But we already knew that we were dealing with institutions with an extraordinarily rich corporate legacy. Our first pair, Cadbury Schweppes (SST) and Unilever (non-SST), were long-established global companies in consumer packaged goods. Venerable Cadbury Schweppes had transformed itself from a small family-owned producer of confectionery (founded in 1831) and another of mixers (1792) into a combined force that had challenged global giants such as Mars, Nestlé, Coca-Cola, and PepsiCo. Before its recent break-up and sale of the confectionery side to Kraft, it had turned itself into the world's largest confectionery company and third-largest soft drinks outfit. Comparator Unilever, the product of a 1929 union of Dutch Margarine Unie and British Lever Brothers, is the world's third largest food company, behind Nestlé and Cadbury's new owner, Kraft. Its personal care businesses compete with the likes of Procter & Gamble and Reckitt Benckiser. For years, Unilever has been a byword for global reach and solid performance while never seeming to achieve its full potential.

An important part of the history of the UK supermarket industry has been the struggle for dominance of our second duo, Tesco and J Sainsbury (branded and commonly referred to as "Sainsbury's"). From small beginnings in 1932, Tesco, our SST, evolved to transform itself from discount supermarket operator into one of the world's most successful and admired retail giants. By 2012 it was the world's third largest after Walmart and Carrefour. In its rise, it displaced comparator Sainsbury's, for decades synonymous with quality and the British way of life, as the UK's top grocery chain. With more than 150 years of history behind it, Sainsbury's, founded in 1869, is the UK's longest established major food retailing chain, and has long embodied the virtues and failings of a company dominated by its founding family.

The third pair, Smith & Nephew and SSL International, were both mid-sized companies in medical devices and related products. Neither of them is a household name, although two of SSL's brands – Durex and Scholl – are. Today's Smith & Nephew bears no relation to the original provincial dispensing pharmacy that bore its name in 1856. Since then, it has transformed itself on every dimension to become a global player in four specialist high-tech markets – orthopedic reconstruction, orthopedic trauma and clinical therapies, endoscopy, and advanced wound management – with listings on both the London and New York stock exchanges. Despite a strong recent record, including significant strategic and structural change, comparator SSL International, the oldest of whose component companies dates back to 1909, ruled itself out as an SST because of substandard performance during most of our research period. In 2010 it was acquired in a £2.5 billion deal by Reckitt Benckiser. (Before deciding on SSL we also considered Smiths Group as a comparator for Smith & Nephew, interviewing a number of executives before coming to the conclusion that SSL was a better match industrially.)

Figure 2.2 depicts the annual financial performance of the three pairs of companies. In terms of financial performance, the figure shows that Cadbury Schweppes easily outperformed Unilever in every one of the 20 years covered except 1985, when it was slightly behind. In a different pattern, Tesco started the period behind the consistently high performance of industry leader Sainsbury's before catching up in the middle and then taking its rival's place as undisputed industry champion. Tesco's dominance over Sainsbury's has only increased since 2003. The third of our SSTs, Smith & Nephew, substantially outpaced SSL International in performance in every year but one, 1995, when it lagged marginally behind.

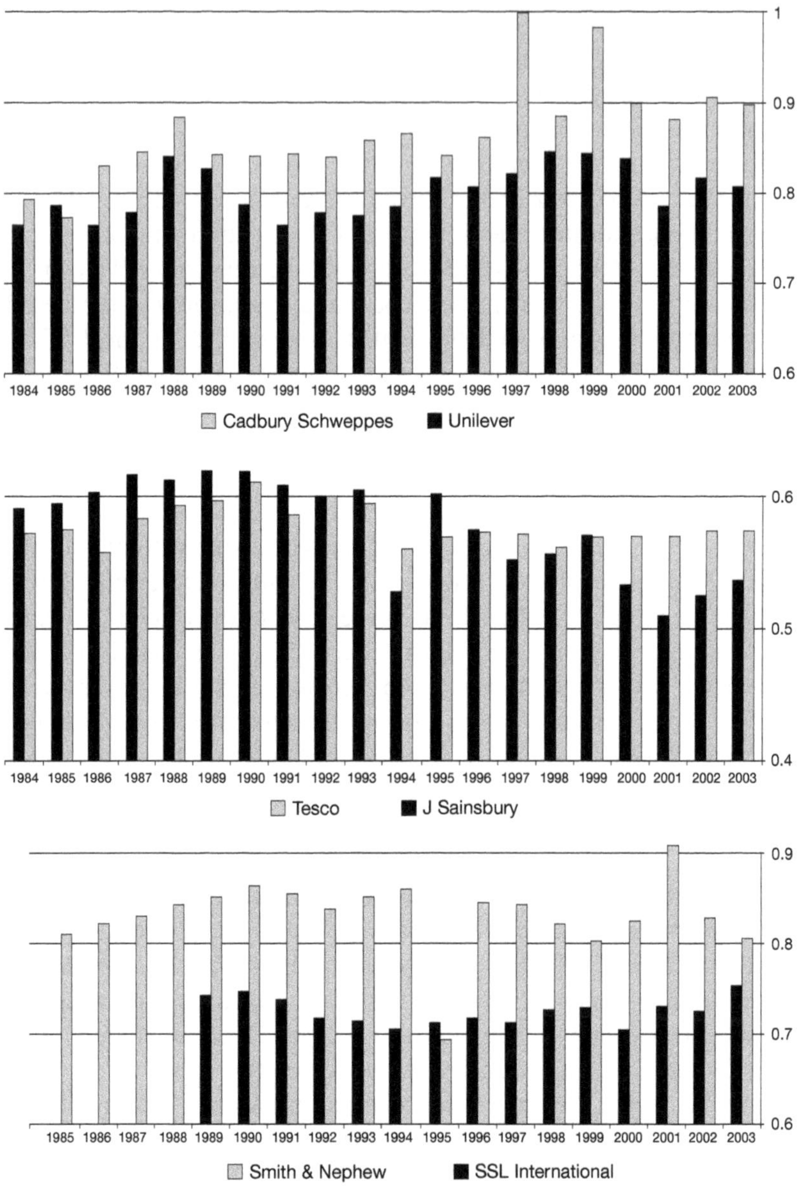

Heights of bars show performance relative to the annual international industry frontier. 1.0 = frontier performance that year. The average values differ across the three sectors because of the performance of international competitors. Tesco's and Sainsbury's scores are relatively low because in their sector, supermarkets, Japan's 7-Eleven had outstanding performance nearly every year, defining the frontier at a very high level.

FIGURE 2.2 | Financial performance of the six companies

STAGE 3: EXPLAINING STRATEGIC TRANSFORMATION

Although we believe that our means of getting there, particularly the use of frontier analysis, has some novel features, establishing our cast-list of long-term SSTs and their comparators was only the preliminary skirmish. With stage 3, we reached the central point of the exercise and the most challenging part of our research: interrogating the history of the three pairs of companies to reach general deductions about how patterns set in the past, sometimes nearly invisibly, condition present outcomes.[13] We therefore need to describe our approach in some detail. (Readers for whom the methodology is unimportant can skip to Chapter 3.)

Our first step was to collect everything we could find about each of the company's strategies, structures, and corporate, business, and industry models from day 1 onwards. For this, we used a wide range of secondary sources, including business histories, public archives, annual reports, company magazines, and press reports, as well as extensive interviews with current and past executives. Figure 2.3 gives an overview of the research method and dates for all three stages.

Collecting the data

Looking at corporate milestones through a historical lens puts them in a radically different light. Take, for example, the undisputedly successful transformation of Tesco since 1994. In the press and elsewhere, Tesco's renewal is usually ascribed to the talents and drive of senior managers, especially Terry Leahy, its CEO from 1997 to 2011, under whose aegis the company developed and put into operation a radically different customer value proposition in the mid-1990s. We do not deny these talents, but we were looking for deeper underlying causes: how had Tesco approached other turning points in the past, were there similarities in the approaches, and if so where had they originated? Where we could see a convincing reinterpretation of history for one company, we tested it on the other five to see if it could help to explain what had happened to them. After several such comparative cycles, we found one particularly compelling theory, the role of traditions, which we earmarked for further investigation in the next research phase.

To gather the primary information, we conducted detailed interviews with 46 active and retired executives from the six companies. Half the interviewees were former or current chairmen or chief executives (Table 2.4) – a truly impressive list.

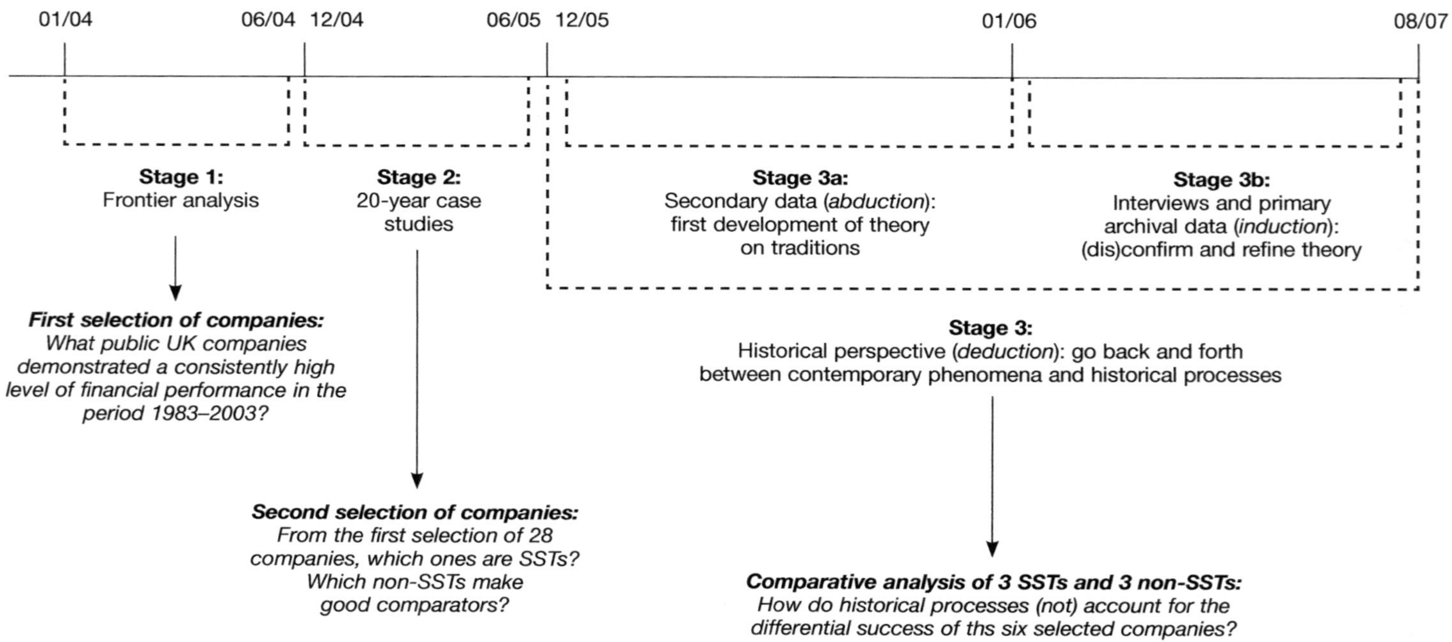

FIGURE 2.3 Research method and date

TABLE 2.4 Executives interviewed from the six selected companies

Company	Role at time of interview
Cadbury Schweppes	Chairman
Cadbury Schweppes	Chief Executive
Cadbury Schweppes	Chief Human Resources Officer
Cadbury Schweppes	Former Cadbury Board Director
Cadbury Schweppes	Former Chairman
Cadbury Schweppes	Former Chairman & Chief Executive
Cadbury Schweppes	Former Chairman & Chief Executive
Cadbury Schweppes	Former Chief Financial Officer
Cadbury Schweppes	Former Chief Financial Officer
Cadbury Schweppes	Former Company Secretary
Cadbury Schweppes	Former Head Consultant
Cadbury Schweppes	Former Managing Director
Cadbury Schweppes	Former Managing Director Beverages
Cadbury Schweppes	Former Schweppes Board Director
Sainsbury's	Former Board Director
Sainsbury's	Former Chairman
Sainsbury's	Former Chief Executive
Sainsbury's	Former Financial Control Manager
Sainsbury's	Former Marketing Director
Sainsbury's	Former Marketing Executive
Sainsbury's	Former Research Manager, Property
Smith & Nephew	Chief Executive
Smith & Nephew	Former Chairman
Smith & Nephew	Former Chairman, Former Chief Executive
Smith & Nephew	Former Deputy Chief Executive
Smith & Nephew	Former Deputy Chief Executive
Smith & Nephew	Former Group Technical Director
Smith & Nephew	Former President Endoscopy Inc
Smith & Nephew	President S&N Inc.
Smith & Nephew	President Wound Management Inc
SSL International	Former Board Director
SSL International	Former Group Managing Director
Tesco	Chairman
Tesco	Chief Executive

Company	Role at time of interview
Tesco	Former Chairman
Tesco	Former Chief Executive
Tesco	Former Customer Service Manager
Tesco	Former Deputy Chairman
Tesco	Former Site Research Manager
Unilever	Former Company Secretary
Unilever	Former Board Director
Unilever	Former Chairman
Unilever	Former Chairman
Unilever	Former Chairman
Unilever	Former Chairman
Unilever	Former Chairman

Like all of us, managers make sense of messy, nonlinear processes by corralling events into chronological and logical sequences that suggest unambiguous and appealing lines of causality.[14] To counter the tendency to retrospective rationalization, we pushed our interviewees to give their thoughts on relatively open-ended questions[15]: "What was the strategy process like when you joined the company?," "Did the process change over time, and why (not)?," "Who wanted and did not want strategic change, and why do you think that was?," "Did strategy intentions and consequences align over time?" For the same reason, and to tease out contradictions as well as similarities in managers' recollected accounts and thus elicit finer-grained explanations, we asked a number of interviewees to explain the same events and processes, in which they had often been personally involved. We could then relate their explanations back to the historical event timelines we had built for each firm.

We took a number of steps to make the perspectives as rich as possible. First, we targeted as many generations of living executives as possible. In practice, we were able to interview four generations of managers at Cadbury Schweppes and Smith & Nephew, and three generations in the other four firms. Second, we aimed to interview managers who had been with their company for a minimum of 10 years, although this was not always possible for the fourth generation. Third, to "triangulate" our interview data, we realized that we needed the views of members, active and retired, not only of current leadership (what has been called the "dominant coalition," consisting generally speaking, but not necessarily exclusively, of the CEO, his or her top management team, and board members[16]), but also of those in "alternative" leadership coalitions, sometimes with very different opinions, waiting in the wings. This was a very important distinction, as we shall see. We began by interviewing those most obviously wedded to the dominant, "official" version of transformation attempts, whether successful or not, before consulting those who might have different views. Identifying who belonged to which grouping required access to observers, on both the inside and the outside, with an intimate knowledge of company workings.

In addition to many hours of top-level interviews, we were fortunate to be granted access to several private company archives, providing us with an invaluable direct source to supplement, and sometimes counter, managers' retrospective rationalizations. Gaining access to interviewees and private archives was very time-consuming. It took three researchers more than 18 months to convince company leaders that supporting the effort to interview different generations of managers and releasing their private archives was in both our and their interests. Company archives included board meeting notes covering the whole post-World War II period, and in the cases of Unilever and Smith & Nephew the entire 20th century. Researchers are hardly ever allowed to consult full board and group management minutes of the last 20 years, so this was an extremely rare privilege. We were the first noncommissioned researchers – and only the second research team ever – to gain sight of Unilever's most recent records. We also received unprecedented access to group management executive minutes at Smith & Nephew, providing a less formal, more detailed description of management discussions at the highest levels over the last three decades.

Finally, our visits to retired managers proved doubly useful, some of them having kept notes and minutes of their own on board and executive discussions going as far back as the 1950s. This proved especially useful in the case of Cadbury Schweppes. While incumbent managers were reluctant to permit full access to sensitive official archives, retired generations had no such hesitation in letting us consult their own private records.

Analyzing the data

How are deep patterns to be uncovered in the contextual profusion of the kind of material we had assembled? Our analysis relied on three strategies. First, we took an approach that was comparative and historical, and used multiple cases. To take the last first, analyzing more than one case permits a "replication" logic in which each one can be thought of as an independent experiment capable of confirming or disconfirming emerging conceptual insights.[17] Comparison is important because the resulting agreement and difference in their different ways provide insights enabling us to become more specific about causality.[18] The joint method of agreement and difference allows for insights into what are the necessary causal conditions for an effect to occur. For instance, we found a remarkable pattern of mobility in our three SSTs, but not in our non-SSTs. Furthermore, we found that the occurrence of remarkable patterns of mobility – for instance, the young Adrian Cadbury's promotion against seniority rules in the family – preceded transformational changes in all three SSTs. By contrast, absence of such mobility ushered in and accompanied a long period of drift.

Moving back and forth between efforts to identify and describe historical processes and the consolidated results of all of them, that is, the present,[19] prevented us from succumbing to the tendency to overemphasize either *change* on the one hand (which is what you see when you focus only on the present) or *continuity* on the other (the result of an exclusive focus on the past).[20] Another advantage of this research strategy is that it serves to frame a set of patterns of cause and effect that is both specific enough to be relevant to contemporary questions, and general enough to be relevant across different historical episodes. For instance, we found evidence of a small number of order-generating traditions in our three SST firms going back (more than) 50 years, and across four generations of managers. Other studies tend to focus on much more recent phenomena, one successful generation of leaders, and one specific type of arguments. The latter can engender less timeproof generalizations or conclusions, as in the case of a recent book on Nokia's strategic agility.[21] This is all the more the case when insufficient attention is paid to disconfirming or comparative evidence.

In practical terms, we started by framing comparative research questions to get a first feel for the capabilities and processes that differentiated SSTs from non-SSTs. Subsequently, we hypothesized that these capabilities and processes were institutionalized phenomena, the origins of which lay way back in time. By going back and forth between contemporary and historical findings, we were able gradually to open the black box of institutionalized phenomena. For instance, how do we explain Terry Leahy's very modest, almost "ordinary" demeanor compared with John Sainsbury's style of grand leadership? Going back in taken-for-granted time horizons allowed us to understand how prior acrimonious leadership disputes induced the gradual emergence of such a modest leadership style in Tesco.

A second analytical strategy involved the triangulation of secondary archival data and primary data in order to increase the dependability of our findings across the six companies studied.[22]

We also employed a third analytical strategy. Arguably, strategy can change structure as much as structure can change strategy.[23] To ensure transparency and consistency, we therefore analyzed our findings in a predetermined order. First, we studied the emergence of *structural* changes. Second, we studied which groups in the company, if any, undertook what *strategic actions* to improve the fit between corporate and business models. Finally, we analyzed the impact of companies' strategic initiatives on the *emergence of complementarities*, in particular the fit between industry archetypes and corporate and business models.

Lastly, we confirmed our interpretations by conducting a workshop with three of our interviewees: Clive Butler, a former board level executive director of Unilever, David Malpas, a former managing director of Tesco, and Sir Dominic Cadbury, a former chairman and chief executive of Cadbury Schweppes.

Confirmatory analysis of transcripts[24]

The personal interpretation of qualitative research always carries a risk of researcher bias or misinterpretation. So we also used a second, statistical methodology to confirm or refute the differences that we found between the SSTs and their comparators. Since we had rich accounts of the strategy development of the firms from generations of managers, we subjected these accounts to careful textual analysis. We were particularly alert to signs of what we described in Chapter 1 as "organizational ambidexerity" – the ability of a firm to be good at both business as usual and exploring new avenues, whether in strategy or organization. We provide a more technical description in a Methodology Appendix at the end of this chapter.

So we took the findings from the historical analysis, added findings from others' research on organizational ambidexterity, and created a list of characteristics that might describe a firm capable of both exploiting current capabilities to achieve a financial success, while exploring how it might develop new strategies based on new capabilities. We then employed the services of a researcher not previously associated with the project to reanalyze all the interviews and identify where managers were talking about any of the characteristics we had identified. He employed the following protocol:

- The interview transcripts consisted of everything from invitations to have coffee to telephone interruptions. For the purpose of this analysis, the researcher removed anything that was not related to explaining the processes of strategy development.

- The interviews were then broken down into time periods by decade. The interest here was to see if there were differences between the early stages of the firm's development and the period we were particularly interested in, that is, 1984–2003 (the subject of stage 1 of our study).
- The researcher then identified for each of these periods how much of the interviewees' time was spent explaining the strategy development of the firm in terms of each of the characteristics identified above. He did this by coding "chunks" of transcribed text from the interviews according to their match with the characteristics. In effect, what the researcher was looking for was what the interviewees most emphasized as explanations of the firm's strategy development.
- Samples of this coding were also undertaken by one of the authors of the book as a check for consistency.

We found this analysis especially useful in two respects. First, it enabled us to check whether the findings from the historical study corresponded with the findings from this "textual analysis." Second, since our findings (discussed in the chapters that follow) flagged up the importance of the evolution of management processes over time in these firms, we wanted a systematic check on the extent to which the managerial processes at work in the period 1984–2003 were the same as or built on the earlier managerial processes we had identified.

The results of this analysis are shown at the end of Chapter 7 as "The legacy of the traditions."

SUMMARY

From beginning to end – research design through three research phases to textual analysis – the study took us 5 years to complete. By itself, developing a research methodology robust enough to give us confidence in our eventual conclusions took 2 years. But the effort was worth it. By the end of the period of study, we had gone a long way to confirming that there are firms that had reinvented themselves without being obliged to do so by severe financial crisis in the 20-year period, even if, as we had suspected, they were rare. While "gold medalists" resembled "bronze medalists" in that they did all the same operational things but just a little better and faster, in some other respects they differed markedly – and those underlying differences, with origins located deep in the past, sometimes three or four generations back, were the reason that our three transformers had escaped the pull of drift and creeping obsolescence to which the nontransformers had succumbed. We look in detail at the individual company histories in Chapters 3, 4, 5, and 6.

METHODOLOGY APPENDIX

This appendix details our methodology for the frontier analysis and for the transcript analysis.

Frontier analysis methodology

Normal approaches in strategy and management (and indeed industrial organization in general) rely on comparisons between mean cross-sections of firms (as would be the case with regression analysis or analysis of variance). Population ecology studies rely on survivorship analysis that does not distinguish between levels of survivorship. More qualitative assessments have suffered from a problem of ex-post sampling problems, the most famous case of which is *In Search of Excellence*.[25]

Frontier analysis

Our approach is based on what is called "frontier analysis," which has a long tradition in economics and operations research, particularly for estimating production functions and for benchmarking activities. Frontier analysis is based on the simple logic that it is the extremes of distribution of the data that are of interest. In the case of production, this is the minimum cost associated with a volume of output (not the mean cost). In our case, it is maximum performance. Two approaches are used. One, called data envelopment analysis (DEA), is a linear programming approach that allows for the assessment of multiple outputs and can handle small samples, but suffers from the fact that it is nonparametric.[26] Stochastic frontier analysis is a parametric approach that accounts for the stochastic character of the data but requires larger sample sizes and can accommodate only one dependent variable.[27]

For this study, we chose to use DEA as a means of creating a sample of "frontier" performers. DEA was chosen because it allowed us to make use of multiple measures of performance and impose a more stringent set of criteria that required firms to be extreme on more than one dimension of performance. This was critical in our case because our reliance on DEA and secondary data meant that we could have made errors in selection if we had used a limited number of performance criteria. The output of interest to us was the *performance efficiency* of a firm, where performance efficiency was measured across multiple criteria and based on a comparison with a global industry peer set.

Figure 2.1 earlier shows an example of how such a performance measure is calculated for a situation with two output measures (space precludes us from going into much greater detail). The maximum efficiency measure is 1, and numbers below 1 can be roughly interpreted as percentage deviations from the frontier. Empirically, efficiency is measured as a radial projection from the origin to the nearest point on a plane in the space defined by the dimensions of performance. Frontier analysis puts heavy demands on the quality and comparability of data. Hence, we estimate frontiers on an industry-by-industry basis using comparable measures of performance (for example, excluding taxation, depreciation, and other factors that would be distorted by different accounting standards across countries) (see Figure 2.1).

The logic for the use of DEA in management research is outlined in a number of papers[28] and can be justified with recourse to resource-based and capabilities thinking.[29] The resource-based theory and dynamic capabilities approaches place emphasis on the unique, path-dependent, causally ambiguous components of a firm's structure as a major determinant of *long-term strategic* performance. However, tests of these theories traditionally rely on analysis that compares the mean performances of different cross-sections. DEA, by emphasizing extreme performance, is more in line with the logic of current strategy theory.

Selection of firms

The logic is that a firm is being benchmarked against not just other firms' performance in any given year, but any firm's performance in any given year. Therefore, each combination of firm and year is a potential frontier performer against which other firms are being compared. This creates several complications for which adjustments needed to be made. First, the performance measures must all be computed in comparable terms (such as adjusting for currency changes and inflation) and based on criteria for the industry. Second, where an industry shows changes in average performance efficiency over time, we need to adjust the distribution to account for such temporal patterns. For example, the telecom industry showed no change in average efficiency until around 2000, when the average firm's efficiency declined. Figure 2.4 shows the example of Reuters in the publishing industry, which was excluded based on criteria 2 and 3. Even though it was a frontier performer in 1999 and had quite good performance at times (the average performance efficiency in its industry being 0.65), this performance was erratic, with a significant collapse over the 4 years 2000–2003.

One problem of time period selection is sensitivity to start and end dates if the measure is the total or the average change from start point to end point. (We are all familiar with how managers and fund managers select periods to maximize reported performance.) The frontier technique avoids this problem by taking an annual (or other period) approach such that performance can be viewed as a pattern over multiple years, and with each year's performance independent of previous ones (that is, the technique does not look at change from the previous year). It estimates annual deviations from the frontier. Each deviation can then be plotted to show how far a company is from the frontier each year, thereby establishing a picture of performance over the entire period (see the example in Figure 2.4).

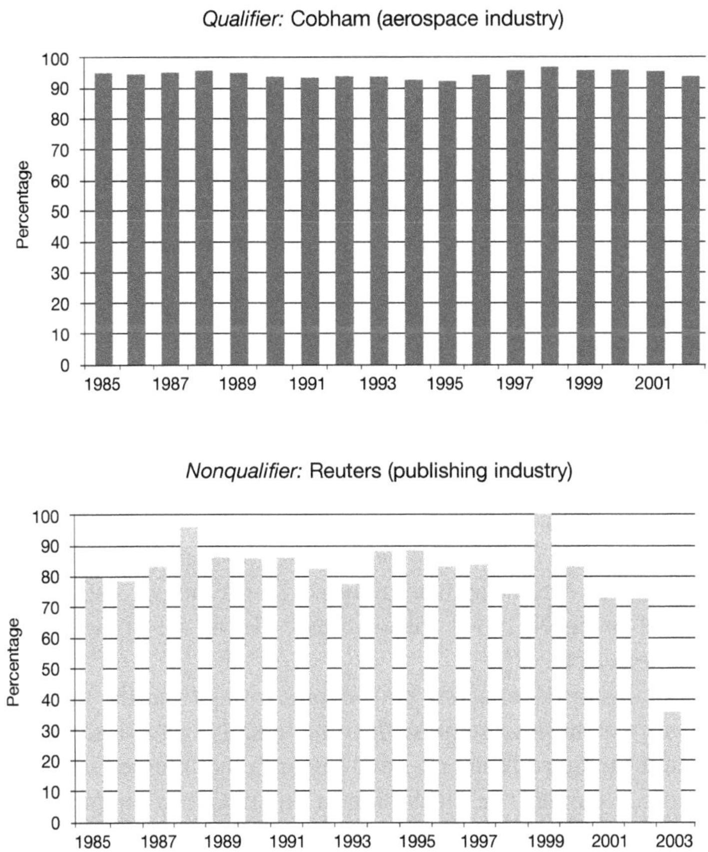

FIGURE 2.4 | Examples of annual deviations from the frontier – a qualifier and a nonqualifier as long-term superior performers

Annual deviation from the frontier

Once the performance frontier had been created for a particular industry, each company's "deviation" or distance from the frontier for any year was calculated. As we were estimating the performance frontier for 20 years, we were able to plot each company's performance relative to the frontier over time. This approach is illustrated in Figure 2.4 for two companies. The first company, Cobham, in the aerospace industry, easily qualified on the three criteria, as illustrated by the bar chart of their deviation from the frontier. In every year, Cobham was above the 90th percentile of performance relative to the frontier. In contrast, the second company, Reuters, in the publishing industry, shows the power of observing annual deviations. Reuters performed very well for the 15 years from 1985 to 1999, indeed being the frontier performer with a value of 1.0 in 1999, but it then went into rapid decline, falling below 0.4 by 2003. Hence, it easily failed both criteria 2 and 3. The Reuters example shows how examining the annual deviation from the frontier reduces the sensitivity to start and end dates for measures of performance over a total time period. Reuters was indeed a superior performer until its change of strategy in 2001 to diversify into Internet-related businesses. Similarly, Vodafone might be at risk of dropping off the list if the analysis were extended through 2006.

Transcript analysis

Personal interpretation of qualitative research always carries the risk of researcher bias or misinterpretation. So we also used a second, statistical methodology to confirm or refute the differences that we found between the SSTs and their comparators. Since we had rich accounts of the strategy development of the firms from generations of managers, we subjected these accounts to careful textual analysis. To do this we used a standard procedure of using NVivo 8 software to code all the content of the 46 interview transcripts.

While the historical analysis built explanations from the data itself, in this analysis we chose to begin with some tentative propositions from the management literature based on prior research that seemed to be relevant to our research theme. The discussion in this chapter summarizes this. In particular, one theme in the literature was of special interest. The idea of "organizational ambidexterity" is that businesses need to be simultaneously capable of managing the *exploitation* of existing capabilities as well as the *exploration* for new capabilities on which to build their future strategy. This literature seemed particularly appropriate to our research interests. However, as noted in this chapter, most of what is written on organizational ambidexterity lacks a historical perspective. We were therefore interested in to what extent the ideas in this literature (1) were to be found in the interview transcripts, and (2) corresponded to our historical analysis.

We recruited a research assistant not associated with the data collection and historical analysis to reanalyze all the interview transcripts in terms of the ambidexterity literature. We employed concepts related to three key organizational features found in that literature: the organizational structure, the organization's leadership, and the organizational culture/context. The coding scheme consists of three types of codes:

- *Codes that were directly adopted from the ambidexterity literature.* These codes and their definitions were directly adopted from the ambidexterity literature.
- *Codes that were altered or added based on insights from the historical analysis.* Our historical analysis allowed us to refine some of the ambidexterity codes or provide opposites to those codes. *It is important to note, however, that, in order to avoid bias in coding, the researcher who undertook the coding had no familiarity with the historical analysis.*
- *Codes that were added based on our own insights during the coding process.* During the coding process, we made continuous refinements to the coding scheme in two ways: (1) by refining codes in order to build subcodes that provided explanations more closely aligned with the transcript data, and (2) by creating "free codes" for passages that seemed to be relevant, but for which we did not have any *a priori* developed codes from the ambidexterity literature.

We employed these codes as a basis for making sense of the transcripts. We systematically read all the transcripts and noted where passages from these transcripts corresponded to the codes we had created. We developed coding procedures to limit the effect of potential biases associated with the nature of the data and the data analysis techniques employed. Rather than coding all the interviews for one organization first and then moving on to the next organization, we alternated between organizations. This encouraged us to take a relatively objective stance toward what was said in the interviews, and reduced the impact that a previous interview would have had on our interpretations if it had come from the same organization. We did not expect the organizations in our sample to perfectly represent opposite poles on the coding dimensions we developed. Therefore, we allowed all concepts to apply to both sets of organizations. However, we expected that the extent to which a concept applied to a particular set of organizations would differ.

Our primary interest in this analysis was not to establish if a particular transcript corresponded to our codes, or indeed if the transcripts pertaining to one organization did so. Our primary interests were twofold: (1) to establish whether there was a pattern of differences between SST firms and non-SST firms, and (2) if there was, to uncover to what extent and how this corresponded to the explanations derived from the historical analysis.

Part II

What We Found

CHAPTER 3

The Three Successful Strategic Transformers: The Beginnings

How did Cadbury Schweppes, unlike Unilever, manage to develop a coherent and leading portfolio in both branding and geographical terms from the 1980s onwards? Why has Smith & Nephew been able to refocus its R&D and marketing practices on high-margin healthcare niches in the US, in contrast to SSL International, which has been forced to retreat to a purely consumer business? Why did Sainsbury, in stark contrast to Tesco, struggle to renew its customer value proposition, develop a non-food business, and expand geographically?

In this and the next chapters, we demonstrate that conventional media and business interpretations of important developments at Tesco, Smith & Nephew, and Cadbury Schweppes are at best partial, at worst severely misleading. Careful historical analysis shows instead that the roots of these companies' success are to be found more than 50 years ago and not just in more recent, "radical" changes in management, business model, structure, or culture. In fact, when considered historically, these latter changes are not that radical at all, but quite logical extensions of developments that started in the 1950s and 60s.

All six of our companies possessed their own model of success, a dominant logic imbued by their founders at the start of our analysis after World War II. In what follows in Chapter 3, we explain the dominant logics of the successful transformers and the management processes that developed from World War II to the late 1970s. In Chapters 4 and 5, we then explain the developments and eventual breakthroughs over the next two decades for Cadbury Schweppes, Tesco, and Smith & Nephew. In Chapter 6, we compare these developments with what happened in our comparators, that is, Unilever, J Sainsbury, and SSL International.

In this chapter, we will show how the three successful strategic transformers first developed their dominant logics, then created room for alternative developments, and eventually allowed the emergence of alternative business models.

DOMINANT LOGICS

Before their merger in 1969 Cadbury and Schweppes were very different companies, following very different dominant logics. For one thing, while Schweppes had split management and ownership as early as 1834,[1] Cadbury Brothers remained a predominantly family-owned and family-directed company[2]: indeed, until the merger its chairman had always been a direct descendant of John Cadbury. It was no ordinary family either. The Cadburys stood out by virtue of their active Quaker background, their century-long roots in Birmingham and Bournville, and their very own management style, dubbed "Cadburyism"[3] – a paternalistic blend of harmony and worker welfare very different from North American scientific management. All in all, Cadbury was a very rooted British company that abroad too followed the flag, setting up branches almost exclusively in the Commonwealth.

Schweppes, by contrast, was a somewhat rootless, London-based creation in the image of its founder Jacob Schweppe, an immigrant who lacked strong British, family, or religious ties. Schweppes' sole "glue," as it were, lay in its 20th-century predilection for recruiting ex-members of the Royal Air Force as managers. Indeed, after World War I, Schweppes had become known as something of a "military base."[4] In contrast to Cadbury, Schweppes quickly shed many of its family connections. Jacob Schweppe sold most of his interests as early as 1799, and in 1834 ownership changed hands again. Although the descendants of the purchasers, particularly the Kemp-Welch family, would remain associated with the company until 1950, Schweppes would be run in an increasingly detached fashion. In 1897 the company went public, and in 1919 the Kemp-Welch family relinquished the chairmanship. The new chairman, Sir Ivor Phillips, coupled the old model of financial opportunism with a greater emphasis on geographical expansion. Under Phillips' direction, which lasted until 1940, the dominant logic of Schweppes was *to expand internationally through financial opportunism*, in particular by extending the shareholder base. When Phillips stepped down as chairman in 1940, the company had more than 2,700 ordinary shareholders.

Cadbury's historical dominant logic, by contrast, could be described as *enterprising and fair, but conservative*. The enterprise, clearly reflected in Cadbury's role in turning the British into the world's biggest chocolate consumers (largely thanks to the launch of the iconic Dairy Milk brand), was an active and explicit part of the company's Quaker values, in which "candour, freedom of speech ... a spirit of toleration and liberty ... are the dominant notes."[5] The emphasis on fairness, manifest in both the paternalism with which the company treated its employees and its insistence on product quality, came from the same origin. Cadbury had campaigned against both slavery and alcohol, as well as the adulteration of the product. The company's reluctance to venture into areas beyond its core competences, meanwhile, testified to an innate conservatism.

A much younger company than Cadbury and Schweppes, Tesco in the early 1950s remained a one-man band, recognizably still the descendant of the price-conscious "market stall" for the London East End working class that it had been at its birth. With founder Jack Cohen still firmly in charge, *pile it high, sell it cheap* was the unchallenged dominant logic, and *retailing is a people business*[6] the only acceptable philosophy. Subsequently, Cohen would be recognized as "one of the really great businessmen," the creator of a huge business. At the time, however, nicknames like "Sir Save-a-Lot," "Slasher Jack," the "barrow-boy," and the "Guv'nor" spoke eloquently of a management style variously qualified as "cavalier" and "seat-of-the-pants," and a business model that could be summed up as "always keep your hand over the money and be ready to run."[7] Not surprisingly, market leader "John Sainsbury would have been as rude as hell about Tesco ... Sainsbury would've said there are no standards here, he would've said there was no honesty with the customers."[8]

Finally, Smith & Nephew, in strong contrast to Tesco and Cadbury, had undergone a profound shift of focus since its founding in the 1850s. Founder T.J. Smith had started out supplying hospitals with cod-liver oil. His nephew H.N. Smith smartly moved out of cod-liver oil into bandages, effectively turning the company into a textiles concern, consolidating the move with the acquisition of sanitary-towel manufacturer Sashena in 1912. Diminution of family control in the first decades of the 20th century laid the foundation for the incorporation of Smith & Nephew Associated Companies in 1937.

Behind their willingness to experiment, founder and nephew remained true to a consistent dominant logic to which they both contributed: *to compete by spending less on technological innovation than their rivals while generating proportionally higher sales through superior entrepreneurship and customer relationship management.*

T.J. was certainly both "entrepreneurial" and technologically savvy, combining close relationships with pharmaceutical bodies with a thoroughly international outlook. Witness his successful approach to cod-liver oil, which he sourced from Canada and refined in Norway. T.J. began the shift into textiles by going into surgical dressings, a move that was enthusiastically prosecuted by his nephew H.N. Like his uncle, H.N. was happy to bring in technology from elsewhere (for example, Germany, the most advanced healthcare market in the interwar years) rather than commit the company to expensive and risky research. Steadily expanding the textile business, he also made a number of acquisitions. But what really differentiated the two men was H.N.'s greater proficiency in selling and marketing to the medical profession mainly imported products that he subsequently exported to the Commonwealth.[9] H.N. relinquished control of the parent company to non-family members in the 1930s. Despite a waning family influence, the trends set by T.J. and H.N. were to leave a lasting imprint on the company.

ROOM FOR ALTERNATIVE DEVELOPMENTS

During the 1950s and 60s several trends combined to push our champions into new dynamics of transformation of a largely unintended nature. Small but significant changes to established corporate patterns and routines at Cadbury and Schweppes, Tesco, and Smith & Nephew, broader changes in the UK political economy, and leaders' growing confidence and ambition, all played a part. Among the corporate changes, the most significant was the emergence of challengers to the prevailing dominant logic: a professional accountant and some argumentative family members in Tesco; a stubborn R&D engineer and "boffin" at textiles-oriented Smith & Nephew; a less cautious, more risk-taking family member as chief executive at Cadbury; and two men with a professional rather than an RAF background at Schweppes. The major changes in the UK political economy were the loosening of post-World War II price and exchange controls, the increasing openness of domestic industries to US-driven competitive dynamics, and the rising affluence of customers. The "big" ideas were Adrian Cadbury's dream of turning a largely UK-based company into an international player and chairman Watkinson's propensity – compensation, perhaps, for an abruptly terminated political career – to think in grandiose terms; Jack Cohen's desire to shine in the media headlines; and at Smith & Nephew, chairman George Leavey's penchant for the grand gesture.

Cadbury and Schweppes: the route to an unlikely merger (World War II – 1968)

As national champion of British chocolate, operating in a less than cut-throat industry, Cadbury could have been excused a little complacency. In the first half of the 20th century, managers had come to view other companies less as competitors than as organic parts of a comfortable chocolate-industry ecology that had evolved for the comfort of all. Only Nestlé was considered a real competitive threat. It was in this climate, under an old-school chairman, Paul Cadbury, that new man Adrian Cadbury began to make his way in the company.

Adrian had joined the company in 1952, somewhat unexpectedly becoming personnel director in 1958. In that capacity, he helped set up the "Beeches training course" to increase the transformative potential and mobility of "bright younger managers from around the company, world-wide." While doing so, he was struck by the idea that "there was the possibility of doing a good deal in the way of the [needed] reorganisation," by using these bright young men to set up "a small commission … to study our internal and external organisation." There were two pressing problems. First, Cadbury was experiencing "high labor turnover and serious dissatisfaction in the factory … because of the greatly increased complexity of the factory and organisation since WWII." Interdepartmental recriminations made it hard to agree on the causes, which in Cadbury's opinion were to be found in not any one department "but our own internal organisation, which was not capable of carrying out what was asked of it under the conditions of 1960." This linked with a second problem: the difficulty of finding time in the board "to discuss how our present organisation functions or what our long term intentions are."[10]

Adrian found the results of the Beeches course encouraging enough to suggest that "three or four of our senior staff … might work out a blueprint for the future," paying particular attention to factory management, the Bournville office structure, and the relationship with other group companies.[11] Even if an improvement plan took time to implement, "[it] would have a great effect on morale in the factory and enable us to work the present system to the best possible effect in the meantime."[12]

Adrian's proposals anticipated growing awareness on the board that the internationalization of fast-moving consumer goods markets could spell the end of the comfortable national product oligopolies. Alternative archetypes of organizing were already on the horizon – on the one hand, there was the Mars model based on international mass-manufacturing facilities for an increasingly diversified portfolio of, first, snack foods and chocolate candies, and later main meals; on the other, there was the Coca-Cola model of international brand marketing, supported by an international franchising network. Both the Mars and Coca-Cola archetypes would eventually prove to be relevant to the merged Cadbury and Schweppes.

But how did this merger come about? Schweppes' financial star had waned somewhat in the interwar period. With the ascent of Frederick Hooper to the chairmanship in 1948, however, the company's fortunes appeared to be about to change. Having learnt his trade in Schweppes' more energetic subsidiary Rose,[13] Hooper brought a new marketing shrewdness to the company. Reared in a more vigorous, less old-fashioned culture, Hooper pursued a new "sales orientation," going for "anything that could add to the Schweppes profit."[14] He also brought renewed geographical ambition, pursuing expansion in both Europe and the US, shrewdly using the services of Commander Edward Whitehead, an "engaging walrus" who became chairman of Schweppes USA in 1952, to open up the US market.[15] Yet despite Hooper's efforts, as Dominic Cadbury explained:

> Schweppes was very vulnerable at that time to the growth of nonreturnable bottles, private label and the strength of the supermarket chains. The factories, production and distribution structures were geared to the higher margin returnable bottles sold through the licensed trade.

The Schweppes board did, however, leave room for one unprecedented development: the emergence of two senior executives with a professional rather than an RAF background. Managing director in waiting Basil Collins and future finance director James Forbes had also come up through the more unconventional ranks at Rose. With their insistence on, respectively, longer term strategy and a greater degree of financial professionalism, Collins and Forbes were instrumental in steering Schweppes in the direction of, first, diversification into foods, and later the search for a complementary merger partner. After a largely unsuccessful foray into jams and jellies, chairman Hooper retired in 1964, to be succeeded by Harold Watkinson, a former Conservative defense minister, who had just been sacked in Prime Minister Macmillan's infamous "night of the long knives." Together, the triumvirate concluded that, the domestic soft drinks market being largely saturated, overseas expansion was key to Schweppes' future. The snag was that, as Forbes insisted, Schweppes' capital base was too lean to allow for such an expansion – and the 1968 acquisition of Typhoo Tea only accentuated the problem.[16] A longer term solution finally emerged in autumn 1968, when Cadbury – well padded, cash-rich, domestically strong – was identified as a complementary merger partner. The companies began talks soon thereafter and came to an agreement in January 1969.

Clearly, the very "long-term oriented" Cadbury family was categorically not about to adopt Schweppes' opportunistic focus on sales at all costs. For the Cadburys, only the long term really mattered, and year-to-year fluctuations were much less significant.[17] So what prompted the merger with such an "alien" counterpart? One element was the Cadbury board's decision to go public in 1962, bringing increased pressure to respond to the shorter term needs of institutional investors. Crucially, directors also started paying attention to the views of younger family members and managers. These voices were arguing for strategic change on two fronts. Adrian Cadbury believed the company needed nothing short of a change in competitive identity that would position itself "not as a chocolate firm but as a food company,"[18] while some of the younger managers were arguing that the Mars model of mass manufacturing was the way forward.[19]

Another development would give more urgent impetus to the board's willingness to countenance change. In an increasingly open UK economy, Cadbury was suddenly an acquisition target. The first result was an unprecedented change to family succession patterns: to his own "great surprise," Adrian, the youngest board member, was appointed chairman. The memos on diversification and manufacturing changes that Adrian "had been pushing … at the board" had had their effect, if indirectly: he had won "the support of the non-family members of the board, who saw more clearly perhaps than the family, the need for change."[20]

There was a new window of contestability in the company, and Adrian seized the moment to exploit it. He quickly brought in more outside help, this time in the shape of management consultants McKinsey, to "help the board formulate its long-term objectives and strategy, and then to develop the form of organization best suited to attain these goals."[21]

By this time, a number of companies were courting Cadbury with a view to acquisition or merger: Consolidated Foods, General Mills, and Mars in the US, along with British groups such as United Biscuits and Cavenham Foods. Meanwhile, Cadbury was pursuing the US-based Campbell Soup Company.[22] In the end, all these options came to nothing, and as a last resort Cadbury was left with Schweppes, Cadbury's almost exact opposite – a non-family company with a secular, "gin and tonic" reputation and an "over-lean" financial structure.

Of course, antithetical could be read as potentially complementary: while Schweppes viewed Cadbury as "over-fat" and overmanned, Cadbury was conscious that Schweppes had the acquisition experience and "decision speed" that it itself lacked – steeped as it was in a "lumbering," consensus style with special committees for almost any task. There were other complementarities. Geographically, Cadbury's expansion was limited to the "low growth areas" of the "old Commonwealth," while Schweppes had achieved some position of strength in Europe and even the US – "strong growth areas." Cadbury products were winter-oriented and Schweppes ones much more summer-oriented. Finally, Schweppes chairman Watkinson "was very concerned about being taken over ... and they'd been growing a foods business for the same sorts of reasons as us."[23] Beyond these considerations, several of our interviewees conceded that there simply was not much time for rational analysis of the pros and cons of a merger.

Tesco: first cracks in Cohen's governorship (World War II – 1963)

After the war, it became harder for Tesco's founder Cohen to run the expanding and modernizing retail business on his own. Up till then, UK food retailing had consisted of independent grocers and cooperatives rather than multiples – retailers with 10 or more stores.[24] Thanks to resale price maintenance legislation, food manufacturers held great bargaining power on the supply side. With the end of the war, this situation changed rapidly, first with the erosion of resale price maintenance, and then with the rising affluence and mobility[25] of a society eager to shed its postwar sense of austerity in favor of US-style consumerism. US concepts of first self-service and later supermarkets became increasingly popular, benefiting the multiples with their superior financial capacity to invest in the new retailing concepts and reap economies of scale.

If not a laggard, the Guv'nor's continuing urge for absolute control ensured that Tesco would not be a retail pioneer either. Yes, Cohen had taken the company "public" in 1947, setting up a corporate board in the process, but this did not mean he had any intention of relinquishing control. He was chairman and by far the majority shareholder – his 922,910 shares compared with 16,715 held between them by Albert Carpenter and Thomas Freake, Cohen's co-directors. Nor was there much contestability of management decisions. After continuing protests at Cohen's refusal to brook interference with his individualistic marketing and production methods,[26] Freake resigned in 1950 – some say he was sacked, "on the grounds that decisions with which [Cohen] was in disagreement had been made without reference to him."[27]

This sudden event would usher in small personnel changes with significant long-term consequences, albeit altogether unintended and unforeseen by Cohen. In 1951 Edgar Collar joined the company. A qualified accountant with extensive retailing experience, Collar as "financial wizard" would prove invaluable in both implementing a proper corporate model of financial control and opening up the board's decision processes to disagreement and contestation. Having known Cohen for some years, Collar was well prepared for the latter's trading exuberance, and although he was unable to curtail all Cohen's trading and acquisition excesses, his influence on the company was described by several fellow managers in the most complimentary terms: "He was a man that Jack Cohen couldn't dictate to. He kept him and everyone else in their place ... His expertise really started the company's post-war expansion. Mr Collar laid down the ground rules for larger stores, and kept a tight rein on finances."[28]

Collar's example emboldened one of Cohen's sons-in-law, Hyman Kreitman, to champion his own alternative ideas.[29] Kreitman joined the company before the war, and the board in 1947; by the 1950s he could see that his father-in-law's "pile it high, sell it cheap" market trading methods were rapidly becoming antiquated. It was time to heed new developments such as self-service. Cohen would later claim that he was the pioneer of US-style self-service in the UK. In fact, without Kreitman's insistence on substantial investment in the new methods,[30] Tesco might have missed the opportunity altogether. By 1955 four-fifths of Tesco stores had been converted to self-service, and Tesco had regained the trading momentum it had lost since 1948.

But there was more to it than the move to self-service. The scrapping of building licenses in 1954 triggered a property and takeover boom in which Cohen was a characteristically enthusiastic participant. With Burnards, bought the next year, he acquired a highly professional management team that was well versed in the cut-price business model that Tesco formally espoused but had lost its focus on after the war.[31] Burnards thus provided Tesco with the means to tighten up its trading policies. But it did much more too. The arrival of Arthur Thrush added an invaluable dimension of acquisition and retailing expertise to Tesco's management.[32] Thrush, entirely unpremeditatedly, would function as the mentor of the "management trainees" who joined the company after 1959. The first of these was Ian MacLaurin – although the title *"management trainee"* was a misnomer, given the lack of anything resembling a Tesco training program. When MacLaurin arrived, Tesco, although still basically operating on the market-stall principle, was performing well.

Two years later, in the teeth of Collar's dire warnings of overstretch, Cohen pushed through the acquisition of Williamsons, an old-fashioned, ill-managed enterprise that had recently been taken over by a group of speculative property developers headed by David Behar. The addition of the talented Behar to the Tesco board was one of two good things to come out of the Williamson purchase, the other being Cohen's extremely reluctant concession to Collar and Kreitman of the need to call in outside specialists to design a proper warehouse system.

Still, Collar and Kreitman were dissatisfied. As with self-service, it was hard to convince Cohen to invest in the new supermarket format, even though other multiples such as Sainsbury's were already forging ahead. Again, it was Kreitman, with strong support from Behar and aided by Thrush's expertise, who finally committed Cohen to an investment program in supermarketing by the early 1960s.[33] The effort proved so draining, however, that Kreitman resigned in the process. Cohen took advantage of Kreitman's temporary departure to make two momentous decisions. Against Collar's and Kreitman's advice, he bought the northern multiple Irwin's to complement the existing southern portfolio, allowing him to boast that, with almost 400 stores, Tesco was the first to have gone "national." Equally important, Cohen persuaded his second son-in-law, Leslie Porter, to join the company.[34] With a background in textiles rather than food, and only too familiar with the family dynamics, Porter was initially reluctant, only accepting when promised that he could launch his own non-food division, which became known as "Home 'n' Wear."

Cohen did leave some room for others to initiate changes. Kreitman eventually came back. Collar managed to bring a measure of financial discipline to the "unruly" company strategy. Ironically, by focussing entirely on his own agenda of cheap diversification to fuel volume growth, Cohen left space for others to anticipate industry developments, thus inadvertently sowing the seeds of greater contestability and mobility.

Smith & Nephew: much ado about the R&D boffins?[35] (World War II – 1962)

Since its incorporation in 1937 Smith & Nephew Associated Companies (SANACO) had effectively operated as a conglomerate, with chairman H.N. Smith taking an increasingly hands-off stance and delegating many of his powers to other board directors running their own subsidiaries. The conglomerate form would also suit Smith & Nephew well as a transitional device in its search for a clearer competitive identity in the subsequent decades.

Before the war, Smith & Nephew had often looked to Germany for technological innovations – for example obtaining the British rights to Elastoplast bandages from Lohmann, and licensing much of the manufacturing process for Gypsona bandages from other German companies. Later the company was quick to reap the windfalls of Germany's wartime defeat. Thus, chairman George Leavey quickly snapped up Herts Pharmaceuticals, previously a subsidiary of Beiersdorf, largely to get hold of its research unit. Britain was a technological laggard in healthcare; only after 1945 did it become common for a company to have its own research laboratory.[36] In the case of retail chemists such as Smith & Nephew, the move often owed more to fashion than a real belief in home-grown R&D.

No one on Smith & Nephew's board really understood the logic of research. Although the board's view was that, in strictly commercial terms, the rewards of research were rarely commensurate with the cost, time, and effort that went into new drug production, Frank Moore, Herts' boss and a close associate of Leavey, was given the go-ahead to set up a combined Smith & Nephew Research as a separate company in 1952. But priorities chopped and changed. In retrospect, there had been a real possibility of building up a pharmaceutical company in the early 1950s, but the board's strategy had been too confused to take advantage of it. Only in 1956 was a subcommittee formed to address pharmaceutical policy. Although the recommendations of this committee resulted in a separate pharmaceutical subsidiary, the message again was muddled. It was deemed too risky for the subsidiary to specialize in antitubercular drugs, its old core product line, as their prices were tumbling worldwide. Moreover, the research budget and philosophy of the board with regards to pharma was not commensurate with its diversification and growth aims; even struggling companies such as ICI had a pharmaceutical research budget bigger than Smith & Nephew's entire pharmaceutical turnover.[37]

The pharmaceutical research effort, such as it was, now sat rather uncomfortably in a company whose management focus was mainly on textiles, dressings, and feminine hygiene, a focus that came to be problematic. This became brutally evident in the 1950s, when George Whittaker's idea of turning Smith & Nephew into the main provider to the UK's National Health Service (NHS) of any textile-related product was shot down by Health Minister Enoch Powell, who bluntly pointed out that sourcing was cheaper from Poland. It became still clearer in the early 1960s, when a downturn in the market[38] forced textiles director Kenneth Bradshaw into a wholesale rationalization of the group's textiles operations.

The reason why research, a textiles subsidiary, and several other unrelated subsidiaries could live under one roof at Smith & Nephew was that they operated independently. But if research and textiles were not significant profit generators, where did Smith & Nephew's profitability come from? The answer was consumer products: plaster of Paris bandages, the Elastoplast brand, sanitary towels,[39] and Nivea moisturizing cream, a highly lucrative legacy from Herts Pharmaceuticals that even its previous owner had grossly undervalued. Unfortunately, the Smith & Nephew board did not fully understand the logic of Nivea as a toiletry rather than a cosmetic. Despite this lack of understanding, and unaided by any high-profile marketing effort, Nivea soon contributed almost as much to Smith & Nephew's consumer sales as Elastoplast.

EMERGENCE OF AN ALTERNATIVE MODEL

In the three companies, what started off as small changes to established patterns in the 1950s and early 1960s were now coalescing into a full-blown alternative model of transformation. Alternative leaders – Adrian Cadbury, Kreitman, Thrush, and Porter at Tesco, research champion Don Seymour at Smith & Nephew – now wielded considerable boardroom influence, even though the old guard – Harold Watkinson, Jack Cohen, and George Whittaker (and later Kenneth Bradshaw) – men moulded in the old dominant logic, were still in control.

Unlike those at the top, these leaders in waiting (or "shadow leaders" as we think of them) could see that the relationship between the corporate center and the business units was changing and needed to be encouraged. The clash between the old and the new led to emotional and acrimonious boardroom debates, acerbated by the old guard's tendency to think "big." The alternative leaders gradually opted to combine their formal work on the board with a more improvisational, informal type of leadership. Although it was hard to confront the old dominant logic head on in the boardroom, it was easier to fashion an informal framework of thinking challenge behind the scenes, even if, almost by definition, this would incorporate a type of intentionality that was piecemeal and emergent in character. In fact, this became a strength, accommodating both the continuity of the old dominant logic – and financial performance – and the anticipation of a new dominant logic – and a better financial performance – in an environment of rapidly changing competitive conditions.[40]

As well as championing a diverging commercial logic, the new "alternative dominant coalitions" fostered a more tolerant human resources approach, sheltering a new generation of champions from outright authoritarianism. All this led, not necessarily intentionally, to the emergence of four crucial new traditions in the three companies: traditions of continuity, anticipation, contestability, and mobility. Most noteworthy is that their making involved a minimum of "blood-letting" and formally driven changes. Instead, they evolved out of an improvised process of informal conflict and accommodation and movements of personnel that organically and gradually translated into formal transformations. These improvisations were not so much devoid of logic than unusual: they implied an uncommon combination of "thinking big" and tolerance for failure on the part of the dominant coalition (a first generation of leaders); a receptiveness to innovation and a willingness to wait for "happy accidents" by an alternative dominant coalition (a combination of first and predominantly second generations of leaders) waiting in the wings; and urgency and new insights on the part of champions of alternative logics (the emerging third generation of leaders).

Cadbury Schweppes: the emerging "long view" (1969–79)

For the odd couple, Cadbury and Schweppes, there was no honeymoon period. After they merged in 1969, it took a decade before a post-merger dominant logic emerged: a business model combining conservative entrepreneurship in core confectionary and beverages competences with a corporate exercise of financial control. The road to this new logic was painful, however – which is perhaps not surprising since the merger almost amounted to a clash of civilizations. Whereas the Schweppes executives of that time described Cadbury as a company run by enterprising "choirboys" and "teetotalist" Quakers, Cadbury executives saw Schweppes as "gin and tonic drinking Londoners" with a "short-term cowboy approach."

The first post-merger board was headed by archetypical Schweppes man and ex-politician Harold Watkinson. He had the vision to see that Schweppes needed a partner to remain independent and that Cadbury would be that partner.[41] Emotions ran high, however, during Watkinson's reign, largely because of his board's focus on profitability and short-term issues. Still, some of that short-term focus on results may have been exactly what Cadbury needed.

Thus, in the first 5 years of the 1970s the focus at the main board level was on cost-cutting and profit improvement. It was not a particularly successful period, however, Watkinson's grand international ambitions perpetually in conflict with the then managing director Adrian Cadbury's loathing of excess and more cautious approach. As a result, most of

Cadbury Schweppes's moves in the first part of the 1970s were small in scale and had little impact on its overall performance. As Dominic Cadbury explained:

> The Company became too thinly spread across four major consumer sectors which now included Health and Hygiene with the acquisition of Jeyes. In each sector we were faced with larger world class competitors and had brand leadership in only two of them with the Cadbury and Schweppes brand. We had strategically outgrown our strength and needed more focus.[42]

Clearly, the merged company was a new experience for everyone. Rather remarkably:

> the rationale for the merger didn't depend on a purge of top management and there were no enforced redundancies. Some executives enjoyed the new atmosphere and flourished and some didn't and left, largely of their own volition. In the early days the pressure from the main board was on the individual businesses to improve results, leaving their Boards to select and promote their management. It didn't take long for the more able people to emerge and form the future top management team. The process was evolutionary. It was clear from the beginning that Adrian would take over as Chairman when Harold Watkinson retired and the most able Schweppes member of the original main board, Basil Collins, would become the Group Management Director with the title being changed to that of Chief Executive.[43]

Meanwhile, faced with a mediocre financial performance and an evaporating organizational focus, an alternative group of new-generation Cadburyists emerged in the shadows of the main board. Critical of the short-termism that had come to dominate the company, it advocated a return to core competences and values. It involved people as disparate as the MBA-holder Dominic Cadbury, the engineer Peter Gregory, and the self-made Mike Gifford, who had been recruited from ICL as financial director of ailing Cadbury Schweppes Australia. Their version of Cadburyism seemed to be a combination of the old Cadbury "long view" with the "Schweppes "value for money" orientation. Board members such as Adrian Cadbury and Basil Collins gave background support to these new champions.

In many ways, however, it was Gifford who embodied the happy accident that Cadbury and Collins were waiting for. In a company split culturally, politically, and economically, the Australian company was unique in that it was managed as one. In this Australian microcosm, Mike Gifford developed a new logic of financial control. The accident came when, after a brief spell as chief executive of the now rejuvenated Australian firm, Gifford asked for a move to the UK. Collins and Cadbury agreed, little realizing at the time the impact that Gifford's tough new logic would provide.

Gifford was a handful. One colleague commented, "He was very rough on a lot of people at different times," regardless of their Cadbury or Schweppes background or their formal status. He would routinely "rubbish" board proposals he disapproved of, but Adrian Cadbury tolerated such directness with a resigned, "I can cope with one like you on the Board, but not two," acknowledging that while Gifford added nothing to boardroom harmony, he had the great merit of being a "strategic thinker" and "teaching the whole of the Cadbury Schweppes group balance sheet management."[44] Colleagues recall his standpoint as one less concerned with "what does the accounting code of the time require me to do?," but rather with "what makes economic sense." "He also demanded robust financial justification for investment decisions and "taught us to sweat our assets and aim for a 25% return on all operating assets."[45]

What is more, world economic developments presented Cadbury Schweppes' new-generation leadership with an inviting opportunity to fulfill international growth ambitions and complement the "value for money" model by entry into the US. Aided by a strong pound, with Collins and Adrian Cadbury in the driving seat, in 1978 Cadbury Schweppes passed a milestone with its first significant US confectionery acquisition: Connecticut-based Peter Paul. At a stroke, Peter Paul gave Cadbury Schweppes a 10 percent share of the US confectionery market. Domestically too, decisive action was necessary: increasing competition in the confectionery industry had cut Cadbury's share of the UK chocolate market from 31 percent in 1975 to 26 percent in 1977. Under this prompting, Cadbury's management accelerated the shift to a Mars-style centralized low-cost, mass-production organizational structure.

Despite the sharper corporate focus, relationships on the board remained strained after Watkinson's retirement, largely due to Cadbury mistrust of the group managing director, ex-Schweppes man Basil Collins. Collins, for his part, was suspicious of a return to old-style Cadbury values, and in 1982 retrospectively wrote:

> I have to tell you ... there has already been expressed considerable misgivings as to the possiblity of what is referred to as a 'reversion to consensus management' and to blurred or shared responsibility at the top.[46]

Tesco: difficult family relationships and the emergence of an "alternative board" (1964–76)

By the mid-1960s, Tesco's corporate decision-making processes were beset by family strife. Difficult family relationships – involving Cohen, his daughters, and his two sons-in-law – intruded into the home as well as the boardroom:

> throughout the 1960s and 1970s, the rows came home to Cohen's flat, the daughters talked to the mother, and there was a whole sort of family aspect ... Tesco wasn't only run in the boardroom, it was run in parallel with domestic family issues.[47]

After Collar's death in June 1963, Cohen saw his chance to reassert his dominance over the board, and in particular the Tesco vice-chairman and holding company managing Hyman Kreitman. Kreitman was a cautious man, patiently awaiting the opportunity to carry through his plans for integrating all the group businesses into a single corporate whole without incurring Cohen's wrath. The latter remained an acrimonious and divisive presence, however,[48] continually testing Kreitman's patience as if goading him to resign, and in one episode causing him such frustration that they reportedly almost came to blows.[49]

The family disputes were a distraction in a retailing industry where competitive pressures were mounting and which was increasingly consolidating around new supermarket, and, from the end of the 1960s, out-of-town[50] and hypermarket developments.[51] Tesco's immediate answer to new industry developments was still very much more of the same: much of Tesco's growth during the 1960s and early 1970s came through often "unruly" share-based acquisitions that were all about expanding Tesco's buying power in the wholesaling spirit that had characterized Cohen's operations since his barrow-boy beginnings. Hence the acquisitions of Charles Phillips and Asdega, companies with even smaller stores than Tesco, to the embarrassment of Kreitman, who wanted to invest in larger superstores; Cadena, a bread and confectionery company, in 1965; and finally, in one of Cohen's biggest deals, the 217-store Victor Value chain in 1968. Kreitman's and Thrush's reaction was that the Victor Value stores were too small and would put an enormous burden on group management resources, particularly since Tesco had many management problems of its own. But Cohen's decision carried the day. Not surprisingly, the Victor Value takeover "very nearly brought Tesco to its knees."[52]

Tesco's happy accident was Leslie Porter's Home 'n' Wear division. Cohen respected the tougher manner of his second son-in-law, who had always refused to be part of the older man's machinations, preferring to concentrate on building his non-food operation at a distance. MacLaurin and David Malpas later dismissed Home 'n' Wear as an expensive diversion from investment in the core business of food. But in the context of the developing "traditions of transformation," it was a godsend, providing a vehicle to channel alternative top management dynamics and open up the company to managers from outside the family.[53] Home 'n' Wear was also an inspiration and test-bed for future ideas: own-label products, one-stop shopping, out-of-town developments, and even standardized price lists and customer services. It was because of Porter's insistence on expanding non-food that Tesco started buying bigger properties than Cohen deemed necessary for foods alone.[54] As a cash cow,[55] non-food propped up Tesco's earnings when food sales were depressed and provided the wherewithal to invest in new retailing developments.[56] Inevitably, as Porter's stature in the company grew, he would also cross swords with Cohen – on one occasion literally when the pair "grabbed the Wilkinson swords that decorated the boardroom wall and clashed like duellists."[57]

Fortunately, there were one or two non-family board members who were able to remain aloof from the strife. One such was Arthur Thrush, who as well as being an outstanding retailer had both an eye for young retail talent and the ability to shelter it from the board shenanigans. Thrush made it his job to mentor new management trainees, beginning with the very first one, Ian MacLaurin. MacLaurin was appointed director in 1970 and in 1973, aided by Thrush's support, became managing director. But MacLaurin was by no means the only beneficiary: by the late 1960s Thrush had artfully promoted what some, with the benefit of hindsight, termed "an alternative board."[58] Based on the criterion described by one former Tesco executive as "can he or she solve a problem that no-one else can?," Thrush – with the help of MacLaurin – had identified the next generation of Tesco management, among them David Malpas, Mike Darnell, and John Gildersleeve at headquarters level, with others such as Brian Williams and Colin Goodfellow as senior directors of Tesco Stores. Significantly, all these people owed their loyalty as much to their mentor as to the company that employed them.[59]

Another notable boardroom survivor was Daisy Hyams. Hyams worked for Tesco for a remarkable 51 years. By 1965 she had become chief controller of Tesco's food-buying operation.[60] Importantly, Hyams – Tesco's very own purchasing Iron Lady – had done much to turn buying into a professional, centralized operation – a timely response to the growing power of a diminishing number of manufacturers and the rising importance of centralized own-label organizational capabilities. Even if not completely successful, this was no small feat in the light of Cohen's enduring influence. Cohen still commanded considerable loyalty with store managers, who loved him for his price-busting and "buncing," not to mention his nod-and-a-wink "I don't mind if you're making a bob for yourself, as long as you're making two for me."[61] Many store managers – especially in unconverted smaller shops – effectively ran their own profit center and often ignored attempts at inventory and price standardization, making it hard for Hyams to achieve her goals.

Finally, there was David Behar, who from the acquisition of Cadena onwards was allowed to concentrate on property development. With Behar, Tesco had acquired property development expertise that, in the teeth of Cohen's position, and improvisationally at first, would help Tesco realize the ambitious property development plans that other retailers, not least Sainsbury, did not have the know-how or inclination to pursue. Not only would Behar provide decisive opposition to family directors on the issue of Green Shield Stamps – a Cohen legacy that hampered investment in larger, out-of-town stores – but he was also one of the first to react against Cohen's attitude to local planning authorities – another Cohen legacy from which the company took more than a decade to recover. Finally, as a MacLaurin ally, Behar helped to bring John Gildersleeve, an outstanding property location expert, safely though the Tesco system.

Tesco was a conglomerate in all but name: all of the "alternative directors" or shadow leaders effectively ran their own divisions, greatly enhancing their ability to experiment and improvise with new ideas behind Cohen's back. Apart from Cohen, only Kreitman was "prowling around the group."[62] At one point, however, this arrangement seriously backfired. After the substantial acquisition of Irwin's in 1965, Cohen decided to set up a separate operating company, Tesco Self Service, to manage the northern stores. Managing director of the northern operating company was Jim Grundy, described in Cohen's authorized biography as "a quick-thinking very experienced executive" who "applied his mind to the special requirements of supermarkets and to staying with the leaders in the supermarket race."[63]

As it turned out, northern England was the testing ground of one of the biggest threats to Tesco's sustainable advantage: the out-of-town hypermarkets, one of whose pioneers was the Leeds-based Asda.[64] Asda's strategy was to open out-of-town supermarkets in abandoned warehouses selling a wide range of non-food as well as food items at very low prices. Some of Asda's stores had a staggering 50,000 square feet of selling space – 10 times greater than Tesco's average store in the north. Asda had chosen its territory well. Northern customers had always been more price conscious than those in the south. And northern planning authorities were considerably more sympathetic to the development of large stores than their southern counterparts. From Tesco's headquarters in the south, where hypermarket developments met with strong resistance from consumers and planners alike, this was not at all obvious. Convinced as Grundy and Cohen were that Asda's out-of-town superstores were a temporary aberration, Tesco continued opening stores of little more than 4,000 square feet. In the north, however, things were changing rapidly, and by the end of the 1960s the profits of Tesco North had all but disappeared.[65]

In the end the northern fiasco, as it came to be seen, was another happy accident. It enabled Mike Darnell, one of the new standard-bearers, to take responsibility for and learn from the failing northern distribution function. And it led to MacLaurin discovering Malpas, who was employed in the north. MacLaurin and Malpas shared a unique experience as area directors that would prove determining for Tesco's future. They both had been "in charge of branches and could run a classic grocery business … away from the rows between Kreitman and Porter … because these did not really matter to the business at the branch level."[66] This formative experience greatly enhanced the pair's capacity, and desire, to envision a more productive relation between the center and the retail business units, and start experimenting with Tesco's new destiny: out-of-town hypermarkets.

In 1966 a self-congratulatory annual report statement noted that Tesco had come out top of a league table of Britain's fastest-growing companies. By the early 1970s, however, performance was beginning to suffer. Remedial action had already being taken. Realizing that Jack Cohen's outdated philosophy had to be killed off once and for all, Kreitman and Porter combined forces to get Cohen appointed as life president and push through a centralization of the group as a whole. After a brief reign as chairman, Kreitman in his turn resigned in 1973, to be succeeded by Porter. Porter proved to be a very effective chairman. MacLaurin, the new managing director, had the backing of the Young Turks – Malpas, Darnell, Gildersleeve, and others – presciently assembled by Arthur Thrush, enabling him in defiance of the Old Man to close more than 200 smaller stores between 1973 and 1979[67]: "as we couldn't get rid of them wholesale, we just closed a few down each week without telling him."[68] As a last throw, Cohen reportedly tried to oust Malpas, who was "recognized as an absolutely outstanding retailer,"[69] but MacLaurin stood firm and refused.

Smith & Nephew: "managing by argument" and R&D "against all opposition" (1963–79)

Insiders described decision-making at Smith & Nephew in the 1960s and 70s as "management by argument,"[70] "managing by fear," and "be as rude as you can to each other."[71] Proceedings were so acrimonious that chief executive George Whittaker ascribed to them his heart attacks and eventual retirement in 1967. The boardroom acrimony had much to do with the fact that strategy in Smith & Nephew came down to two things: personalities and a less than visionary concept of financial profitability. Under Leavey's chairmanship, the three most important personalities were Whittaker, the marketing-oriented Stephen Steen, who was in charge of consumer products, and financial controller Leslie Long, who together made up the company executive committee. Other board members from 1961 were Don Seymour, the research director, and Kenneth Bradshaw, who ran the textile division. These leaders had a hard time finding common ground. One problem was that, in defiance of the executive committee's mission to draw up a corporate plan and work with 5-year budgets for each division,[72] the company was still managed as an "entrepreneurial production-orientated business." There "was no coherent, obvious thread between what these businesses did." There were "strong personalities pushing for their particular areas of interest."[73]

Another important bone of contention was the role of textiles in a company that increasingly saw itself as part of the healthcare industry – a label with a quite different meaning than in contemporary usage. For instance, while Seymour had understood that it had been agreed to halt textile expansion in response to the recession in that market, the board voted to acquire denim manufacturer Tatham in 1962, a decision in which Seymour was the only dissenter.[74] A year later the board complained that the company's pharmaceutical R&D spend was not producing adequate revenues to support rising research costs. By 1966 Smith & Nephew had withdrawn altogether from the synthesis of antitubercular medication, in effect ending any ambitions it might have had to become a pharmaceutical player.

Smith & Nephew Research had more acceptable results from its plastic and polymer research program – even though, apart from Seymour, still "no-one understood the strategic role of R&D for the company."[75] Serendipity was at the heart of the process. It all started with the "failure" of the Clopay "Tip Tops" project in 1958. As ever, seeking inspiration in the US, Seymour had introduced Whittaker to an innovative plastic fingernail covering developed by the Clopay Corporation in Cincinnati. While Whittaker had little understanding of the technical processes involved – based on injection moulding and the extrusion of polymers – his entrepreneurial instincts prevailed and Smith & Nephew duly launched Clopay's nail products as "Tip Tops." Unfortunately, nails covered in Tip Tops cracked, and the product had to be quickly withdrawn. But because the product had sold well initially, Whittaker let Smith & Nephew's new plastics R&D group live for another day. This decision would prove momentous, as the Tip Top technology, together with Smith & Nephew's more traditional Airstrip and film technologies, would ultimately be the keystone to Smith & Nephew's most successful R&D innovation ever, OpSite. A breathable film technology patented in 1969, OpSite would lay the basis of Smith & Nephew's later claim to be a world leader in surgical dressings.

OpSite would prove a revolutionary step in surgical dressings to aid wound healing processes.[76] Although the convoluted way in which the product came about is a story in itself, in hindsight a special strength of the Smith & Nephew research effort was its sheer breadth and multidisciplinary nature, combining a number of disparate disciplines, all of them eventually coalescing in the company's core competence in "wound care." As a result of these unpredictable and sometimes serendipitous developments, it would ultimately be recognized that "S&N's soul resides in the research department,"[77] although this was not an insight that would become widespread until the end of the 1970s.

Don Seymour's determination to keep Smith and Nephew Research going showed not only determination, but also foresight:

> I think it's fair to say that some of his efforts in developing new generation medical products started to differentiate us in the 60's from our traditional competitors and were, perhaps, the beginning of the high tech medical group that has evolved today.[78]

He took advantage of the independence that came with conglomerate organization to build an alternative platform for change, at a distance from the old dominant coalition centered on textiles.

Although the real magnitude of Seymour's achievements, including his early focus on US innovations, would not be recognized until the end of the 1970s, there had been a previous strategic turning point. In 1968, with Smith & Nephew's share price stagnating, Unilever made a takeover bid. In the emotionally charged contest that ensued, Smith & Nephew fought off the bid, which had the unintended consequence of bringing to the fore a new personality in the shape of Kenneth Kemp, Smith & Nephew's very own financial wizard.

Kemp was known as "Mr 20% because he believed in delivering consistent high returns to shareholders in good times and bad."[79] He became chief executive in the same year. He speeded up the process of professionalization, calling in Professor Roland Smith to deliver seminars on corporate strategy from 1969 onwards. As a colleague of the time explained about Kemp's intentions, Smith & Nephew would not be led by entrepreneurs who, as one past executive put it, "did before they thought" but by "enlightened entrepreneurs, who first think and then do." To bring added discipline, Kemp introduced a 20 percent annual growth target for new investment. In 1972 a reorganization of top management to complement the financial changes and dispel some of the board acrimony followed, in which Kemp and Bradshaw became joint deputy chief executives, with the pair adding respectively the executive deputy chairman and chief executive of operations roles arguably as a classic way of trying to resolve their conflicting views. In addition, the pair gained greater powers, while the official management executive was degraded to the status of an advisory forum.[80]

These developments were timely, since the 1970s would be marked by increasing pressures on margins and volume. Of most concern was the NHS, the firm's main UK account, which in the wake of worldwide recession was becoming more demanding and cost-conscious. At the same time, international competitive pressures in the healthcare industry were mounting as niches became less fragmented and the healthcare industry consolidated. Again, with the benefit of hindsight, the emergence of Kemp was a turning point. Kemp in due time became not only informal chief executive, but also an ally of Seymour, promoting him to deputy chairman and boosting his intent to turn Smith & Nephew into a sophisticated medical technology company with a strong base in the US rather than a confused industrial conglomerate with a Commonwealth legacy. As a result, Seymour was able in 1979 to convince the Smith & Nephew board to acquire in the US, followed in the same year by the purchase of Anchor Continental, a South Carolina-based manufacturer of pressure-sensitive tapes.

Significantly, Kemp also became an ally of the new marketing director, Alan Fryer. Before Fryer's appointment in 1973, there had virtually been no link between financial, research, and marketing logics within the group. As Fryer gained clout, a more coherent and complementary logic would slowly emerge, most notably in terms of how consumer products would function as the cash cow to fund a better balance between research, sales, and geographical expansion. A corporate focus on marketing was sorely needed: "We were running into difficulties [since] growing profits at 20 percent without that investment in marketing was difficult to achieve, particularly in the consumer market place."[81] With the benefit of hindsight, the emergence of corporate marketing as a strategic discipline fitted snugly into the alternative platform for change envisaged by Seymour. That is, the marketing of consumer products would generate enough cash flow for those periods when research did not come off. Again, however, it would take another decade for this marketing insight to become part of deliberate board strategy.

Meanwhile, the directors still considered Smith & Nephew to be an industrial conglomerate, happily encompassing products as diverse as denim, toiletries, wound management items, plastics, and pharmaceuticals. Lacking a clear sense of its own identity, the company was prone to jump on industry bandwagons, as it did in pharmaceuticals – with near-disastrous consequences. Compounding the error of treating Nivea as a cosmetic, in 1971 Smith & Nephew launched a flurry of acquisitions in the cosmetics and hair care market.[82] Since acquiring Nivea in 1951, Smith & Nephew had done little in the way of extending its product and geographical range. Despite the fact that by 1961 Smith & Nephew controlled some 40 percent of all general-purpose skin cream in Britain, the board had never seen much strategic value in Nivea, and extension would have meant high promotional costs and risks. Nevertheless, tempted by what it saw as the industry's growth potential, in 1971 it bought Gala, a medium-sized British cosmetics firm with a substantial presence in the US – a market where the UK could not sell Nivea. Unfortunately, Smith & Nephew was out of its league, its deficient pharma legacy rendering it entirely unable to handle Gala's brand management and research needs. Ominously, from 1976 Smith & Nephew started incurring heavy losses, especially in the US.

Chapter 4

The Three Successful Strategic Transformers: Developments

As early as the 1950s Tesco, Smith & Nephew, and Cadbury Schweppes started developing traditions of transformation: traditions of continuity, anticipation, contestation, and mobility. By the late 1970s only a few remaining sources of inertia stood in the way of these traditions becoming an integral part of the strategic transformation process. A few catalyst events would provide the tipping point: Tesco's 1977 Operation Checkout, Cadbury Schweppes' 1978 Long-Range Plan, and Smith & Nephew's 1978 launch of OpSite. These events precipitated a significant generational and cultural shift.

As one generation succeeded the other, emotional acrimony between particular individuals gave way to contestability and leadership pluralism. The best new-generation people came to the top, partly because the new leadership systematically promoted the champions of the previous period to senior management positions, and partly because the new-found dynamic convinced the less able people to hasten their retirement or departure. The new leaders did not relinquish the improvisational management style adopted in the previous period. In an era of rapidly changing competitive dynamics, an improvisational management style was a great asset, especially since improvisation was based on shared traditions of transformation.

Three generations of leaders accepted living side by side. The oldest generations – Adrian and Dominic Cadbury at Cadbury Schweppes, Porter and MacLaurin at Tesco, and Kemp, Kinder, and later Robinson at Smith & Nephew – focussed on ensuring the *continuity* of the companies. This new sense of continuity allowed for a more coherent combination of thinking big and tolerating failure. Meanwhile, the oldest generation respected the greater ability of new leaders to *anticipate* changes – Williams, Schadt, and Sunderland at Cadbury Schweppes; Malpas, Darnell, and Gildersleeve at Tesco; Robinson, Fryer, Blair, and O'Donnell at Smith & Nephew. This respect was reciprocated: up-and-coming leaders settled for gradual changes, and waited for happy accidents to accelerate their transformation initiatives. Finally, the first two generations gave space to a third generation of champions to engage in sufficient *experimentation* – champions such as Brock and Stitzer at Cadbury Schweppes, Leahy and Penny at Tesco, and Dick, Suggett, and Sparks at Smith & Nephew.

TESCO: "GETTING FOOD RIGHT" AND THE CHALLENGE OF REACHING THE TOP LEAGUE

How did the new Tesco team of chairman Leslie Porter and managing director Ian MacLaurin differ from its predecessors? Molded in Cohen's era, Porter could still be somewhat "rough trade," to MacLaurin's discomfiture. But Porter managed several things his father-in-law was unable to, notably getting rid of Green Shield Stamps in 1977 and, more importantly, by "distancing this family stuff,"[1] creating space for MacLaurin's new retailing team of David Malpas,[2] Mike Darnell,[3] John Gildersleeve,[4] and senior retail managers such as Alan Besbrode to assert themselves. As Terry Leahy put it, "formally Leslie was in charge," but in reality he remained "a little bit remote."[5] Malpas said: "He was often portrayed by people as a thoroughly bad chairman, [but] he wasn't actually. He was thoughtful about the business and prepared to let the executives actually get on and run it" – including developments put forward by the alternative leadership "like our investment in logistics and our investments in the new stores."[6]

Significantly, Porter allowed MacLaurin's team to develop an entirely different approach to property. Under Cohen and Kreitman, Tesco had acquired a retail cowboy reputation with local planners, which MacLaurin worked hard to dispel.[7] Beyond planning, Tesco had a culture that was driven more by property than retail values. The upside was that, unlike Sainsbury's, Tesco had a tradition of employing people with a real property nose, starting with Francis Krejas, who was the head of property, and including MacLaurin, Malpas, and Gildersleeve: "They were all capable of running property companies, not something you normally get in retail businesses."[8] All that was needed to turn the happy accident of Tesco's comparative strength in property into a real strategic weapon was a more customer-led focus. Brooding on this, Malpas came up with the idea of a site research unit to make more strategic location decisions. But there was still doubt in his mind. Remarkably, it was Porter who helped him overcome his uncertainty. "It was Porter who insisted we get our site research on to a properly organized basis," acknowledged Malpas. "After one or two false starts we managed to set up a unit which became the envy of the trade in the end."[9]

From 1982 institutional investors asked Porter to admit nonexecutive directors to the board. This fanned the winds of change – and certainly "strengthened considerably … the position of MacLaurin and Malpas."[10] But even before that, Tesco's maturing tradition of contestability was starting to tell: it slowly but surely compelled the factions to accept the principle of "respectful difference" – cognitive instead of emotional conflict, paired with a measure of dispersed leadership. By the mid-1970s the company had also quietly developed a tradition of mobility – an informal human resource process that enabled capable problem-solvers to rise to top management functions very quickly. The tradition had been jumpstarted with MacLaurin, mentored by Arthur Thrush, and would continue with Malpas, who in turn brought on newer champions such as Leahy.[11]

It was Operation Checkout that crystallized Tesco's developing traditions into a real launch pad for change. MacLaurin had launched it in 1977 with Porter's blessing, incurring disapproval from "experts" in the retail trade in the process. The aim of Operation Checkout was to restore Tesco's price-cutting image and improve its market share – both of which it did. But beyond boosting turnover,[12] Operation Checkout had so many and such pervasive unintended consequences in the shape of knock-on changes to logistics, distribution, and property investment processes that it effectively destroyed the possibility of linear planning or indeed comprehensive control by a dominant coalition. Rather, it spurred Tesco's management to trust and embrace the improvisational processes emerging out of constructive conflict between the different generations of leaders. In Leahy's words:

> It depends which side of the story you tell it from. The old guard would say 'you're probing high risk'; but certainly something needed to be done and we the young guard got the chance to do it in the late 1970s and early 1980s.[13]

This was the deeper and usually unseen outcome of Operation Checkout.

How did it all come about? First, Operation Checkout revitalized the price leadership logic on which the company had been founded – a logic that had become somewhat blurred in the preceding decades.[14] Crucially, the message served as the company's central thread of continuity and reference point for change. Second, by laying bare logistics and distribution problems that almost brought the company to a standstill, Operation Checkout broke the last resistance to large-scale investment in centralized facilities to overcome the difficulties. It helped that the resulting top-line success gave Tesco some welcome financial room for maneuver. But other challenges had emerged on the horizon: the pressing imperative to invest in out-of-town hypermarkets now that building licenses had become easier to obtain;[15] the need to move upmarket with the customer base; and the necessity to shift into own-label before suppliers could exploit increasing concentration and bargaining power to get in first.

The big challenge to Tesco's comprehensive investment program was, however, bringing together the company's warring wholesale (property-oriented) and retail (customer-oriented) cultures into a platform that would allow for contestation and pluralism rather than conflict and cliques. According to Malpas:

> The wholesaling part wasn't remotely interested in the main quality goods or stepping out to buy in quantity its own label products. What it wanted to do was to buy things cheaply and sell them as dearly as they could.

Ultimately, the combination of a tradition of contestation and a new customer focus – the basis of the reinvigorated tradition of continuity – overcame Tesco's dysfunctional legacy: "The division of cultures, in particular the wholesale culture, died away by 1980, because we were becoming truly customer facing,"[16] notably with the development of own-label products. The tradition of contestation was also becoming established. For example, by the mid-1980s a then junior manager was able to give a highly challenging presentation to the Tesco board about the possibility of a price war triggered by the entry of overseas competitors. He was told after the meeting by David Malpas that it was a sign of how well the board had come on that he was able to challenge them and discuss this.

Another spur came from the tradition of mobility that solidified remarkably quickly in the wake of the new growth dynamic. The old guard who had blocked the promotion of managers able to meet the new challenges saw the writing on the wall. People who had been comfortable in a smaller company "found that the business was growing in a way they couldn't really cope with and so they simply hastened their retreat," enabling up-and-comers such as Michael Darnell to take the business forward. Darnell, made distribution director in 1982 at Malpas's instigation, "masterminded all of the transformation of our logistics from a couple of grocery warehouses and a small proportion of centrally delivered goods to a properly organized whole logistics package."[17]

During the 1980s Darnell would find himself at the intersection of several important trends, all of which would serve to increase the coherence of Tesco's competitive position. Before becoming distribution director, Darnell had run the non-food Home 'n' Wear business. Under Porter, Home 'n' Wear had had come to play an "increasingly important role in the company's plans," especially in respect of the move away "from the smaller high-street supermarket"[18] and the acquisition of larger strips of out-of-town land than were necessary for a food business alone.[19] Moreover, since the late 1970s Home 'n' Wear had hosted a number of seminal experiments, including the introduction of credit purchases[20] and own-label products,[21] centralized distribution,[22] one-stop shopping, and the shift from comparison to convenience lines, all of which anticipated subsequent changes in food retailing. Armed with this experience, from 1982 Darnell, again at Malpas' urging, took on food. By that time, the wholesale–retail divide in Tesco's food business was fast disappearing,[23] allowing Darnell to make several distribution improvements.[24] From 1986 the pace picked up. With momentum firmly behind central control and fresh foods, the company launched a major overhaul of its distribution and logistics, including the construction of seven superdepots,[25] the first indication that Tesco was ready to take on the role of retail pioneer rather than copycat.

A move to category management – among the first in the UK – was in part another unintended consequence of Operation Checkout. A few days after the launch, MacLaurin wrote to all suppliers and instructed Daisy Hyams and her buying team that there were to be no more outside deals. With Cohen's tradition of opportunistic wheeling and dealing finally laid to rest, Malpas and Pennell began rationalizing the Tesco range, opening the way for centralized buying, stock control, and category management, with all that entailed for Tesco's suppliers and its own line management. Tesco's buying team could now bargain with suppliers on its own terms. By 1985 Tesco's financial position had improved to the point where it was able to launch a successful £145 million rights issue to finance the capital spending program. Success breeding success, Tesco in 1987 renewed its attack on Asda's northern heartland by buying Hillards for £228 million.

Compared with Sainsbury's, Tesco's change processes in the mid-1980s were informal, unpredictable, mobile, and rapid. According to a senior manager at Sainsbury who was close to several Tesco insiders:

> At Tesco, there actually was a delegation of power ... It was a very unpredictable process, very informal, very mobile, people coming together. There was a lot of chatting around and no clear hierarchy, and decisions were made very fast. And that's something we were very aware of at the time ... our [Sainsbury's] processes were very cumbersome in comparison.

Viewed retrospectively, all these initiatives appeared to be part of a logical sequence of change starting from Operation Checkout. But in fact there was no grand vision: the aims of Operation Checkout went no further than price-cutting and market share. Yet Tesco was the only retailer able to carry them through in such a coherent and self-reinforcing manner. Why? There were two main reasons. First, the changes built on and strengthened a pre-existing transformation platform based on the four traditions. Second, the capacity for improvisation that matured during the 1980s emerged from the same division of labor between three generations of leaders focussing on complementary types of strategic intentionality – continuity, anticipation, and experimentation.

By the end of the 1980s all the unintended consequences of Operation Checkout had so successfully coalesced into a "completely logical policy" that consumer perceptions of Tesco had fundamentally changed.[26] Some contemporary retail analysts even argued that Sainsbury's slogan "Good food costs less at Sainsbury's" could equally stand for Tesco.[27] Two figures underlined such assessments.[28] Tesco had gone from 21 percent of own-label grocery sales to 41 percent in the period from 1980 to 1992, compared with Sainsbury's modest advance from 54 percent to 55 percent. And by the end of the decade, Tesco was opening more new superstores than its rival. Good though the figures were, however, the bigger picture remained that, while Tesco had moved up a league, it was not the UK's retail leader. The 1980s had been too good to Sainsbury's for that, with profits growing at a compound annual rate of 30 percent up to 1985 and continuing at an impressive pace thereafter. Sainsbury's operating profit margins were consistently higher than Tesco's, although the latter had managed to close the gap somewhat by 1992 – 7.09 percent to Sainsbury's 8.71 percent.[29] Finally, under the much admired leadership of John Sainsbury, the company had expanded in the US, a feat Tesco did not feel ready for at all.

But even while they were converging in performance, the two companies were drawing apart in the way the traditions played out. Similar in importance to the decision to abandon Green Shield Stamps, Operation Checkout was the catalyst for banishing the inertia that hindered the embedding of Tesco's traditions of continuity, anticipation, contestation, and mobility.

Now that the alternative leadership of the preceding period had merged into the dominant coalition, a new coherence and sense of anticipation emerged in Tesco's transformation processes. As one generation succeeded another, emotional aggression between individuals slowly but surely gave way to a more generalized acceptance of cognitive difference and plural leadership. The best new-generation people rose to the top, partly because the new dominant coalition systematically promoted the champions of the previous period to senior management positions, and partly because the new-found dynamic convinced less able executives to move on or retire.

Strikingly, far from relinquishing the improvisational management style they had cultivated in their previous roles, the new generation embraced it. Why? Improvisation had become a successful habit; its appropriateness was enhanced by rapidly altering industry and political economy changes, and its effectiveness was enhanced by the embedding of traditions of transformation throughout the company. In the process, the piecemeal improvisational styles of the previous period knit together into a coherent thread that was at the heart of a re-energized company DNA.

As part of this central thread for strategic change, three generations of leaders were able to weave their own variation on the original "pile it high, sell it cheap" success formula, including the founder's willingness to experiment in the name of customer satisfaction. The older generation under Porter and MacLaurin focussed on continuity with an up-to-date version of the existing success theme, combining thinking big with willingness to tolerate failure. At the same time, they respected the greater ability of new alternative leaders – Malpas, Darnell, and Gildersleeve – to come up with future-oriented versions. The respect was reciprocated: alternative leaders settled for a gradual change of direction in anticipation of happy accidents that would in time speed up transformation. Finally, both coalitions gave space to a third generation of champions such as Terry Leahy and Nick Penny to experiment with new and fresher versions of the strategic model.

CADBURY SCHWEPPES: "VALUE FOR MONEY" AND THE CHALLENGE OF INTERNATIONAL FOCUS

The new "long view" that had emerged by the mid-1970s was an improved, financially sharper version of the old Cadburyism, with Adrian Cadbury, the new chairman, as its philosophical leader. After Watkinson's departure, Adrian Cadbury wrote *The Character of the Company*, which became the foundation of Cadbury Schweppes' purpose and values in subsequent decades.[30] While Adrian was the spiritual leader, Dominic Cadbury embodied the new generation of alternative Cadburyists most clearly. Although an inheritor of the Cadbury long view, Dominic set himself apart from the old family guard with his sharp identification with the US, manifested in a Stanford MBA and his predilection for sharper financial performance measures.

The new Cadburyism could not have emerged without the best of Schweppes' legacy rubbing off on it – and Dominic knew it. By and large, however, the new champions remained suspicious of ex-Schweppes people, even after Watkinson left, and to some extent vice versa. It was not until Dominic Cadbury took over from managing director Basil Collins in 1983 that the divisions were finally overcome. By then, "we were a united board, and we had got over the post-merger political difficulties of having either the Cadbury or the Schweppes man run things."[31] This is not to deny that decision-making had substantially improved under the Collins–Adrian Cadbury regime. There was less political meddling and a greater acceptance of legitimate differences. Moreover Collins and Adrian Cadbury, although not always in agreement, had built a good working relationship.

In retrospect, the watershed for both the relationship and the company's leadership processes as a whole was 1978. To backtrack, against the backdrop of a sharp decline in market share and trading profit, Adrian Cadbury's 1976 chairman's statement announced a renewed emphasis on core businesses and better operating performance. This was itself a reflection of the "new Cadburyism" represented and driven by Dominic Cadbury and Peter Gregory, who, as director in charge of rationalization, was becoming a real alternative influence. Management consultants were called in who, not unexpectedly, judged the company's return on assets as inadequate.[32] As competition in confectionery intensified, Cadbury's share of the UK chocolate market fell from 31 percent in 1975 to 26.2 percent in 1977, strengthening management resolve to accelerate the shift to an organization based on Mars-style, low-cost centralized mass production. Yet these were only organizational changes. Where would the strategic momentum for further strategy development come from?

In retrospect, it was the 1978 long-range plan that set transformation in motion, albeit largely unintentionally. The plan itself encompassed no more than a set of operational goals: a large capital investment program, combined with a major headcount reduction and a rationalization of production sites and product lines. But the chain of events it triggered would prove sufficiently unpredictable for Collins and Adrian Cadbury to ditch detailed planning in favor of the new ideas and skills of emerging leaders. One such leader was Michael Gifford. When Collins approved Gifford's request to swap his position of chief executive of Cadbury Schweppes Australia[33] for that of group finance director at UK corporate headquarters, he had no idea how serendipitous the switch would be. Gifford instantly picked up the ball where Adrian Cadbury had left it, philosophically speaking. In a matter of months, growing consciousness of the significance of productivity and brand improvement had cohered into a clear dominant logic of "value for money," putting a premium on leading international brands that could be supported by a financially focussed operation that combined manufacturing, distribution, and marketing.[34]

Gifford's ability to synthesize the new Cadburyism with the old Schweppes financial focus was timely, coinciding as it did with two other developments, both of which would spur the company to raise its sights: Dominic Cadbury's determination to get into the US confectionery market, and improved relations with the unions. Spurred on by resurgent sterling, domestic "winters of discontent," cheaper share prices in New York, and a more receptive American acquisition climate, Cadbury Schweppes took the plunge in 1978 and bought Connecticut-based Peter Paul.

Although the acquisition, hampered by inadequate distribution, would eventually be considered a failure, the accompanying learning process would prove far more important than the actual purchase. Via Peter Paul, the board experienced at first hand the extreme upside and downside potential of the vibrant US fast-moving consumer goods market. Most important, it made the board abundantly aware of the need to combine its "value for money" financial logic with international brand-building and the integration of the distribution–marketing–production operating system. This was true for both the soft drinks and the confectionery arms. By the time Dominic Cadbury took over from Collins as chief executive in 1983, the company's growth was increasingly nondomestic, a market evolution that, with a time lag, would be matched by the opening up of a still very British board to outside membership.[35]

The arrival of personnel director Derek Williams in 1975 was another transformative event. Williams' experience with trade unions at British Leyland Motor Corporation – where he had spent the previous 5 years – helped him settle immanent disputes at Cadbury's. A sort of respectful difference set in between the unions and Williams.

Williams and Gifford were final proof that Cadbury's traditions of both contestation and anticipation were in good working order. Even in the late 1970s it was clear that the pair's efforts to get a grip and their injection of energy were channeling larger changes in the UK political economy[36] that would transpire with the election of Margaret Thatcher. Both men were promoted in 1980. The tradition of mobility was also at work.

In the same year, the pair was joined by another emerging leader when Dominic Cadbury took over as managing director of UK confectionery. In confectionery, Cadbury had a solid and well-functioning platform for change, but problems on the Schweppes side ran much deeper. According to John Sunderland, "The Schweppes drinks business was run on the basis of very outmoded industry practices both in distribution and manufacturing. That was less the case on the confectionery side."[37] To spur the Schweppes side into change, Derek Williams was promoted to managing director of the drinks division in 1984, and director in 1986.

Cadbury's two-speed development could be accommodated because, since Collins' time, the group had been effectively streamed, allowing confectionery, soft drinks, health and hygiene, food, and beverages to evolve their own strategies under the group umbrella. On the confectionery side, "Operation Fundamental Change" was launched in 1982 as the second phase in the turnaround process kick-started by the 1978 long-range plan.[38] The relation between the confectionery and soft drinks streams now was one of healthy competition, with the chocolate people arguing that the chocolate production process was superior, while the Schweppes people boasted that a McKinsey study had demonstrated that Schweppes manufacturing was the only part of the global business that had shown real improvement.

A new element in group strategy since 1980 was to grow core markets in the US[39] – a reflection of the group's greatly raised international aspirations. Resources were to be made available to this end, including for acquisitions "where appropriate." At the same time, the company's position in the US was also strengthened organically by the arrival on the scene of Jim Schadt in 1981. As one colleague described him, Schadt was "One hundred percent American, intelligent, congenial, ambitious." He modernized and took forward the tiny US "Schweppervescence" base built by Commander Edward Whitehead. He also steadily built up a strong staff organization and a strategy nimble and far-seeing enough for Cadbury to avoid the fate of most other small soft drink companies in the US, that of falling victim to PepsiCo and Coca-Cola's great distribution and bottler squeezes of the 1980s and 90s.[40] Ultimately, Schadt would allow the beverage stream to punch above its weight, ensuring that Schweppes would be strong with bottlers around the world. Bolstered by success in reversing the steep international market-share decline of Schweppes Tonic, he also made cogent suggestions for reorganizing confectionery as well as soft drinks on a more global basis – as it turned out, a key element in Cadbury Schweppes' transformation into a credible international player.

In the years 1978 to 1985 the overall productivity at Cadbury Schweppes improved by 75 percent. But these were only piecemeal improvements. Williams and Schadt could not have made the impact they ultimately did without a serendipitous event that started as a moment of crisis in 1985. As we have noted, the direction of Cadbury Schweppes' transformation had already been set by 1978. Unfortunately, as is often the case, stock market perceptions lagged well behind. In 1985 depressed profit indicators joined negative perceptions of the group as a family-run backwater that was failing to exploit its worldwide brand portfolio to bring matters to a head.[41]

The US confectionery business was to blame for much of the 18 percent fall in first-half profits that year. The US management's efforts to push sales by offering extra credit to food brokers turned out to be based on a substantial overestimation of consumer demand. Investors and media commentators took it as a sign that Cadbury was "playing out of its league."[42] With its 8 percent of the US chocolate bar market, Cadbury Schweppes was being squeezed out by the US giants Hershey and Mars, which together accounted for 70 percent. In September 1985 the unthinkable happened: Cadbury Schweppes had become a takeover target. Sure enough, a predator emerged in the shape of General Cinema, which bought 8 percent of the business in a first action and then took advantage of a stock market tumble in 1987 to add 10 percent more.

In retrospect, General Cinema was the happy accident Cadbury Schweppes needed. As one executive explained:

> General Cinema was helpful ... because they made us focus more and faster. We finally stopped trying to be a conglomerate, we stopped trying to be a Unilever and we became a very focused confectionery and soft drinks business.

Dominic Cadbury led the drive to focus on core businesses and competences – doing in practice what management gurus Prahalad and Hamel in 1990 would popularize in theory.[43] The US management was sacked and Schadt[44] put in charge. The board then took the first steps toward reorganizing the management structure on a global basis.[45]

In 1986 Cadbury Schweppes disposed of the health and hygiene and foods businesses using the proceeds to acquire Canada Dry and the license to produce and market Sunkist, two leading soft drink brands.[46] Ironically, cash resources did not only come from divestments: as Dominic Cadbury explained, "The share price had shot up because of the takeover threat which in fact assisted us with some of our acquisitions. This, combined with improved performance, made us a much more expensive acquisition for anyone else to contemplate."[47] General Cinema had provided the company with the incentive it needed to play the long game at its own pace.

General Cinema provided the momentum for other focus initiatives, some emerging in entirely improvisational fashion, happily boosting the legitimacy of alternative leaders and champions. This was the case with Coca-Cola Schweppes Beverages (CCSB), the company's joint-venture bottling company with Coca-Cola. After 2 years of negotiations, Cadbury Schweppes won agreement to combine Coca-Cola and Schweppes brands in a joint company owned 51 percent by Cadbury Schweppes, creating the largest carbonated soft drinks bottling operation in Europe.[48] The aim was to pool resources to boost the brands' market share and profits, each company franchising its brands to CCSB, which would produce, distribute, and sell them.

CCSB came about when Williams picked up on a December 1984 lunch date with Coca-Cola. He immediately spotted an enormous opportunity. On the one hand, he knew that his focus on squeezing the business was not a long-term strategy. On the other, he saw that the deeper reason for the meeting was the malaise within the Coca-Cola arrangement in the UK. The brands Coke and Diet Coke were very strong – they were number one in the world. Yet all the sales statistics in this country were much lower than statistics elsewhere. What Coca-Cola needed from Cadbury Schweppes was its already operational UK infrastructure and local management expertise. Williams saw an opportunity and convinced Dominic Cadbury that the company should take it.

Williams and Dominic Cadbury took chances – including giving up a 30-year distribution agreement with Coke's great rival, PepsiCo.[49] Coca-Cola's relative malaise in the UK gave Schweppes a margin for maneuver, allowing it to take a majority stake in the venture despite entirely disproportional asset figures. Williams was appointed managing director. Because the joint venture had been started on the basis of a handshake rather than legal and operational detail, it had a difficult first year. As Dominic Cadbury explained:

> Pepsi were understandably furious and wanted the earliest termination possible. We had to change horses to Coca-Cola in a very short time and ran into serious administration difficulties during the first year of the new company.[50]

From 1987 onwards, however, CCSB grew very fast, at one point making more money than the beverages stream.

Under Williams, who was allowed to run CCSB in a rather independent fashion, CCSB would be crucial to Cadbury Schweppes' transformation, not just because it was a cash cow, but also because it provided critical mass and a platform for Dominic Cadbury to go global in the 1990s. At the same time, it allowed the company to renew its traditions of contestation and mobility. CCSB became a vehicle for testing the transformational and improvisational capabilities of up-and-coming people. Among a number of bright sparks promoted out of CCSB into the corporate hierarchy was John Sunderland, who learned his trade under Williams in the 1980s, first as a director of Schweppes and then as CCSB marketing manager.[51] Sunderland developed a knack for "the vigorous exercise of performance discipline, getting the best people in and getting those who did not deliver out, in a Cadbury Schweppes way." His reputation as "someone who delivers" got him noticed by Dominic Cadbury, earning him promotion to managing director of the newly acquired confectionery companies Trebor and Bassett.[52]

This brings us to the key changes on the confectionery side of the business during and after the General Cinema episode. Schadt's counterpart on the confectionery side was David Wellings. Wellings had worked for Cadbury in the 1960s before leaving to work in senior executive positions elsewhere. In 1986 Dominic Cadbury invited him back to take over as managing director of UK confectionery. Wellings' arrival was an important move. Having worked at senior level for several American companies, he had no inferiority complex about US business and was less bashful than other senior managers about making ambitious acquisitions and setting his sights high.

Under his leadership, the confectionery stream stepped up the pace of change through what one senior manager termed "rapid incrementalism." This culminated in several important focus decisions. Having failed to make significant progress in the US, Cadbury Schweppes' US confectionery business assets were sold and brands franchised to Hershey Foods in 1988. The funds released benefited both beverages and confectionery. In 1988 construction began on what was the largest soft drinks plant in Europe, with the aim of extending CCSB's leadership in every aspect of the UK market.[53] In confectionery, Chocolat Poulain SA became Cadbury Schweppes' first major acquisition in the continental European confectionery market. Bassett and Trebor following in 1989, the companies being merged the year after.

In part thanks to Wellings, the UK's status as the international base for Cadbury's confectionery business was unchallenged. Outside confectionery, Wellings would also play a pivotal role in squashing the spread of any inferiority complex to beverages. In particular, he pressed hard for the acquisition of Dr Pepper/7Up, the vehicle of Cadbury's great US breakthrough in the mid-1990s. But more than the anticipatory capabilities of a few leaders, the Dr Pepper/7Up story, like CCSB, reflects the company's growing trust in its ability to improvise.

The acquisition of Dr Pepper/7Up proceeded stepwise, in stop/go fashion, over a period of 10 years. It started in the most unplanned way imaginable. Hugh Collum,[54] who had taken over as group finance director from Gifford in August 1986, was called into Cadbury's merchant bank and given the opportunity of participating up to 20 percent in the first leveraged buy-out of Dr Pepper. He had only 36 hours to take a decision whether to spend $18 million to buy 20 percent of Dr Pepper, and only one other director could be reached. But Collum took the decision to go ahead. This kind of improvisational decision-making had become ingrained in Cadbury Schweppes' nature by the 1980s. Undoubtedly, it was the acceptance of dispersed leadership and willingness to let those leaders, best able to embrace accidental opportunities, to take decisions that would enable the company to keep pace with fast competitive changes.

As the 1980s ended, Dominic stepped up his efforts to build critical mass in beverages. In 1989, as Adrian Cadbury stepped down as chairman, Dominic boldly relocated the beverages headquarters, including Canada Dry and Sunkist, from London to Stamford, Connecticut, thus bringing together the entire drinks portfolio of under one roof.[55] Although the decision to relocate was overturned in 1991, it did have an important mobility effect. First, Mike Clark, who as vice-president, general counsel, and secretary for the US company had played a major role in all its mergers and acquisitions activity, joined UK corporate headquarters in 1988 as secretary and chief legal officer.[56] This was an unprecedented move, in terms of nationality professional experience and recognition of a shift from organic to acquisition-based growth.[57] David Nash, previously responsible for acquisitions and mergers at ICI, became group finance director in 1987, while corporate positions at Schweppes International were increasingly filled by North Americans such as John Brock and Todd Stitzer, who not only had acquisition integration experience, but were also learning "judo strategy" skills to neutralize the cola behemoths and their US distribution system.[58] The new generation of leaders imbued corporate headquarters with a new sense of confidence and dynamism.

Brock[59] and Stitzer had already made their influence felt in the organization, the former as Schadt's right-hand operations man, the latter as the top legal manager in the US[60] after Clark's departure to London in 1988. With Schadt, Brock and Stitzer helped to steer the soft drinks business in the direction of "healthier, non-Cola drinks" – and thus exploit a unique opportunity to outflank Coke and Pepsi in their home market, the biggest and most dynamic in the world. As a lawyer, Stitzer recognized that, under the terms of US competition regulation, neither of the cola giants could buy additional carbonated soft drinks. Knowing this, Cadbury bought Canada Dry and Sunkist in the confidence that, building on the Schweppes heritage, it could create a business capable of becoming the number one US non-cola beverages business and distribution system. Culminating with the Dr Pepper/7Up acquisition, it did just that.[61]

Was Cadbury Schweppes just lucky to have the likes of Williams, Schadt, and Wellings, and later Sunderland, Stitzer and Brock, make the contributions they did? That seems improbable. How and why did the company attract and then retain such highly ambitious people? The short answer is that Cadbury Schweppes possessed traditions of transformation that set it apart. By the late 1970s and early 1980s, the force of these traditions was starting to tell. They provided the platform for a transformation that was largely self-driven – and arguably would have occurred with a different management too, since under pressure from the tradition of mobility, less dynamic and competent elements fell by the wayside or felt compelled to move on.

Clearly, the pace of the process was accelerated by Dominic Cadbury, a leader "who probably was ahead of his time" in his conviction of the need to "abandon the conglomerate form"[62] and early willingness to embrace the dynamic benefits of improvisation despite its corollaries of unpredictability and plural leadership. The process that developed during the 1980s was not just about change, that is, anticipation, contestation, and mobility. It was equally about a rejuvenated tradition of continuity. Translating the dominant logic into one hands-on catchphrase ("value for money," "focus," "managing for value," "route to market") provided successive generations of leaders with a simple theme to guide their own change initiatives. It was of course understood that the theme entailed more than the catchphrase: in terms of process, dispersed leadership; in terms of context, the need to accept less than perfect change, including setbacks, in anticipation of a happy accident, and as part of the long game. In terms of content, the catchphrases were shorthand for a Cadbury Schweppes that combined financially focussed operations with conservative entrepreneurship and a core portfolio of worldwide/regional/local leading brands. Clearly, the theme developed coherence over time, more slowly in confectionery than in soft drinks. Whereas the period up to 1985 had belonged to the new Cadburyists, the late 1980s and first part of the 1990s were contrastingly the era of the "new Schweppes" people, with Dominic Cadbury coordinating and facilitating the two streams.

Almost any story of transformation involves sacrifice, and so it was with Cadbury Schweppes. It became clear in the early 1980s that two of the most charismatic change agents were out of step with the new sense of continuity. One was Gifford. Mike Gifford was widely admired for his drive and imagination, but it was felt that the position of chief executive required a steadier hand. Even his admirers agreed. When Gifford was passed over in favor of Dominic Cadbury, he duly left.[63]

So too did Jim Schadt. He had failed to convince the board to acquire the whole of Dr Pepper/7Up. His other reason was that, for reasons of continuity, Dominic had decided to transfer the soft drink headquarters back to the UK.[64] All in all, Schadt's primary US viewpoint and immediate demands were no longer in synch with Cadbury Schweppes' long-term priorities. So he too departed.

What was the balance sheet of Dominic Cadbury's decade in the driver's seat? By 1992 CCSB held the lion's share of the UK soft drinks market. Cadbury Schweppes led in the block chocolate and assortments sectors of the UK chocolate confectionery markets, while Trebor Bassett was number one in UK sugar confectionery. But the world was larger than just the UK. In the international food and drink manufacturing industry, in which it was now categorized, Cadbury Schweppes felt tiny, even in the UK, where it ranked only seventh in market capitalization, ninth in sales, and sixth in profit just against domestic competition. Worldwide, Cadbury Schweppes was up against much bigger operations in the shape of Coca-Cola, Nestlé, PepsiCo, Kellogg, Danone, and Heinz.[65] In June 1993 the *Financial Times* noted:

> Cadbury Schweppes thinks it suffers from a perception problem. 'People today want an uncomplicated, two-word description of everything,' says Mr Dominic Cadbury, chairman. 'But if you are more than national, yet less than global, you are an uncomfortable animal to describe.'[66]

During this period, Cadbury Schweppes still lagged behind comparator Unilever in terms of business performance, yet judged by the maturing traditions of transformation, the gap in Cadbury's favour was widening all the time. Not without difficult decisions and conflict, the result was a virtuous circle in which the traditions raised the company to a new level, which attracted ambitious new executives who further built on the traditions, and so on. The traditions were now part of the corporate DNA.

With the 1978 long-range plan as the catalyst, the new habits combined with a rapidly changing competitive dynamic to spur the coalition of the "old guard" to step out of its comfort zone and embrace a transformation that became self-reinforcing through both the consequences of planned actions – the happy accidents – and deliberate action, including the removal of roadblocks in the form of those uncomfortable with the new regime. And yet, like Tesco, the company maintained its own identity. Over the period, new players improvised increasingly confident variations around the familiar tune, which in turn emerged subtly different – but it was still recognizably the distinctive Cadbury Schweppes theme.

SMITH & NEPHEW: SHIFTING SANDS – WHO'S REALLY IN CONTROL?

It was during the era of Eric Kinder as chief executive that Smith & Nephew's traditions of transformation gained maturity and achieved their self-driven character. Whether he entirely intended this or not, on his watch all generations of change agents came to frame their efforts around the same simple theme – entailing an acceptance of the principle of leadership pluralism, reflected in a division of labor between a dominant coalition focussed on the existing business model, alternative leaders willing to countenance change, and up-and-coming executives eager to pursue it.

Officially, Smith & Nephew was headed up by Kinder and chairman Kenneth Kemp. But in practice, the forward momentum was provided by the technology-oriented John Robinson and Alan Fryer in the medical division, joined later by Jack Blair, the US orthopedics chief who came with the Richards Medical Company acquisition. It was Robinson and Fryer who dismantled the conglomerate Smith & Nephew Associated Companies and split the components into two divisions: consumer products, comprising Elastoplast, Nivea, and textile products such as cotton wool; and healthcare, grouping R&D-intensive medical goods. As part of the same process, the cosmetics subsidiary Gala was sold off in 1980.

In terms of strategic focus, Robinson brought a strong determination to put more emphasis on R&D and product innovation, which would ultimately lead to a number of important customer-centered innovations, including OpSite IV3000 (patented in 1982), Dynacast (1986), Allevyn (1987), and IntraSite (1988), as well as a ground-breaking powder-free glove (1987). Meanwhile, Fryer – another ex-Unilever man – was developing a more sophisticated marketing structure. Fryer was a realist:

> Clearly, we could not have an international consumer business, we were far too small compared to the likes of Procter & Gamble or Beiersdorf. We had no on the ground presence in the United States or mainland Europe.[67]

Instead, he concentrated on turning consumer products into a cash cow, buying time for Robinson and Kinder to build a longer term strategy for the high-margin medical devices market. His strategy included acquisitions, Smith & Nephew buying the well-managed UK toiletries company Albion in 1989, partly for its complementary brands and partly for its additional manufacturing capacity.

The first effects of Fryer's wisdom were evident in Kinder's US strategy. Smith & Nephew had virtually no US market share, and for many observers the company's growth policy there did not appear "desperately strategic."[68] One disaster involved the loss of a big chunk of the US market for OpSite, the group's ground-breaking breathable technology. Unintentionally and counterintuitively, however, the fiasco would help to transform Smith & Nephew from a mainly British company best known for Nivea and Elastoplast into a major player in the US market for high-tech medical devices, through the vehicle of its largest US acquisition, Richards Medical Company, in 1986.

The back story to Richards Medical involved two other US purchases, Anchor Continental in 1979 and Affiliated Hospital Products in 1985. Anchor would provide a beachhead into the US – but at a price. The decision to remove OpSite distributorship from Johnson & Johnson in favor of Anchor had been taken from the UK, based on an inadequate understanding of US distribution arrangements.[69] Soon Kinder was reporting that Smith & Nephew Inc. was suffering unexpected problems on the changes in the distributorship of OpSite and had sharply reduced profit estimates. The extra margins from these changes were seriously reduced by anticipated sales shortfalls. In response, Kinder stressed the necessity to discuss the development of sales through Affiliated Hospital Products at the earliest opportunity. The protection and promotion of OpSite profit in both the UK and the US were of vital importance. Affiliated Hospital Products could not work miracles, however, and by 1985 the situation was fast becoming disastrous, especially since the OpSite patents were coming to an end and the royalty stream was in danger of drying up. These blunders encouraged the competition to get its act together, resulting in the permanent forfeiture of a large chunk of Smith & Nephew's US OpSite market.

Despite its role in the disaster, Robinson considered Affiliated Hospital Products to be the crucial US move. As well as boosting R&D and marketing synergies worldwide, Affiliated Hospital Products gave Smith & Nephew a platform without which it would not have been able to buy Richards Medical. Richards was not just a base in US medical devices. Through its businesses in orthopedic implants, trauma, and arthroscopy, it effectively focussed Smith & Nephew's transformation into the high-technology, high-margin, surgically oriented areas that would in the 1990s be the company's mainstay.

Initially extremely unhappy, the OpSite debacle thus turned into a happy accident. First, it helped to revitalize Smith & Nephew's historical customer relationship strengths, effectively barring as acquisition targets any company that could not point to excellent customer relationship management, R&D, and marketing. Richards Medical and later acquisitions such as DonJoy, Ioptex, and United Medical all possessed these qualifications. Beyond that, the larger lesson was the urgent worldwide need to improve Smith & Nephew's marketing strengths. Finally, it underscored the need to integrate R&D and marketing requirements at a corporate level, which was done via a research steering group set up in 1989. The group would be moderately successful in its immediate aim of realizing the financial benefits of integrating R&D and marketing strengths worldwide. In the longer run, however, it would speed the shift toward a transformation platform focussed entirely on high-tech, high-margin medical devices.

CHANGES ALL AROUND ...

As technology champion, Robinson effectively took on some of the chief executive's decision-making role. His hand could be seen, for example, in the progressive marginalization of "Kinder's baby," the Smith & Nephew textile division. In exercising this power, Robinson was greatly supported by Fryer, who in 1986 was promoted to the group management executive. Barely settled in his new position, Fryer announced that "inadequate leadership" required a series of management changes in the UK and Europe.

In a series of resulting appointments, the most important was that of Christopher O'Donnell as managing director of the healthcare division in 1988. O'Donnell had developed his skills at Vickers, where he had learnt to differentiate between noncore products and "nuggets," and to shed the former as a means of investing in the latter.[70] Shaped by this experience, O'Donnell's views did not sit well in the unfocussed group of the Kinder era; in fact, they did not entirely fit in Robinson's more centralized structure either, although he did not make this plain at the time.

Lacking authority to put into practice more radical proposals, O'Donnell concentrated on winnable battles. First, he was struck by how primitive and out of date Kemp's model of financial control now seemed. The problem lay with unresolved issues deriving from Smith & Nephew's conglomerate past, with board members competing on rather than coordinating their growth strategies. The most glaring example was the institutionalized practice of divisions attempting to make profit on the back of intracompany transfers. What triggered the eventual adoption of O'Donnell's proposals for better corporate cash management was their coinciding with the group management executive's desire to implement just-in-time manufacturing in response to a strong destocking trend among retailers.

In fact, both Fryer in marketing and Blair from the US orthopedic side were making a similar argument. Testifying to the increasing Americanization of the portfolio, Fryer came by the late 1980s to realize that the only way to meet Kemp's 20 percent profit growth target, apart from being good at the bottom line, was to get the top line going as well. Thus, in 1989 Robinson invited division heads to complete strategic reviews giving – real – best and worst estimates for 1990 and 1991 profits and sales.[71] When the unsatisfactory figures came in, Robinson urged the need to develop strategic thinking to overcome the profit shortfall in the longer term.

Influential though Robinson had become, it was inconceivable he could shift the "immovable object"[72] of Kemp's financial target before his formal appointment as chief executive in 1990. Then again, Kemp's 20 percent was more functional than some made it out to be. It provided the company with a simple and continuous theme, a tradition of thinking big and an assumption that seeking new avenues of growth occasionally meant tolerating failure. All that was needed was to reinvent the tradition in a more contemporary shape by marrying high financial return targets with a top-line marketing and sales strategy. And that gradually came to pass. As CEO, one of Robinson's first actions was to import a new finance director, Peter Hooley, to introduce a fresh model of financial control and resource allocation, together with overall budget targets for sales, profits, and cash.

The OpSite problem had convinced O'Donnell of something else:

> You can't make marketing and selling decisions for the US based in the UK. You've got to have management that you really understand, are competent and you trust. So you have to have the locus of decision making in the US.[73]

In fact, by 1987 Kinder had already sanctioned the setting up of a US business development group, officially in recognition of the global significance of that market.[74] Informally, however, most people knew that the real reason for granting unprecedented autonomy to the US business unit was altogether less visionary:

> Richards was successful from the start (more so than the UK divisions). This allowed the senior management, notably Blair, to more or less say to UK headquarters: 'we're doing better than you, so you can't teach us how to do it.'[75]

Blair had a point and found Kinder more amenable to his ideas than Robinson. Just before his retirement as chief executive in 1989, Kinder proposed a management structure consisting of three geographically based business development and one research group, all reporting to the company management executive.

Robinson also listened to Jim Dick, one of the new international marketing men promoted by O'Donnell. A turning point came in a 1991 budget meeting. After Dick had presented growth estimates of 14 percent, achieved largely on the back of new products, Robinson "in front of Chris O'Donnell said 'well, that's great, but it's just not good enough … I want you to go away and tell me why it can't be more, what's getting in the way, what are the obstacles.'" Jim Dick saw this as an opportunity to formalize a view that had been taking shaping for some time: that the problems were to do with geographical constraints on marketing, the country barons, the lack of group financial incentives, different notions of profit contributions, and "a lot of people want[ing] to do their own strategy, yet we're facing global competition."[76] O'Donnell quickly agreed, and out of the presentation grew the powerful idea of "centers of excellence," product-based divisions where marketing and R&D, rather than manufacturing, were the key activities.

Despite Robinson's tireless support, the centers-of-excellence concept would only be fully accepted after his retirement as chief executive in 1997 – a failure that some saw as evidence of indecision, conflated by "a horrible climate with shareholders [that] developed … All the shareholders had the sense that this company was going nowhere."[77] But behind the scenes, was Robinson's era really such a time of indecision? A different reading would be that Robinson was ahead of his time: even in the Kinder era, he anticipated and acted on the changes that were needed. What is probably true is that he had too many groups on his back – national barons, Blair and the US faction, business commentators, and shareholders. Yet, true to the heritage, he reinforced the central corporate theme: Smith & Nephew as global provider of high-tech, high-margin medical instruments, imbued with strong financial discipline and distinctive customer relationship management skills. A general acceptance of constructive conflict and plural leadership allowed an alternative dominant coalition to come to the fore, where they nourished and built on the improvisational style that had been their making. Improvisation had become the new "way things are done around here."

CHAPTER 5

The Three Successful Transformers: Breakthroughs

In the early 1990s business commentators were still casting doubts on the prospects of our three transformers. Thus, in the same period from 1992 to 1994, the *Financial Times* could describe all three as "stuck in the middle" strategically. Cadbury Schweppes was neither a national nor a convincingly international player. Tesco was not a leading discounter, but nor could it be called a high-profile quality provider. And Smith & Nephew's pretensions as a supplier of global, high-margin medical devices was undercut by a hard-to-shift image of a slow-moving peddler of bandages and creams.

Yet by focussing on immediate end results, business commentators blinded themselves to these companies' most compelling competitive asset: their superior platform for transformation. Over several decades, all three companies had built traditions of transformation that in the 1980s coalesced into a simple but highly effective model. This model interwove a long game of incremental change with a key dynamic capability: the improvisational flexibility to turn problems unanticipated by the leaders of the time into catalysts for change – "happy accidents," as we call them.

There were three strands of change in strategic management. In terms of content, everyone worked on a variation on the same success theme. In terms of context, the companies institutionalized a division of leadership in which a dominant coalition ensured continuity while a shadow leadership anticipated new contexts, and thrusting Young Turks experimented with possible future ones. In terms of process, individuals pursued their own incremental initiatives in the confidence that, jointly, the company could turn unexpected events into a means of accelerating transformation across the board.

Although the latter was largely internalized and understood rather than officially formulated, structure followed strategy. In stark contrast with the imposing control structures developed by the likes of Unilever, Sainsbury's, ICI, Mars, Coca-Cola, and PepsiCo, our three transformers were characterized by undersized, much smaller headquarters and short lines of communication. So by the mid-1990s a new "can do" dynamic had emerged. And a fresh generation of alternative leaders would use it to propel their companies from the position of ambitious follower to world leader.

CADBURY SCHWEPPES: AN "UNCOMFORTABLE ANIMAL" COMES OF AGE IN "THE LAND OF GIANTS" (1993–2007)

The problem with Cadbury Schweppes, suggested the *Financial Times* in 1986 in the wake of its US confectionery woes, was that it was "playing out of its league."[1] It returned to the theme in 1992 when, in line with its rivals, the company's confectionery business was particularly hard hit by recession. Cadbury was an "uncomfortable animal," opined the *Financial Times*, straddled between national and international pretensions: having passed up the opportunity to extend its minority stake in Dr Pepper/7Up in 1991, "[it] has outgrown the UK but lacks a convincing international expansion strategy."[2]

There was, however, more wisdom in that decision than outsiders realized. One problem was cash. With the General Cinema prop to the share price removed and interest rates soaring on both sides of the Atlantic, the era of cheap acquisitions was over; joint ventures were now a more realistic aim. A less obvious impediment was that the confectionery executives who now dominated headquarters were somewhat awed by their giant competitors – Mars, Hershey and Nestlé, as well Coca-Cola and PepsiCo – a daunting roll call of competition for any company in the world. Up-and-coming Schweppes people, such as John Brock, Todd Stitzer, and Bob Stack, had no such self-doubt, but having suffered criticism after the failure to acquire Dr Pepper/7Up in 1991, they were in no position to assert themselves against the confectionery majority who had believed that building critical mass would be more of a struggle in beverages than in confectionery. It was fortunate that in the Coca-Cola Schweppes Beverages (CCSB) joint venture, which had grown beyond all expectation, the company had a vehicle for upping the tempo (with significant support from Coca-Cola) in response to recession. In 1992 CCSB was consolidated into the beverages stream in the hope that its growth dynamic would spill over to the latter, and £80 million was invested in marketing support for soft drinks brands.

Still, the question remained: where would the company find the confidence to make the leap from uncomfortable animal to giant among giants? The key question for Dominic Cadbury was "how to be different … how can we become a [top] tier-company, although we are not a [top] tier-company in scale."[3] What was needed was an alternative leader who combined the sense of continuity of the confectionery side with the "can do" spirit of the beverages stream. David Wellings would be that man because of his achievements after returning to the company in 1986. Back in the fold, he had proven his leadership qualities on the confectionery side, first by promoting the Bassett and Trebor acquisitions and later by expanding the confectionery business away from traditional British Empire markets.

One of Wellings's close collaborators was David Kappler, another insider with outside experience. Kappler had joined Cadbury in 1965 as an accountant, leaving after a spell at the increasingly marginalized Jeyes affiliate to become finance director of candy sugar company Trebor in 1984. When Cadbury bought Trebor in 1989, Kappler came with it. He rapidly moved up through the ranks, becoming finance director of Cadbury UK in 1990. Kappler told us:

> We bought all sorts of companies in all sorts of countries around the world. Some were good buys, some of them not so good buys, but we didn't have this old restraint that it had to be chocolate. We were allowed to go into sugar candy and even one or two chewing-gum businesses. In summary, we in Confectionery, felt more confident.[4]

The pair were duly rewarded with promotion to group positions, Wellings taking over as chief executive to Dominic Cadbury's chairman in 1993, while Kappler had to wait 2 years longer to make group chief financial officer. It was a bold choice, Wellings eclipsing larger figures, some of whom had been with the company much longer, for the top prize. Why? One reason was continuity. As well as having a strong confectionery background, Wellings could also point to a proven capacity to think and act outside the box. He had less "cocoa in the blood" and more "can do," as one contemporary put it.

Wellings announced his intentions from the start: "The aim is very clear. We intend to be part of the big league," he told the *Wall Street Journal*.[5] That would in fact mean turning Cadbury into one of the world's top three chocolate-makers and the leading producer of non-cola soft drinks: transformation. The first steps in that direction quickly followed. Driven by the US unit's plans in beverages and Wellings' confidence, corporate headquarters got bolder and took made bigger acquisitions. Top of the agenda was Dr Pepper, in which Cadbury quietly upped its stake to 25 percent – a strategic move aimed at ensuring it had a seat at the table when the expected consolidation of the US soft-drinks industry took place. When that came to pass in 1995, the company duly jumped on the occasion to acquire the rest of Dr Pepper, thus achieving its much-desired major US breakthrough. At a stroke, Cadbury had taken its share of the US soft drinks market – one-third of the world total[6] – from 5 percent to 17 percent. With 45 percent of profits now coming from the US instead of 15 percent as previously, it had also transformed its profit profile. As important, the fast-growing DrPepper/7Up brands[7] greatly increased the group's leverage with independent bottlers.[8] Finally, Dr Pepper/7Up promised to be very flattering to Cadbury's financial measures because it was a big business that operated on a franchise basis and therefore achieved high returns on a low-asset base.

Although the Dr Pepper acquisition was a shot in the arm for Cadbury Schweppes' dominant coalition, the effect was short-lived. The City's reaction was unexpectedly negative, pushing Cadbury's share price down rather than up. The hostility was partly due to "the dismal record of UK investments in the US" in general,"[9] with the fuzzy structure of Cadbury's "one man and his dog" confectionery stream another contributing factor. But buying Dr Pepper/7Up business brought some much more immediate and basic problems. It had now invaded Coke's and Pepsi's back yard, and the giants quickly responded in kind, squeezing US distribution of some group brands,[10] while Coca-Cola launched a direct attack on 7Up with Sprite. And tension mounted within the CCSB joint venture. To compound the problems, there was concern in the City regarding equity dilution, prompting Sunderland and Kappler to take action to improve discipline in Cadbury Schweppes' financial process.

In the face of these challenges, it was time for the company to take the next step on the transformation road. Wellings had been promoted first among equals in 1993 because, despite being different from the traditional Cadbury mold, he represented a safe pair of hands. Wellings' improvisational "can do" credentials were impeccable. But somehow he seemed to have inherited an imperfect version of the Cadbury "long view" gene, and he now seemed like a transitional figure. According to one observer, Wellings' idea of a long-range plan was "what are you going to do for the week?" More obliquely, Kappler noted that, "As regards these acquisitions, I'm not sure they were individually as carefully analyzed as they should have been, but the building of critical mass, generation of new products and excitement were important."[11] Finally, Wellings' predilection for relatively unintegrated and decentralized growth, while much to the liking of local barons, failed to please the up-and-coming leaders of the powerful US beverage business who had been trying since the early 1990s to persuade him to adopt a more global corporate model, but to no avail.

Their turn would come after the Dr Pepper acquisition – although for reasons that were unanticipated at the time. After a period of reappraisal, it was clear to change agents such as Sunderland, Kappler, and the new US generation that the falling share price and vastly changed perceptions of Cadbury as a competitor could be turned to advantage – that they were in fact a happy accident, a natural catalyst for change in an entirely sympathetic direction. Once Sunderland had been identified as the person best equipped to confront these problems, there was no holding them back. In 1996 John Brock was promoted to head of the beverages stream, Bob Stack replaced the retiring Dick Stradwick as group HR director, and Todd Stitzer became head of Dr Pepper/7Up, the first two gaining board seats in the process.

In the best Cadbury tradition of not standing in the way of the company's future, Wellings retired in 1996 at the comparatively tender age of 55, making way for a new wave of more shareholder-oriented executives headed by another safe pair of hands, John Sunderland. Sunderland was uniquely placed to oversee the next bout of fast evolution in Cadbury Schweppes' long game.[12] Having passed through the marketing and general management ranks of Schweppes, CCSB, and the confectionery businesses, Sunderland was accepted by all groups. After Wellings, a people person, Sunderland's emphasis on facts and figures was welcome. Finally, while firmly rooted in the company's British character, Sunderland was well aware of the need for the board composition to reflect the growing importance of the US market and US shareholders.

By 1997 the financial press again was becoming twitchy. Despite Dr Pepper, the omens for Cadbury Schweppes' global aspirations were judged "not good." In carbonated soft drinks, Cadbury Schweppes lagged a distant third behind Coca-Cola and PepsiCo, while in confectionery it was only fourth to Nestlé, Mars, and Kraft Jacob Suchard. "Taking on arch-rivals like Coca-Cola, PepsiCo, Mars and Nestlé in the cut-throat international soft drinks and confectionery business" was simply beyond it, given the company's "more limited resources" and the fact that "market appetite" for its shares was already satisfied.[13] Investors seemed to agree, with Cadbury's shares underperforming the market by almost 20 percent.

In the face of this tepid reaction, Cadbury Schweppes' management was commendably firm, determined not to be deflected from its twin theme of improvisation around the "long game." Even before the Dr Pepper acquisition, the board had come to the conclusion that critical mass was needed. Becoming the world's biggest confectioner became the new task – this despite the two-thirds share of profits and the growing influence of beverages on the board. But Cadbury Schweppes was blessed with, or had built, remarkable complementarity among its leaders, who included nonexecutives such as Robert Henderson, Tom Hutchison,[14] and Ian Hay Davison with close links to the City. Together they formed a hard-headed, forward-thinking team for whom there was no such thing as a sacred cow, whether in investment, category, or geographical terms.

Already under Wellings, Sunderland had re-energized confectionery's push for international bulk with substantial acquisitions in Canada and the construction of a £75 million factory near St Petersburg with an eye on the Russian market – a venture that unfortunately turned out to be premature.[15] Further expansion took place in Poland, Argentina, and China. After 1996 Sunderland's de facto rebalancing of the group toward confectionery took on a more official quality and developed greater momentum, although the logic was more in the spirit of improvisation than planning.

In 1996 the board sprang a surprise on both analysts and stockholders by selling Cadbury's 51 percent stake in CCSB to Coca-Cola for £700 million, a move designed to focus resources on building the group's global confectionery and soft drinks businesses.[16] Initially well received,[17] the sale would later provoke fears that Cadbury's control over the bottling system had been damagingly diminished. Adding to the confusion, the sale was initially stalled by the European Monopolies and Mergers Commission. Following the not entirely successful bid to internationalize the Dr Pepper brand, in 1998 the group finally ended its 30-year strategy of developing a global soft drinks business by selling its beverage brands outside the US, France, and South Africa to Coca-Cola for £1.1 billion.[18]

Cadbury's ruthless long-game logic was at work here. Although profitable, the non-US businesses were unsustainable in the long term because Cadbury Schweppes lacked distribution clout.[19] Instead, the proceedings were used to invest in a more effective distribution strategy based on its own bottling network,[20] which included taking a 40 percent stake in the largest US independent bottler, the American Bottling Company. In 1998 Sunderland gave his fiat to the extension of the Dr Pepper/Seven Up licensing agreement, as well as a security-enhancing new bottling contract with the Pepsi Bottling Group.

Although improvisation played a part, these reshuffles in the beverages and confectionery streams were based not on gut instinct but on Sunderland's signature "Managing for Value" program, launched in 1997. At the time, the program was considered to be just another variation on Cadbury's "value for money" tradition. Only later would it become a fashionable mantra in the fast-moving consumer goods industries – as in Unilever's "Path to Growth," for example. The downside of Sunderland's anticipation of the industry curve – as seen with Dominic Cadbury a decade earlier with core competences – was that there was no taken-for-granted industry discourse for change agents to rely on. Rather, to gain resonance and momentum, they had to unite several fledgling alternative developments within the company.

The first had been initiated by Sunderland as managing director of Trebor Bassett. The integration of Trebor and Basset was no instant success – in fact far from it.[21] But rather than writing it off as a failure, Sunderland was encouraged to use the sugar confectionery subsidiary to pilot Managing for Value in prototype form.

A second fledgling development was discontent with the lack of financial discipline in the relationship between corporate headquarters and the business units: "There was very little discipline about the process. We were not tough enough on people and standards."[22] To remedy this, Sunderland made strenuous efforts to change the culture to one "where the primacy of the shareholder within our stakeholder constituency was made very clear to the organization, and where the disciplines of return on capital, incentive schemes, and letting the best people have the best jobs were more prominent."[23] Managing for Value was much more than a variation on the value for money theme. It was a vehicle for distinguishing between core and noncore brands and geographies and fostering operational integration between the former and divestment of the latter.[24] As Kappler put it, "Managing for value also was a strategic process to help us determine in which market sectors we should put our efforts, and which ones we should either be milking or withdrawing from."[25]

The third and final seed of Managing for Value germinated in Bob Stack's Executive Development Program. Taking a leaf from Adrian Cadbury's original young executive programs, Stack, with the encouragement of Dominic Cadbury, established a new program in 1992 to address two group-level management challenges. The first, articulated by the US beverages managers, was the failure of the group's two streams to act as real global businesses. As one senior executive put it: "In fact [Cadbury and Schweppes] were anything but global, they were operating as a global portfolio of companies ... there were no global brand initiatives." The second was a concern about local financial reporting: "everything was very independent and individualized, apart from having to deliver a bottom line profit objective."

From these two preoccupations emerged a series of events: CEO conferences, targeted at top management, and younger executive development sessions, targeted at "high potentials." Initiatives developed from interactions between the two levels – not always to Wellings' taste – for example regarding the desirability of expressing a group "vision." Moreover by 1996, with Sunderland now installed as CEO, Stack was running a controversial program around management quality – a subject firmly ruled out by Wellings. Moreover, Sunderland agreed to carry out an external assessment of Cadbury Schweppes' top 200 people globally, positioned as a "development exercise."

Ultimately, Managing for Value may have been even more important for the boost it gave to the traditions of contestability and mobility than for the actual outcome – a vastly increased share price and a more top-line-oriented dialogue between corporate headquarters and business units. Many in the development program were promoted several times. Richard Verne went on to run Cadbury's bottling operation, Kappler became finance director, and Todd Stitzer would make it all the way to CEO.

In 2000 the executive chairman and long-standing face of the company, Dominic Cadbury, retired, to be replaced by a relative outsider, Derek Bonham, in a nonexecutive capacity. This gave Sunderland room to take on a leading strategic role, a necessity now that the second phase of Managing for Value was about to begin.[26] One of Sunderland's first acts was to reorganize senior management to give more emphasis to strategy by separating operating responsibilities from strategic development. The result was the move of several US leaders to corporate headquarters. John Brock, MD of beverages, became chief operating officer, a new post, with unprecedented responsibility for driving performance in both confectionery and beverages through a single operational organization. The two-stream concept was abandoned in favor of a flatter geographical organization, including larger regional reporting units. Henceforth, the heads of all regional beverage and confectionery units were to report directly to Brock in a bid to increase group-wide operational synergies.

At the same time, the other rising US star, Todd Stitzer, was made chief strategy officer, another new position, reporting directly to Sunderland.[27] Stitzer's strategy team focussed on the second part of Cadbury Schweppes' historical success theme: maintaining the vitality of the long game by revitalizing the center's acquisition capabilities and thinning out the noncore portfolio. Stitzer had long experience of bedding in acquisitions and brands, and it would serve Cadbury well – as did his far-sighted commitment, dating back to the 1980s, to healthier noncarbonated drinks, a trend that the world was about to follow.

In September 2000 Cadbury Schweppes made a decisive move in this direction by acquiring Snapple. Seventeen other beverage companies followed, for a total of £6 billion. Under Stitzer, Cadbury Schweppes' drinks portfolio also shifted from around 80 percent carbonated and 20 percent noncarbonated to a 50:50 split. It was a move both timely and clever, simultaneously anticipating the price war that Coca-Cola and PepsiCo would unleash in response to the shrinking carbonated drinks market and consolidating its position in the US bottling system. The strategy also worked to fend off the new threat of global food and drink corporations such as General Mills and Unilever in this market.

Meanwhile, the arrival of Brock and Stitzer in London proved a turning point. For the first time in its history, Cadbury headquarters developed a real sense of co-ownership of strategy with the US subsidiary. Just as important, it created powerful complementarities, Stitzer's strategic role complementing the more hands-on operational skills of Brock in more ways than one. Like Stitzer, Brock was, as one colleague described him, an analytical heavyweight, but his special skill was in integrating businesses geographically, first in the US and increasingly on an international scale. Ultimately, Brock would become recognized as an "expert globaliser in the beverages industry,"[28] while Stitzer would focus more on regional and on marketing aspects.

Stitzer had to call on his strategic and marketing instincts sooner than foreseen. The only way Cadbury could achieve volume growth in the mature and highly competitive UK confectionery market was by stealing market share. Mars, Nestlé, and Cadbury Schweppes were effectively locked into a form of "Red Queen" competition, compelling them to run faster just to stand still. To maintain their existing market positions, they had to increase investment, which could not be justified in terms of financial returns. Still more uncomfortable, this form of competition increasingly applied to the entire Western world, where Cadbury Schweppes was pitted against Hershey Foods, Philip Morris, and Nestlé in a race to acquire the few remaining large independents. Cadbury's long game of becoming the world's biggest confectioner was in dire need of a shot in the arm. The company lagged behind the likes of Nestlé in the emerging Asian and Latin American markets, while its strengths were in mature Western markets with their increasingly health-conscious customers and governments.[29] Its joint bid with Danone for Nabisco having failed, Cadbury Schweppes had to look for expansion not only beyond its core Western markets, but also outside its core chocolate and confectionery sectors.

As ever, fortune would eventually smile on Cadbury, which always seemed to have alternative leaders in reserve. Realizing the magnitude of the problem, Stitzer had commissioned a study of the confectionery markets to see "whether there was a different way to skin the cat." It turned out that there was, and it came in the shape of chewing gum, which "had been the fastest-growing, highest-margin segment of the confectionery business for the last five years."[30] So Stitzer set about acquiring gum companies, first Hollywood in France, and then Danish Dandy. Dandy gave Cadbury access to markets in Turkey, Argentina, and China and made Cadbury the second largest player in the European gum market.[31]

But Stitzer's masterstroke was yet to come. With Sunderland and the rest of the top team, Stitzer had been eyeing an even bigger prize: Adams, whose key gum brands Halls, Trident, Dentyne, and Bubbas gave it a substantial footprint in Latin America and Asia as well as the US. When parent Pfizer finally made up its mind to sell Adams in 2002, Stitzer's team was well prepared. Stolen from under the nose of Cadbury's giant competitors at $4.2 billion, Adams Confectionery was the group's biggest acquisition and the vehicle of confectionery's breakthrough as a global leader, at a stroke making Cadbury the joint number one confectionery company in the world.[32]

The timing of the Adams acquisition coincided with appointment of John Sunderland as chairman. Who would succeed him as CEO? After Mike Gifford and Dominic Cadbury, Derek Williams and David Wellings, Frank Swan and John Sunderland, Cadbury Schweppes again applied its continuity/anticipation trade-off principle to decide: the most visible change agents often are not the most appropriate CEOs or chairmen. This time the choice was between Brock and Stitzer. Brock was seen by some as more senior, but as John Sunderland explained: "John was more operational. Todd was more strategic." He also had experience in legal, operational, marketing and strategy. Stitzer got the nod. Brock subsequently left to become the CEO of the world's largest brewer, InBev.

The new CEO had little time to celebrate his promotion or the mega-deal he had just helped to seal. As with Dr Pepper, the aura of the Adams acquisition quickly faded. Investors had reacted badly, suspecting that Cadbury had overpaid and would find it hard to integrate the ailing Adams businesses. In a matter of weeks, Adams had become what Todd Stitzer described as a "life or death issue."[33] It threatened to cause an enormous loss of value if it were integrated into the old, loose global model, so the incoming chief executive team was faced with a litmus test of its barely commenced tenure.

Fortunately, Cadbury's tradition of anticipation came to the rescue, which would ultimately turn the Adams mini-crisis into a happy accident. Stitzer and his team "had been thinking for a few years about changing the old [aspirational global] model by forming regional reporting units, separating operational from strategic responsibilities, reducing business units, and so on."[34] Their earlier reluctance to force the changes[35] now paid off, Adams providing a much more natural catalyst. "At that point, it was clear to everyone that Cadbury Schweppes had to take these kinds of decisions," says Stitzer. "There certainly was productive debate," but more importantly, "there wasn't a lot of unproductive debate." The "last remnants of the old [local baronial] culture" were about to be swept away as Stitzer and Stack put all their effort into finding "people who could perform to a higher standard."[36]

The bout of accelerated transformation triggered by the Adams acquisition came under two headings, each corresponding to one of the two pillars of Cadbury's long game: "Fuel for Growth" was a variation on the old "Value for Money" theme of product delivery, while "Smart Variety," the idea of disseminating all the good ideas around the world, was a variation on the dynamic capability theme of acquiring and integrating core categories and geographies. By July 2004 the crisis was over. Analysts were expecting first-half pretax profits of between £350 million and £378 million, and the dip in the share price after the Adams acquisition had been reversed as the market turned upbeat about Adams and Stitzer's strategy.[37]

It was not all change at Cadbury, however. In a move designed to signal his commitment to Cadbury's heritage and tone down his "Yankee" outsider image, Stitzer in 2005 announced a £40 million investment in the Bournville plant to meet growing demand for Cadbury's Dairy Milk.[38] Then, claiming his place among the major architects of Cadbury's long game, Stitzer in rapid succession announced the sale of the company's European beverages division, the full acquisition of the Dr Pepper/7Up bottling group,[39] and finally, in March 2007, the plan to split the group into two separate businesses.[40] Under the plan, Cadbury would sell off the soft drinks business to focus on confectionery. To complete the picture, Stitzer promised to reduce the headcount by 15 percent by 2011 to boost top-line margins that were lagging those of rivals Hershey and gum- and mint-maker Wm. Wrigley.

By 2007 Cadbury Schweppes was able to present a superb long-term track record to the world. From being an undersized UK competitor, the company had transformed itself into a true global leader in two of the most competitive industries in the world without any of the major financial trauma or management upheavals experienced by rivals Mars, Wrigley,

Kraft, Hershey, or Coca-Cola.[41] What's more, it had done it with resources that were much more limited than those of its giant competitors. Over the previous decade and a half, Cadbury Schweppes had managed to bring in and rejuvenate the ailing Adams brands and transform the Dr Pepper/7Up business from a repeated management buy-out target into a major force in the US, in the process returning 7Up to its place in the top five US grocery brands. But the company's acquisition record had not been faultless: the Chocolat Poulain acquisition in the 1980s was ill-judged, for example. But small failures like these were never allowed to become disasters. In addition, the management team became steadily more skilled at managing the tensions between acquisition, integration, and divestment dynamics. Over the period, the company had balanced bottom-line and top-line margins and at the same time integrated and boosted the performance of bought-in brands, in a way that has few parallels. Of its rivals, perhaps only Nestlé has done such a good job of drawing exceptional growth from a legacy of heritage brands – often enhancing their status (as Cadbury Schweppes with Dairy Milk and 7Up) on the way.[42]

In the light of this performance, it was odd to find the financial press in the same year, 2007, accusing Cadbury Schweppes of having grotesquely "underexploited its brand portfolio" and charging Stitzer with being over-conscious of the "Quaker roots and aura of benevolent capitalism which still permeates the company."[43] The immediate reason was a series of mostly minor mishaps,[44] but in June there was a more serious warning with the news that the private investor Nelson Peltz had taken a 3 percent stake in the company. In December, with his stake now increased to 4.5 percent, Peltz issued an ultimatum to Cadbury Schweppes' management, demanding tighter management, higher top-line margins, and a strategy aimed at realizing the brand portfolio's "full potential." Thus began a chain of events that for the first time Cadbury could not finesse into a happy accident, ending with its takeover by Kraft in 2010.

Leaving the most recent history aside, however, what has been truly remarkable in the Cadbury Schweppes story is the way the confectionery and beverages streams balanced each other out, one stream leading the way in using happy accidents to re-energize the traditions of transformation and speed up corporate change, the other holding off overzealous tendencies to corporate control by preserving key improvisational elements such as devolved business unit responses and cultural diversity. Let us review the post-merger history to illustrate this. The Cadbury Schweppes merger and subsequent board dissension turned out to be a blessing in disguise for the confectionery side. From it emerged a new Cadburyism, marrying the "long view" to a "value for money" emphasis at a distance from the old Schweppes guard. The pace of evolution was much faster here than in beverages, where the proliferation of local business units and devolved sense-making were much harder for the new Cadburyists to control. This, however, would soon change.

After another happy accident, this time the takeover threat from General Cinema, the soft drinks business units took up the running as transformer. For the next decade, beverages (including the CCSB joint venture) would lead the way in terms of the emergence of up-and-coming champions and alternative leaders, the development of world and regional brand leadership, and the integration of acquisitions. Under the leadership of a new US team, the beverages stream was transformed into an international player with a tightly focussed transformation platform. Interestingly, the CCSB venture remained independent of soft drinks as a whole, bringing a maverick element into Cadbury Schweppes' corporate decision-making processes. And while confectionery was slow to consolidate its international presence, its unresolved issues around "national baronies" served to avert overambitious control tendencies and keep alive diversity and business-unit animal spirits – such that from 1997 it could again take over leadership of the new Managing for Value theme as well as brand acquisition and integration.

TESCO: A EUROPEAN RETAIL GIANT COMES OF AGE (1992–2007)

Between 1990 and 1993 the UK experienced a sharp economic decline. Output fell and claimant unemployment rose to nearly three million. Although recession had a lesser impact on food retailing than on other sectors of the economy, by summer 1992 Tesco was suffering.[45] With sales growth slowing and margins under pressure, commentators and academics alike were quick to suggest, as with Cadbury Schweppes, that Tesco was "stuck in the middle" between Sainsbury's image of quality and Safeway's price competitiveness.[46] Industry overcapacity had led to a pattern of "Red Queen" competition between the five major retailers, which, having acquired most of the smaller regional chains between them, now accounted for 62 percent of the market. Gaining market share was henceforward a zero-sum game. Further compounding Tesco's problems, Prime Minister John Major's government the same year introduced more restrictive planning regulations for freehold sites, ushering in a new "race for space."[47] In response to these financial pressures, Tesco, Sainsbury, and Safeway all launched large rights issues – with Tesco in particular incurring the wrath of skeptical commentators and investors. If this were not enough, a number of "hard discounters" led by German Aldi and Danish Netto were preparing to cross the Channel, attracted by the high margins racked up by the leading British supermarket groups.[48]

One of the escape routes out of the destructive pattern of domestic competition was to internationalize, which meant challenging the lone European giant Carrefour.[49] With the acquisition of the 90-store Catteau supermarket chain in Northern France, that is precisely what Tesco did in 1992, in a move that was dubbed "the boldest foray yet by a UK retailer into continental Europe."[50] Too small to provide a concerted challenge to Carrefour, Catteau had limited success and Tesco divested the chain in 1997 – but not before a team led by David Reid, deputy chairman with responsibility overseas development, had extracted some valuable lessons from the experience.

The first lesson was that Tesco would be better off focussing on less mature markets such as emerging Eastern Europe, where to differentiate itself from Carrefour and Walmart it would strive to be even more sensitive to local differences. A more surprising takeaway was that Tesco had gone to Europe with the wrong store format. Instead of the original superstore template that worked so well in the UK, the company found that it had to use the hypermarket format to succeed abroad. In other words, Tesco needed to reinvent Porter's legacy of combining food and non-food in a one-stop shop. Yet another happy accident was in gestation. With a flexibility far removed from Sainsbury's command-and-control instinct and structures, Reid's team reimported its foreign learning to reinvent the UK business.

Reinventing the position of non-food in Tesco's customer value proposition provided a promising way ahead – but only if the destructive domestic competition could be faced down first. In response to changing demographics, eating, and travelling habits – as well as planning restrictions – MacLaurin and Malpas brought back the concept of town-center stores in the shape of Tesco Metro.[51] Yet, as they were well aware, this was only a partial answer. Where was the "big picture" response that would somehow enable them to turn the macroeconomic crisis into a happy accident? Was there an alternative leader in the house who could think differently enough to get the company out of its rut?

This is where Tesco's traditions of contestation and mobility served it well. Tesco had a much more questioning and challenging culture than its competitors, not to mention a leadership process that was rather open. People recruited from Sainsbury or Marks & Spencer were surprised at the lack of hierarchy, simple lines of communication, and the authority they were given.

It helped that Tesco's dominant coalition, MacLaurin to the fore, had a very good astuteness in terms of the ability to put together people with different points of view. The core team of MacLaurin, Malpas, and Reid strikingly exemplified this. MacLaurin was seen as someone who understood the front end of retailing and had great execution skills. "Malpas was the 'strategic man,' with great clarity of vision and rigor, while Reid, neutral and measured, sat in the middle, and judged more in terms of commercial and financial rationales."[52] One senior executive added that all the members of the team "had permission to disagree, but once a decision was made everyone was expected to get on the ship."

Not least, their astuteness extended to spotting future leaders very early on – those who could solve a problem no one else could and kept solving problems. One such was Terry Leahy, who was quickly singled out and mentored by Malpas. "The business wasn't doing very well in 1992 and none of us could really understand why, to tell you the truth," Malpas said. It seemed to be stuck in a 20th- rather than 21st-century customer proposition. Malpas decided to spend what turned out to be "a very important day" with Leahy. After visiting a number of Tesco and competitor stores, the penny dropped. As Malpas explained: "We had lost sight of the customer … we simply did not give enough space for customer convenience" – something Leahy had "absolutely picked up on." It was at that moment that Malpas realized that Leahy would be his successor.[53] With the nod from MacLaurin and Malpas, Leahy was quickly propelled on to the board as marketing director, a position that, despite his ambition, he was initially hesitant about "because as marketing director you are bound to get in strategic trouble … it puts a lot of spotlight on you."[54]

But if it was bold to remove a top performer from operational responsibility and give him a clean desk at a time of maximum pressure, it was also shrewd. When Leahy probed the customer relationship, it was "almost like marriage guidance". Loyalty was low because hard-up customers resented the company abandoning its value for money stance in an effort to be more like Sainsbury: "We're angry at you and we're going elsewhere."[55] In a paper presented to the board in May 1993, Leahy proposed that "we should stop benchmarking, stop copying competitors; instead, we should follow customers … unconditionally." In a conformist industry that tended to respond to customers only if it made economic sense or everyone else was doing it, Leahy's proposal of "an unconditional contract with customers" was a radical step. The good news, however, was that "we don't need a new business model … just a lot of small changes." Those small changes would become Leahy's trademark slogan "Every Little Helps."[56]

Even so, Leahy's proposals were tough for the leadership to stomach. What he was putting forward was no less than a return to Tesco's price-conscious roots, matching Asda's prices rather than Sainsbury's, and introducing a new "value" range to compete with rivals' discount lines. All this caused a "big rift" in a team whose whole rationale was the need to boost quality and margins to move away from the original "pile it high, sell it cheap" logic. According to Leahy, MacLaurin and Malpas "initially held back somewhat ... I wanted to move much more strongly in 1993." As they had foreseen, shareholders who had "bought our shares over the last 10 years on a story of 'it's all about improved margins'" were appalled by the new strategy, and the share price plummeted. Perhaps fortunately, Leahy had been too naïve to anticipate the reaction: "If I'd been more worldly-wise I might have been swayed away from it."[57]

Despite the misgivings, Leahy's ideas were in practice absorbed since they fitted so naturally with Tesco's tradition of continuity.[58] As Malpas had warned in the mid-1980s à propos of Aldi:

> When the price war comes, and surely it will, we will cut harder and deeper and more aggressively than anyone dreams possible, because that is what this company was built on and that is what everyone around this board table really knows how to do.[59]

Or as another top executive remarked to us, Leahy's changes "were about reinvention or reinvigoration rather than transformation" – although the "results clearly were transformational." After some anxious months, Tesco could by the end of 1993 see initial signs of success: the company had maintained a price gap of 4–5 percent against Sainsbury and was more than holding its own against the hard discounters.

Rather than rest on their laurels, Tesco's top trio was at the same time playing with another counterconventional notion: the revolutionary idea that customers should not have to queue at the checkout. Breaking with industry custom would cost, they estimated, 10 percent of Tesco's profits. But they did it anyway: "It broke in early 1994 and it was a huge success, so then our trade really was moving strongly."[60] In another pointer to things to come, in the same year Tesco outbid Sainsbury to acquire the leading Scottish retailer, William Low. It was a calculated bluff: David was beginning to outmuscle Goliath.

In 1995 Leahy became deputy managing director, largely thanks to determined lobbying by Malpas:

> I felt very strongly that this beautifully running, well-oiled machine was very much a 20th century machine [whereas] what we needed was a 21st century machine. And that said to me that I shouldn't consider any of the more established board directors to take over from me as MD but that we should look to skip a generation.[61]

One of Leahy's first acts was to introduce Clubcard, the UK's first supermarket loyalty card and the mechanism that would allow Tesco to leapfrog Sainsbury into the number one retail spot. Leahy recalls, "The famous call for Tesco was on the day that Clubcard came out and Sainsbury, our main competitor, said that it was the wrong thing to do … and then we went through the roof in terms of market share and we had a free run of a year or more."[62] The combination of William Low's 10 percent and the free run with Clubcard were decisive. Reflects Leahy: "It's amazing now when you think that in 1993 Sainsbury's market share was much bigger than ours … we flipped that around within about three years."[63]

After a successful 1996, MacLaurin and Malpas retired, leaving Leahy alone at the top as chief executive – to some initial dismay on the part of MacLaurin and others, who would have preferred Malpas to stay on as nonexecutive chairman. Determined to see a generation change, the latter "flatly refused," however, and the others fell into line. Although some analysts saw it as high risk and raised objections, ultimately, as Malpas had predicted, it was not high risk at all: "You can imagine how every year since 1997 I have watched with delight the way that business has come along."[64]

Where would Tesco's new boss find the next round of growth? Planning regulations were becoming more stringent with every year. Meanwhile, mainstream giants such as Carrefour, Ahold, and Walmart were preparing a big international push. Leahy could see that Tesco and Sainsbury's "were in danger of quickly falling into the second rank." He saw no need to alter the core strategy of steady improvement of the retail offer ("Every Little Helps," or, as new marketing director Tim Mason[65] put it, adding "bricks in the wall"[66]), but that was just part of a broader four-element overall strategy. As well as consolidating a strong UK core, Tesco would build up its non-food offer, diversify sideways into retail services such as banking and the Internet, and make itself a force on the international retail scene.[67]

To boost UK growth, Tesco copied Cohen's policy of thinking bigger than the opposition, rolling out new stores and expanding existing ones at every opportunity. It also continued to experiment with formats such as Tesco Metro, Tesco Extra in both food and non-food, and Tesco Express.[68] In the same vein, Leahy launched a banking joint venture with RBS in 1997 and initiated a first foray into online shopping.[69] While the online learning period would last more than 2 years, the distribution and logistics elements were largely improvised – which would have been unthinkable for most companies, including Sainsbury's. Out of these experiments emerged Tesco's distinctive online model, based not on the classic centralized warehouse but on existing stores where Tesco.com employees picked and packed online orders during off-peak periods.[70] Criticism was scathing:

"We had analysts telling us we were doing the wrong thing, people from McKinsey, Andersen, PwC."[71] Sainsbury's went the conventional route, initially delivering from a central warehouse, but by 2003 it was fulfilling customer orders in its stores, like its rival. Tesco had a 5-year start and an expanding user base, however, which made catch-up hard.[72]

Tesco's international strategy emerged from recognition that the UK market was saturated and that domestic retailers were bound to face competition from international players.[73] As ever, undeterred by conventional industry "facts" – by international standards, UK supermarket firms are small and chains find it hard to expand beyond national boundaries[74] – Tesco chose defense by attack. Quickly deciding that Catteau was a long-term underperformer, Reid and Leahy sold it off to focus not only on Eastern Europe, but more ambitiously on further-flung emerging markets such as Thailand, South Korea, Taiwan, and Malaysia. In 2000 Leahy pledged that Tesco would be the "first British retailer to become an outstanding success" internationally – with a portfolio of 70 hypermarkets in Eastern Europe and 60 in the Far East.[75,76] In 2003, anticipating plans to take a stake in a Chinese retail chain, Tesco appointed an Asian expert, Standard Chartered Bank CEO Mervyn Davies, to the board.[77,78] Finally, after much groundwork, Tesco made its boldest international foray yet, launching a new Fresh & Easy superstore format in arguably the toughest market of all, the US.

In effect, in the decade from 1997 to 2007, Tesco's four-element strategy acted as a simple step-up-change program, to be reviewed and redeployed whenever a new threat arose. Thus, when Walmart arrived on the scene in 1999 with its purchase of Asda, "there was a big worry among retailers such as Sainsbury's: 'is this the end of life as we know it? Is this the end of retailing as we know it?,'" a former Tesco executive commented.

Adding to the worries was a full-scale inquiry into the industry by the UK Competition Commission, addressing growing concerns that the majors were ramping up profits by using their market power to squeeze suppliers. Tesco took all these threats in the same stride. The company had a whole series of these step-change programs taking place, so Tesco accelerated everything. As a result, Asda was surprised at how quickly Tesco got those changes through. In the event, the Competition Commission inquiry was less damaging than feared, absolving the supermarkets of making excessive profits and noting that the real price of food had declined between 1989 and 1998.[79] Despite the favorable outcome, the level of critical scrutiny remained intense – but it was something that Tesco, unlike some of its retail rivals, seemed to thrive on.

By December 2004 Tesco had come full circle. It had taken Cohen's original market-trader philosophy, debugged it, and reinvented it as a supremely successful business model. Not only was the company by far the largest UK retailer, but it had also beaten Asda into second place as the price leader. Preferring to trade lower margins for higher volumes, Tesco had made the "pile it high" part come true as well as "sell it cheap," all without repudiating the quality element introduced during the MacLaurin era.

Like Cadbury Schweppes, Tesco is ambidextrous, fusing dynamism with stability, improvisation and flexibility with continuity. It is – at least for the moment, despite hiccups in 2011 and 2012 – a winning combination. Yet a word of caution is in order. As one top executive pointed out, one of the foundations of Tesco's recent success was that "the strategy process is easier now there is absolute clarity on our customer values ... that is our bible." Yet "bible" does not rhyme well with contestation or anticipation.

Before Leahy's ascendancy, the top management team – MacLaurin, Malpas, Reid, Gildersleeve, and others – had been highly diverse, with different characters and aptitudes. On the positive side, since 1997 Tesco's authority structure has been flattened to comprise just five levels of management from cashier to board member. As in the MacLaurin era, no one can say that the Tesco board is composed of clones. Less positive is the fact that, for the first decade of the 2000s, Leahy was the undoubted leader, with insiders commenting that there was only one leader ... and everyone on the board totally bought into the strategy. Has Tesco's challenging culture that began, let's not forget, in physical fisticuffs become a hierarchical one, or in danger of becoming so? How will Leahy's retirement in 2011 affect that culture?

SMITH & NEPHEW: A HIGH-TECHNOLOGY, HIGH-MARGIN COMPANY COMES OF AGE (1995–2003)

Eric Kinder summed up his years at the top of Smith & Nephew (1982–90) as an era of acquisition-led expansion in North American medical products. John Robinson followed (1990–97) with a period of consolidation, with an emphasis on the high-technology end of the industry. Both chief executives saw each other's contributions, as well as those of Alan Fryer, Kenneth Kemp, and Don Seymour, as sequential steps in an historical process from which Smith & Nephew would eventually emerge as a fully fledged global leader in high-tech, high-margin medical instruments.[80]

Almost 5 years into Robinson's tenure, however, the financial press had failed to detect any such logical progression, still seeing a company apparently unable to shake off its image as a slow-moving "peddler of bandages and creams."[81] Shareholders took their cue from another prima facie observation. Taking the group's long failure to make a substantial acquisition as evidence of paralysed decision-making and becalmed ambition, they left the share price where it was.

What would it take to reinject momentum and purpose into Smith & Nephew's trajectory? At a minimum, two kinds of dynamic were needed: alternative leadership and a happy accident. First of all, one or more alternative leaders were required who were close enough to the inner circle of Robinson, Fryer, and chairman Kinder not to endanger continuity, yet who were at the same time able to anticipate a different emphasis as well as distance themselves enough in style and history to bring back into the fold some of Robinson's and Fryer's opponents, as well as eager young fresh thinkers outside the dominant coalition. By 1995 Christopher O'Donnell had positioned himself in this role. As managing director of the medical division, O'Donnell – an "operations guy" by contrast with the production-oriented Kinder and technology-focussed Robinson – had "many runs-in" with Fryer, who nonetheless conceded: "You know, it was absolutely right that Chris should become chief executive."[82] O'Donnell also had a "unique capacity to be onside with everybody."[83]

But even O'Donnell would have struggled to reap results without two happy accidents, one minor and one major. First, thanks to a display of uncanny patience by Robinson, Smith & Nephew had by 1995 been restored to financial soundness. Its balance sheet free of debt, it could now realistically contemplate another round of acquisitions. But Robinson was deliberately making the window of new opportunity much wider. There was a need to encourage change and new ideas, he told the group management executive in January 1995. Decision-making was at risk of becoming hierarchical and conformist, slowing the company down and wastefully rejecting new ideas. To break the group-think, Robinson concluded, "no one person or group" should henceforward have monopoly responsibility for key issues.[84] Instead, strategic decisions should be the result of a "shared process."

Initially, senior managers lacked the confidence to take up this invitation. The turning point was, ironically, a low-risk, nonsurgical acquisition put forward by O'Donnell.[85] Despite the small (£4 million) and "pretty simple" nature of the deal, O'Donnell found himself compelled to do 28 presentations, including five to the full board, to push it through. It was of course "ridiculous" – but, more important than the acquisition itself, it was the incident that "broke the logjam." O'Donnell put forward three more acquisitions, two of which were passed and one which was not, and then other parts of the business started to have the confidence to do that too.

O'Donnell was nonetheless frustrated. "They [the dominant coalition] did not see the bigger picture … they didn't ever get to a clean cut," he complained:

> With 20/20 hindsight, what the Board should have done was say 'we've got all these problems, we'll just tell the market look, as a one-off solution which is going to cost us half a billion pounds we'll sell this business, that business, we'll close all these textile mills and then we'll be able to grow the thing up.'"[86]

Robinson knew what to do, as he had shown with his steadfast commitment to the Centres of Excellence concept. But he was unable to drive it through because he failed get key people on board, notably US orthopedics chief Jack Blair. By 1996 Blair was "totally fed up with the English way of doing things."[87] Jim Dick remembers: "There was some bitterness about how much was being spent on R&D because that was always fiercely protected (by Robinson)." More generally, Robinson's "'one healthcare company' concept was running out of steam … it could have worked, but it was bogged down with US politics."[88]

It took a major happy accident to get O'Donnell's ideas put into practice. Responding to pressure from disgruntled investors, Robinson had nailed his colors to the mast of international expansion. A whole series of investments in Asia followed. No sooner had they been completed, however, than the Asian currency crisis kicked in and the company lost 40 percent of its profits in 18 months – just at the moment when O'Donnell, fulfilling Robinson's prediction, had taken over as CEO. O'Donnell spent most of his first year flying round Asia: "I mean, you could have a good business plan when you got on a flight and by the time you got off, the currency had changed so much the business plan was rubbish."[89] The board's reaction to the crisis was unanimous: there was no way the company could carry on as it had been doing. Fryer recalls:

> Chris had a real dilemma. He had two options. Do we carry on running this Group as we have been in the past? Or do I, in the first six months of my leadership … bite the bullet now?[90]

O'Donnell characteristically chose the second option. With the aid of nonexecutive board members, he convinced Robinson to undertake a complete strategic and manufacturing review, bringing in McKinsey to do the first and PricewaterhouseCoopers the second.[91] What followed was an intensive 6-month review of the company. All supporters of the Centres of Excellence project, O'Donnell, Dick, Blair, and Robinson had long been convinced that Smith & Nephew was trying to do too many things and spreading resources too thinly, a conclusion broadly supported by the review. McKinsey's other conclusions were also no surprise. First, Smith & Nephew should exit the small, nonglobal businesses that were absorbing disproportionate amounts of management resources. Second, as O'Donnell, in particular, had already concluded, the group's diversity made it hard to frame a convincing narrative for investors because the investor public did not really know what business the company was in. Third, McKinsey corroborated O'Donnell's intuition that although the company had excellent technology, "we were spending far too much on that and nothing like enough on selling and marketing."[92]

After 6 months of deliberation,[93] the Centres of Excellence concept was replaced with a fresh initiative centered on strategic business units. Remarkably, by the time the transformation project began, O'Donnell had swung everyone behind it.[94] Some credit must go to O'Donnell's unique people skills here – but the external review undoubtedly gave it needed authority. Without it, "we would not have done the things that we subsequently did," one team member commented, "Not because we didn't know that they should be done, but … we wouldn't have had the ammunition to bring it about."

The change program began in 1998 and lasted 2 years. The defining feature was the adoption of a new management structure and strategy focussing on three strategic business units: orthopedics, endoscopy, and wound management.[95] All the other businesses would be sold off to invest in the core. There was also a restructuring of the businesses, with those that were slated for exit run for cash to plough back into the expansion businesses. The board also signed off the establishment of a new US healthcare division, combining orthopedics and endoscopy, consolidating all US sales and distribution functions in one place. True to O'Donnell's commitment, the "locus of decision-making" for these businesses was placed firmly in the US, where marketing and selling were concentrated.

At the same time, O'Donnell substantially beefed up the sales and marketing effort, focussing more on healthcare sales and education. Finally, to increase the group's market and investor visibility, Smith & Nephew listed on the New York Stock Exchange in 1999. North America was not only Smith & Nephew's largest market, accounting for 45 percent of revenues, but it was also home to both much of the group's product development effort and its major competitors Stryker Corporation, DePuy, and Biomet. It was hoped that the listing would gain Smith & Nephew access to the huge base of American institutional investors and thus help close the gap with these rivals.

It is fair to say that the business unit restructuring was an outstanding success. Spurred on by the launch of key products such as Journey, an innovative knee-replacement system, Exogen ultrasound devices and the Supartz osteoarthritis treatment, Smith & Nephew's share price went through the roof.[96]

Smith & Nephew's once blurred identity came more sharply into focus with every year. In 1999 the company sold the majority stake in its Bracing and Support Systems business to the private equity arm of Chase Manhattan.[97] A year later, it was the turn of the symbolically important consumer healthcare business, including the heritage brands Elastoplast and Lil-Lets and the Nivea distribution business,[98] which was sold to consumer products group Beiersdorf. Finally freed of its sticking-plaster image, Smith & Nephew could be seen for what it was – a high-growth, high-tech leader in a fast-growing global industry.

With the benefit of both better financial disciplines and the investment firepower yielded by the consumer products divestment, Smith & Nephew could go hunting for acquisitions again – but this time concentrating on often small, bolt-on additions that could be swiftly integrated with the existing businesses.[99] "Before Robinson nobody ever met the budget," recalls Alan Suggett:

> What's evolved in recent years under O'Donnell is that budgets are bedrock and therefore you can aspire to more ... because you can go to the City every half year and say 'well, we did what we said we would' ... And that openness with investors gave confidence, not just with people who work for the company but for investors and investment.[100]

In a sense, this marked a return to the old days in which the best technologies were acquired and licensed to help grow the business efficiently. It was again a winning recipe from which Smith & Nephew has continued to prosper. Yet, with the intensified consolidation among orthopedics manufacturers – Smith & Nephew's fastest growing business – the pressure for another transformational merger grew. Although O'Donnell undoubtedly bequeathed to his successors a very healthy operating business at his retirement in 2007, the failure to pull off the other attempted mergers or acquisitions left Smith & Nephew looking vulnerable. Takeover rumors are never far away, suggesting a further transformation dimension still to be achieved.

What key lessons can we learn from Smith & Nephew's transformation history? Investors and business commentators have long mistaken Smith & Nephew's long game of logical incrementalism for dull mediocrity, characteristically ascribing most of the company's post-2000 success to

O'Donnell.[101] Yet despite appearances of a radical break, 2000 is better described as a tipping point, the moment when the "logical next steps" taken successively by Seymour, Kemp, Kinder, Fryer, Robinson, and O'Donnell himself finally cohered into transformation. In other words, as "Mr Global Marketing," O'Donnell came up with his own variation on the old success theme, just as Robinson ("Mr Technology"), Fryer ("Mr European Marketing"), Kinder ("Mr US"), Seymour ("Mr "R&D"), and Kemp ("Mr 20 percent") had done before him. Each new leader found an angle appropriate to his time. The main difference was in the happy accidents – the only reliable way to speed up the pace of transformation – which benefited some more than others: compare the drought under Robinson with the defining accidents that gave O'Donnell his chance at the very start of his tenure.

Of course, by now the underlying transformation theme had undergone so many improvisational variations that at first blush observers might not connect it with the original. But the original is still there. In the end, O'Donnell's philosophy of bolt-on acquisitions, and his combination of British personability with American sales flair are variations on the theme evolved by Smith & Nephew's founding family: spending less on technological innovation (originating in the leading healthcare market of the world – then Germany, now the US) than the competition, while generating proportionally higher financial revenues through superior entrepreneurial initiative and better customer relationship management.

Smith & Nephew's perceived "dullness" disguises a historical capacity to "hit the market" with change announcements while the sun is shining, that is, before investors perceive a change as a massive transformation.[102] This capacity is grounded in Smith & Nephew's traditions of transformation that have allowed the company to stay consistently one step ahead of changes in the competitive environment and thus transform itself at its own pace rather than at that imposed by external pressures. This has resulted in many decades of above-average growth, uninterrupted by bursts of financial trauma, during which Smith & Nephew has regularly outperformed market expectations.

Ultimately, O'Donnell, Robinson, Kinder, Kemp, and Seymour share the credit for developing a simple, continuous thread around which the company could continuously adapt itself, in logical steps 5–10 years apart, without significant external pressure or the trauma of financial crisis.[103] While to outsiders the manner of this transformation sometimes appears worthy but plodding,[104] the reality viewed from the inside was anything but. When a long-serving director was asked at his retirement party in the late 1980s why he had spent 40 years at the same company, he replied that he hadn't, because "every five years it changed completely."[105]

Now, however, Smith & Nephew faces new challenges. Up to 2000 the company's reputation as an unexceptional, middle-of-the-road company was actually an advantage. It gave top management teams the necessary leeway to leave creative tensions temporarily unresolved, in turn allowing for the emergence of traditions of transformation through a historical process unfathomable to any single generation of managers. In its new position of industry leader, Smith & Nephew is facing expectations of an entirely different order. Under pressure to deliver more quickly, the danger is that Smith & Nephew's top management team will respond by cutting short the self-energizing historical dynamic. One of the most critical tensions in contemporary Smith & Nephew is that between British and North American management traditions.

Financial analysts have for some time believed that Smith & Nephew might be more highly valued if it were based in North America. In response, O'Donnell rebalanced the investor base so that, at the time of writing, it is now equally divided between the US and UK. He also laid more emphasis on decentralized marketing strategies and recruitment processes. As a result, most recent top management appointments have been external North American recruits. In 2007 Smith & Nephew announced that one of these, orthopedics president and General Electric veteran Dave Illingworth, would succeed O'Donnell as CEO.

From a short-term financial perspective, all these appointments seem to make sense – after all, US orthopedics has been the mainstay of Smith & Nephew's recent growth and profits. Yet, as we have seen, financial analysts have been notoriously oblivious to the benefits and importance of Smith & Nephew's longer game. Seen in this light, the UK/North America tension is not about patriotism or immediate success, but the deeper historical process that has been a key element in Smith & Nephew's long-term success: its openness to technological innovation and entrepreneurship *anywhere*. In a very real sense, the question is thus the reverse of patriotism: whether to keep the international orientation or, bluntly, to become North American. Before his retirement, O'Donnell acknowledged that if there were some "big acquisition-related change, Smith & Nephew might no longer be British."[106]

Jim Dick puts his finger on the perils of such an ahistorical change. "There is a danger going forward that we become too US orientated, that is financial market-led, instead of international," he warns. "If they're not careful, we'll do the same to the rest of the world as the Brits did to the US. We'll start exporting US culture, and I think we've now got four businesses run by US presidents, and there's a US CEO."[107]

CHAPTER 6

The Three Comparators

In this chapter, we describe the history and strategies of the three comparator companies: J Sainsbury as the comparator for Tesco, Unilever as the comparator for Cadbury Schweppes, and SSL International as the comparator for Smith & Nephew.

J SAINSBURY

Of the three comparators, J Sainsbury was the most direct competitor to its successful strategic transformer, Tesco. Furthermore, J Sainsbury was viewed for a very long time as a superior company. Why did that superiority not last?

Dominant logic

From its foundation in 1869, the Sainsbury brand has been linked with fresh foods and promoted in terms of high quality at lower prices. Founder John Sainsbury's greatest achievement was to associate the family name with the idea that price competitiveness was not incompatible with quality. This translated into several practical policies. One of Sainsbury's earliest was to promote from within, ensuring that even family members could only become managers after rising through the ranks and acquiring training and experience.[1] Quality control and discipline were also enforced, with the founder and his wife Mary often dropping in on stores unannounced.[2]

At first sight then, John Sainsbury and Jack Cohen had little in common apart from entrepreneurship. Whereas Cohen could and did turn a blind eye to ramshackle shops and "sharp practices," John's branches and service had to be as pure as his Dutch butter, and his last words when he died were: "Keep the shops well lit."[3] Whereas Sainsbury took control of the supply chain early on, building privileged supplier relations and centralizing buying and logistics, Cohen was the embodiment of improvisation and opportunism. Nevertheless, in one aspect, Sainsbury not only resembled his rival but outstripped him: the Sainsbury culture and John Sainsbury as a manager were considered by many to be hierarchical and autocratic.

No cracks in Sainsbury's armour (1915–66)

By the beginning of World War I, the Sainsbury chain comprised 122 shops. With the founder's original aim of providing each of his offspring with at least one shop long satisfied, the issue now was succession and the division of roles among the children. John Sainsbury postponed the succession issue as long as possible by the simple expedient of remaining chairman until his death in 1928 at the age of 84. By then, real control had long passed to his eldest son, "Mr John," who in 1915 took over as trading director – a key position at Sainsbury then and in the future. During his 23 years at the helm, the "uncompromising" Mr John built on his father's legacy of control.[4] Drawing on the levers of the central buying and logistics operations in Blackfriars, he extended the food range, doubled the number of shops, and extended the Sainsbury brand franchise from Greater London to the Midlands, East Anglia, and the south.

Like his father, Mr John combined military control tendencies with uncanny retailing instincts that allowed him to spot new trends and opportunities early on. Capitalizing on the quality connotations of the brand, he launched a range of "home-manufactured" cooked meats, sausages, and pies. He also pioneered own-label products such as teas and margarine. By 1930 Sainsbury's position as a cosmopolitan and creative purveyor of high-quality foodstuffs sourced from all over the world was virtually impregnable.

Again mimicking his father, Mr John maintained continuity by remaining chairman until his death in 1956,[5] although passing executive control to other family members much earlier. By then, Sainsbury was selling much more per square foot of selling space than any of its domestic competitors. Rivalry within the third generation had been pre-empted by allocating responsibilities according to inherited positions in the family tree. So Mr John's eldest son, "Mr Alan," inherited the key trading side, while his other son Robert, "Mr R.J.," became chief accountant. Cousin James Sainsbury was made head of manufacturing, while Fred Salisbury, previously personal assistant to Mr John, became the first non-family member of the board in 1941.

Given the strong family traditions, none of the Sainsburys could be expected to play the significant dissenting role performed by Edgar Collar at Tesco. At the height of his influence under Mr Alan, Salisbury was allowed to set only the meat prices. Salisbury had to reckon with the intrusive eye for detail of other family members too: even though he set prices, the judgment of Mr James prevailed when it came to the quality of the meat. Failure to toe the family line was not an option.[6]

In this way, the third-generation Sainsburys entrenched their predecessors' habits of meticulous attention to detail, military-style command and control, and strictly centralized customer service and staff training. Unlike Tesco, where buying decisions were decentralized and "buncing" (sticking higher prices on goods previously labeled at a lower price) and improvised price-cutting were rife, Mr Alan personally supervised the weekly price lists that were religiously followed by Sainsbury's branch managers.[7] Sainsbury's discipline and centralized control stood in stark contrast to the looser rein exercised by all other multiples after the World War II.

Under Mr Alan's leadership, the company embarked on several industry-leading innovations, pioneering the large-scale development of own-brand goods and experimenting with the self-service formats developed in the US. These led to a program of store modernization and development that was to transform the UK retail industry. The central thread that drove these moves was put into words in 1959 as "Good food costs less at Sainsbury's."[8]

Conversion to self-service was initially slower than at Sainsbury's rivals, partly because of the authorities' reluctance to license the larger stores that Sainsbury wanted to build.[9] By 1960 only 10 percent of the company's shops were self-service. By the end of the decade, however, it had not only caught up but was playing in a league of its own. Although only 50 percent of the estate was converted (compared with nearly 100 percent at Tesco and Fine Fare), sales had increased two and a half times, and profits before tax had almost doubled. By 1968 Sainsbury was achieving sales of £4 per square foot, compared with an industry average of £1.50 on much lower overheads. In 1969 Sainsbury's 100 supermarkets were turning over £25,000 a week on average, and the average across all its stores was £15,000. By comparison Tesco, Fine Fare, and Allied Suppliers were able to manage just £4,000, £2,700, and £2,100, respectively.[10]

Perfecting the control model or devolving initiative?

Despite the company's dynamic growth, Mr Alan never relaxed his absolute personal control. By the time he retired as chairman in 1967, the micromanagement of branches and quality had reached extreme levels. After a 2-year interregnum under brother Robert, would the advent to power of a fourth generation of Sainsburys force a break with the past? Mr Alan and Mr R.J. made sure it would not. Officially, they started the succession planning process in 1959,[11] but in reality the process had been pre-empted much earlier. As with their parents, the new generation inherited their positions in the firm and with them their future responsibilities. So when in 1950 Alan's eldest son John D. (J.D.) joined on the trading side, the future chairmanship had effectively been settled. Mr Alan's other two sons, Mr Simon and Mr Timothy, were rapidly directed toward other responsibilities. When David, R.J.'s son, became a director in 1966, he took on the same personnel and financial responsibilities as his father had.

This seamless transition meant that, in the 1960s, the five key board directorships were all occupied by members of the Sainsbury family – and unlike at Tesco, where violent disagreements over Green Shield Stamps drew a line between the dominant coalition and rival Young Turks, at Sainsbury stamps served the opposite function: to weld old and new generations together in perfect agreement. The Sainsburys were usually keen on US innovations, but not this one. In 1963 the third and fourth generations closed ranks, with spectacular success. While Mr Alan launched a fierce attack against the "expensive gimmickry" of stamps in the House of Lords,[12] J.D. led an extensive antistamp campaign in newspapers and with customer leaflets, coupling the new slogan "Honest to Goodness" with the old "Good Food Costs Less."[13] As sales soared, *Management Today* admiringly concluded:

> The 95-year-old firm already had a marvellous reputation for quality. But until the stamp battle broke across the front pages and advertising columns few customers saw Sainsbury as it really is: an efficient, expanding multiple chain which is fiercely competitive ... very profitable and very much in the firing line of the food revolution.[14]

Even in a company as closed as Sainsbury's, the advent of new functional specializations such as computer processing and market statistics made some senior outside appointments unavoidable. Thus, the independent-minded chief statistician Bernard Ramm became a director, along with Mr Timothy, in 1962. After J.D. became chairman in 1969, external appointments were no longer an exceptional event. Ex-Monsanto personnel chief Roy Griffiths in particular would play a pivotal role in the company in the 1970s. But it was hard for J.D. to change Sainsbury's overnight, especially as the board that he inherited was his father's board. Not surprisingly, J.D.'s main strategic thrust was simply scaling up the size of stores and the range and quality of the offer while remaining true to the family mantra of quality and value.

In at least one respect, J.D. did set out to differentiate himself from his father – by calling a halt to the latter's micromanagement, especially the edict that no prices could be altered without the chairman's authority. But the Sainsbury family maintained a huge influence on the business, to the extent that it used to be said that all the important decisions were taken over Sunday lunch. And the board was effectively an operating board. It managed the business rather than took the strategic decisions.

Now, the Sainsburys' single-minded focus often gave the company a powerful advantage, and industry watchers were quick to attribute Sainsbury's success to such qualities as close family control, continuity of management, and a lack of "office politics." All these elements seemed to promote a distinct "long view" rather than an obsession with "bigger profits today or tomorrow."[15]

In stark contrast to Tesco, political correctness applied even to family relationships. Succession planning by family tree and a tacit noninterference pact crucially undercut the very competitive nature of the fourth-generation Sainsburys. Under the overall Sainsbury umbrella, each brother ran his area of the business in his own style – to the extent that there were reportedly three head-office buildings, one for each. Yet if anyone attacked any one of them from the outside, they all came together. For non-family employees, the family adopted a top-down, authoritarian style, and going public in 1973 seemed to make little difference to the way the company was run.

Entrenched attitudes were strong in other areas. For instance, while theoretically accepting the need to keep a close eye on US retail innovations, J.D. refused to take Leeds-based Asda's new discounting model seriously. With far fewer outlets, Asda had the same amount of sales space and offered a wide range of products much more cheaply than Sainsbury's. Yet the north seemed too distant from Sainsbury's home territory for the family to worry about.[16] Nor were the Sainsbury brothers much bothered with Tesco's non-food innovations or Asda's "variety" stores in the 1960s. Their response was simply to reinforce the delivery of their food proposition – where Sainsbury's purchasing power was now so great that its buyers could not have exerted much more control over its suppliers if it had owned them[17] – so why invest, for example, in supermarkets larger than needed for the food range?[18]

J.D. never really believed in non-food as a core retail proposition, and, unlike the situation at Tesco, the rest of the family seemed to agree. It was Griffiths, virtually alone in standing up to the chairman, who voiced concerns about the company's size relative to the competition. Supported by cousin David, who had been sidelined from retailing and was anxious to build a power base, Griffiths worried that, without diversification, Sainsbury "would run out of growth." His arguments were aided by three developments. First, the company was cash-rich and had to do something with its money. Second, in a period of economic instability the government's restrictive attitude to food retailing threatened to crimp the growth of the core business. Finally, British Home Stores had approached the company with a plan for a new hypermarket venture – to which J.D. quickly assented. The signs were propitious: the companies' assets were complementary, and J.D. got on well with the head of British Home Stores, Colin Paterson. SavaCentre, as the new venture was called, had the added advantage of pushing Sainsbury to the forefront of innovations in management information systems.

Meanwhile, developments in the late 1970s – some anticipated, some not – would open a brief window to movement. Internally, three of Sainsbury's most experienced directors fell ill just as brothers Simon and Tim retired. Externally, the retail industry was going through a decade of economic instability and inflating food prices. And as if that wasn't enough, Tesco chose this moment in 1977 to launch Operation Checkout.

Basking in glory, mortgaging the future

John D. Sainsbury and his trading directors were truly shocked by Tesco's Operation Checkout, a shock compounded by Sainsbury's unions going on strike the same weekend. This strike was a major setback that resulted in a significant loss of market share in 1977, and it spurred J.D. into making some important changes. One of them was to make Peter Davis, who had joined in 1976 from Key Markets, Sainsbury's first marketing director. This was a remarkable appointment in that Davis was known to be an independent-minded manager and J.D. had never previously shown signs of valuing marketing as a retail function. Davis was permitted to respond in kind to Tesco's challenge with Sainsbury's equivalent, "Discount '78." An instant success, Discount '78 would project Sainsbury's market share from 8.7 percent to 10.8 percent and push profitability and earnings per share level to unprecedented heights in the decade ahead.

For a while, the understanding between J.D. and Davis, moderated by Griffiths, bore fruit. The 1980s were all about "Good Food Costs Less," and Sainsbury did more than deliver on its promise. Throughout the decade, Sainsbury's structural price position was 2 percent better than that of the competition, including Tesco. In addition, Sainsbury's own-label categories were highly successful, not least because they were widely perceived as offering better value than the brands. Sainsbury seemed to be successfully defying Michael Porter's axiom that a company had to make a choice between leading on price or leading on quality. If Sainsbury's was "stuck in the middle," an uninterrupted run of 20 years of 20 percent profit levels meant it was happy to be there. By 1983 Sainsbury had achieved what was then a remarkable 15.8 percent domestic market share, followed at a distance by the seemingly struggling competition, which included Tesco.

Analysts agreed. Sainsbury seemed to be outdoing Tesco even in activities where the latter had seemed pre-eminent, such as geographical and product expansion. Sainsbury expanded north to Lancaster in 1985, and launched the DYI chain Homebase in 1979 to complement its non-food retail range. In 1987 it took the further step of venturing into the US, buying Shaw's, a retail chain. All in all, the combination of operation Discount '78 and the company's impressive strides in own-label put Sainsbury firmly in the driving seat in the 1980s, and top management basked in success.

Appearances were deceptive, however. Perhaps through overconfidence, the Sainsburys made several strategic and succession missteps that would eventually cost the company its market leadership. The first concerned the leadership of the company. The expected successor to J.D. was cousin David, who by one of the accidents of family history ended up owning four times as many shares as J.D. (David being an only child, J.D. one of four). Yet J.D. did little to prepare David for the position and did not have much time for the non-food ventures, particularly SavaCentre, the terrain on which David had elected to prove himself. Nonetheless, on David's succession J.D. commented:

> the business was so strong and doing so well and had such good people in it, I felt that he [David Sainsbury] would be fine as the chairman and [that] ... he'd follow the old principle: don't fix it if it ain't broke. The company was doing well and of course it would continue to evolve and change, but it didn't need anything radical.[19]

David was not the only one affected. Davis, the marketing champion in an otherwise family- and trader-dominated enterprise, was another. For him, the success of Discount '78 proved to be a two-edged sword. On the one hand, it gained him much credit and legitimacy. But he continued to feel that his path was blocked by Sainsbury family members, and he resigned in 1986.[20]

Davis's departure had the unfortunate side-effect of casting adrift newer marketing recruits, who were now effectively orphaned. "We shall never have a marketing director again," J.D. was widely reported as saying.

Unfortunately, by closing off the marketing route to influence, he had also killed off the prospect of more vibrant traditions of challenge and internal mobility. "John Sainsbury was a towering figure in the supermarket trade," reflected David Malpas, his great rival at Tesco. "Like so many towering figures he didn't concern himself too much about succession and didn't have about him people who were going to argue or dispute with him or have proper debates with him about positions."[21] In short, no other traditions of transformation could emerge to temper the family's overdeveloped sense of continuity. Even Griffiths was unable to provide a counterweight here. With Davis' departure in 1986, and Griffiths' relinquishing of executive duties 2 years later, the potential for contestation and constructive disagreement was to all intents and purposes extinguished.

With hindsight, Sainsbury was compromising its future in other ways. Take property development. Where Tesco's decision-making was bold, devolved, and timely, Sainsbury's was formal, hierarchical, and becoming steadily more cumbersome and uncompetitive. While Tesco's site research unit was making great technical strides, Sainsbury's decisions still relied mostly on J.D.'s intuition. As long as J.D. was around to make those decisions, the negative consequences were limited. But what would happen once "the best retailer of his generation" departed?

In terms of store modernization, Sainsbury's less than impressive record in the 1980s was partly a case of previous success coming back to bite it. Its domination of the rich Home Counties market was so complete that it hesitated to upgrade stores that by the 1980s were small and old. Replacing them would have meant cannibalization – "so it did lead the way for Tesco to challenge them in terms of stores and sites." But complacency may have unwittingly played a part too. As several Sainsbury managers observed, the fact that the company boasted and placed emphasis on a consistent 20 percent annual profit growth affected investment decisions, for example in renewing store formats, overhauling logistical systems, and, as we shall see, the internationalization trajectory.

Untimely awakening: sudden pressure to transform radically

By 1990 analysts were still assuming that Sainsbury's position as market leader was unassailable. "It would be churlish to question [Sainsbury's] medium-term ability to deliver the goods. The group boasts a 12-year record of dividend increases of 20 percent or more. Earnings per share have risen by as much for nearly as long, and there is little sign that the sequence is about to be broken," was a typical comment.[22] Yet, as we have seen, the first signs of decline were already beginning to show. J.D.'s retirement in 1992 would turn out to be far more problematic than even his greatest admirers could have imagined. J.D. had known "so much that he was able to make the decisions perfectly safely … but when he retired he left behind a board without leadership … It found it very difficult to keep the momentum in the business going."[23]

There have been numerous criticisms of David's role as chief executive. But others believe he was effectively crippled by the overhang of succession and recruitment problems inherited from the previous regime. One was the legacy of J.D.'s management style. Under J.D., Sainsbury's attracted people who could work in a highly paternalistic regime. Unfortunately, this meant that they were at a loss with how to deal with David's very different, consensual style. Furthermore, the appointment of Tom Vyner as deputy chairman and joint managing director in charge of UK supermarkets virtually ensured that strategy would remain unchanged: as buying director under J.D., Vyner's position in the new regime would be even more powerful than in the past.

Unfortunately, it did not seem to become apparent to his successors until the end of the millennium how intractable the legacy of J.D.'s insistence on control and continuity would be. One ironic effect was arguably that the significance of the non-food ventures Homebase and SavaCentre was missed. Hailed as great successes internally, they are more plausibly understood as missed opportunities that stopped in its tracks the development of a transformation platform.

Whereas Home 'n' Wear became the vehicle for the development of a real alternative coalition at Tesco and of traditions of anticipation, Homebase was the vehicle of a "cosmetic" alternative coalition rather than a real one. The venture was backed and led by people from the financial side of the business – David, and Dino Adriano, who ran Homebase, with marginal influence on Sainsbury's core trading business. Ultimately, Homebase served to defer transformation rather than advance it, and acted as a vehicle to ensure the noncontestability of Sainsbury's dominant coalitions, including that of David Sainsbury from 1992 onwards. This led to missed opportunities to foster changes in the company's culture, and to provide impetus and the tools to engineer an overhaul of the core food business, even though such an overhaul (not least in terms of larger hypermarkets and new city center store formats) was sorely needed.

Little of this was evident to outside observers in 1992, when Sainsbury's was still highly admired. Was not Sainsbury the most popular and profitable supermarket in the UK, having just overtaken Marks & Spencer with a remarkable profit before tax of £628 million on group sales of more than £9.3 billion?[24]

Sainsbury's market leadership was, however, increasingly deceptive. That it was becoming a retail follower rather than a leader became clearer in 1993, when the company responded to Tesco's "Value" line initiative with wide-ranging price cuts of its own. Several months later it had to admit that margins had shrunk, in consequence of which the pace of superstore construction would slow and the value of some of its properties would be written down. And when Tesco launched the renewed town-center format – Tesco Metro – in 1992, Sainsbury was forced to follow suit with its Sainsbury Central format, albeit 2 years later.

Major investment was also needed in the distribution chain, which had changed out of all recognition since the 1970s, and where Tesco had carved out an enormous lead. Sainsbury's historic superior distribution network were cancelled out by Tesco's improved distribution efficiencies using just-in-time stock picking in near-stockless depots. By contrast, according to Ian Coull, Sainsbury's property development director at the time, Sainsbury was stuck with "big clunky depots which were built for us having two weeks' supply of tinned beans." As a result Tesco's supply costs were 33 percent lower than Sainsbury's, a gap that could only be bridged by major investment.[25] Yet neither David Sainsbury nor his successor Dino Adriano would do it.

In fact, despite his very different management style, David found it hard to break with the legacy of the successful past. As one Sainsbury executive of the time reflected: "He did little to challenge the accepted view that there was nothing wrong with the brand; the company only had to get the operations right." In addition, he pursued J.D.'s international strategy unchanged. Eschewing Tesco's gradualism, Sainsbury had gone straight for the US, the toughest retail market in the world. When the Iron Curtain fell, the mistake was repeated. Like Tesco, Sainsbury eyed Hungary among other prospects but decided it would not be profitable soon enough.[26] Instead of getting the core domestic food business right first, as Tesco had done, Sainsbury ploughed ahead in the US. In 1994 it took a stake in Giant Food, a Washington DC-based chain of 159 stores. As late as 1999, when the company was in clear decline at home, the Shaw's subsidiary was permitted to buy the Star Market retail chain in New England.

The climbdowns continued. Again in 1994 David was obliged to admit that his initial negative assessment of Tesco's new Clubcard initiative was wrong; Sainsbury introduced its own Reward Card soon after.[27] Whereas the 1992 macroeconomic crisis had functioned as a happy accident for Tesco, prompting a period of lively debate and fast evolution under the up-and-coming Terry Leahy, for Sainsbury it was the reverse: having fared relatively well, its leadership saw no reason to reassess its business model. There were simply no alternative voices to be heard.

By 1995 Tesco had officially overtaken Sainsbury as the UK's premier food retailer.[28] But the alarm bells were muted even then, David seeing the necessity only to engage in a few business process re-engineering projects to cut costs. To disperse the focus still further, he bought the DIY chain Texas Homecare in 1995 and converted its loss-making stores into Sainsbury's Homebase format. When Sainsbury had to report its first yearly profit dip for 22 years in 1995, the relationship between David and cousin J.D. – who still had an office and influence at Sainsbury headquarters – had reached breaking point. Even now, however, not everyone was drawing the obvious conclusion: Sainsbury had got itself marooned in the middle, torn between lower price and higher quality.

It was at this point, with the strains nearly unbearable, that David announced his desire to go into politics. As a gesture toward streamlining the decision process, he had previously decided to split the roles of chief executive and chairman. Perhaps unsurprisingly, his choice of successor fell on one of the people most likely to maintain the Sainsbury tradition of continuity, Dino Adriano, general manager of Homebase and who was another manager with a financial rather than a trading background. It was an appointment that some Sainsbury executives did not agree with; for example, Ian Coull remarked:

> I was not in agreement with Dino's appointment as CEO. He was not a natural leader. He was an accountant who had led the Homebase business very well but the size of the Sainsbury's business was on a different scale and I did not feel he was the right man at that point.[29]

Despite lip service to the urgent need for cultural change, deteriorating financial results and continuing brand erosion made Adriano's tenure a short one – a prelude to radical transformation under a more authoritative figure, none other than the returning Peter Davis. Davis's appointment in 2000 was welcomed by City analysts, who felt that Sainsbury had at last achieved what should have been done long ago – bringing in an outsider to "think the unthinkable."[30] Inside the company, too, reactions were positive. Some remembered Davis's struggle to break J.D.'s hegemony on decision-making and invest in brand marketing, others experienced him as "a breath of fresh air," "a brilliant chief executive … strategic … visionary … a great leader."[31] As an outsider with significant insider experience, Davis's strategic assessments appeared to be on the mark. He decided to restructure Sainsbury's property function and sell off Homebase to boost investment in logistics, distribution, and store environment in the core food business. On the other hand, despite a minimal contribution to group cash flow in the 1990s, he elected not to dispose of Shaw's.

Early enthusiasm for the appointment notwithstanding, Davis came with a downside: a lot of baggage from a different historical era. Marked by his experiences in the late 1970s and 80s, Davis perhaps unconsciously mimicked some of J.D.'s traits. Back came the politically correct view that there was nothing fundamentally wrong with the brand: profits, marketing and operating efficiencies were the focus rather than a root-and-branch relaunch of the food business. Historically, Sainsbury's success had been based on the endeavor to be better and more authentic; now it was merely to be more profitable and better marketed.

Profits were elusive, and in the end Davis's 3-year tenure proved to be only slightly less transitory than his predecessor's. By 2004 Sainsbury's cost-to-sales ratio, at 24 percent, still compared badly with the industry average of 18 percent. Although the consensus among industry analysts was that Davis had not been "radical enough,"[32] his appointment was, however, by no means a disaster. He certainly left a more positive legacy for his successor Justin King than he had received from David and Adriano. A measured judgment is that Davis provided the spark that ignited the group's transformation, laying "foundations that the company is benefiting from today."[33]

Poached from Marks & Spencer on the strength of his role in that company's turnaround, King launched the 4-year recovery program "Making Sainsbury's Great Again" in 2004. Beyond setting key sales, cost, and cash flow management targets, one of King's first acts was to do away with Davis's dual managing directors. He brought in fresh blood at board level, poaching new directors from other leading retailers. Other long-standing problems were tackled: to get out of the cost/quality bind, attention was refocussed on the quality of basic food items and premium, health-related Sainsbury brands launched under the slogan "Taste the Difference, Be Good to Yourself." Distribution was reviewed,[34] while the cumbersome headquarters culture was overhauled with a cull of corporate staff. At the same time, King pledged radical improvements to customer service.

Every successful transformation involves a measure of good fortune. King was lucky to begin repositioning the Sainsbury brand at a time when consumer preferences and priorities were moving in his favor. By 2007 Sainsbury was clearly benefiting from the rising demand for higher margin organic produce and from King's recovery program more generally. He had done a good job of refurbishing the company's traditional middle-class credentials. That said, however, has the gap in innovativeness and customer orientation from Tesco narrowed? That seems doubtful. Although under King the chain has breathed enough life into its tradition of continuity to keep up with most of the competition, catching and overtaking Tesco will require more than that. We would argue that, lacking strong traditions of anticipation, contestation, and mobility, Sainsbury can at best hope to keep on terms with the market leader but not replace it unless, that is, Tesco stumbles, and by 2012 some were saying it had. By definition, such traditions cannot be conjured up overnight. Whether upcoming Sainsbury generations have the courage and awareness to develop them remains to be seen.

UNILEVER

In terms of product range, Unilever was never a direct competitor of Cadbury Schweppes, but we chose it as the most comparable British food company.

Dominant logic

Unilever has long been one of the most globalized and diversified companies in the world.[35] Ever since its foundation in 1929, the firm's dominant logic has been a combination of product and geographical leadership, the ambition offset by a prudent policy of making itself too large and diversified (as opposed to efficient and focussed) to fail. Rather than being driven by profit per se, Unilever was driven by a combination of worldwide ambition and a respect for local realities and customs, something that largely holds true to this day. At no point did Unilever seriously contemplate forcing a single group-wide brand denominator on its huge array of brands. To be sure, the center has periodically attempted to assert itself by cutting costs and pruning proliferating brands and geographies – more so recently. Yet Unilever's overall dominant logic has long stood out in the world of corporate giants, let alone the fast-moving consumer goods (FMCG) industry that emerged after World War II. Where did it come from?

Unilever was the product of two successive merger rounds, the first Dutch, the second Anglo-Dutch. In 1927 the Dutch companies Jurgens and Van den Bergh merged to form Margarine Unie. In the second round, British Lever Brothers, of Sunlight Soap fame, fused with Margarine Unie, the result being Unilever. The worldwide financial crisis that hit a month later not only seemed to truly vindicate the merger decision, but also shaped the company's attitudes for decades. Divided, in crumbling markets they stood to fail. United, it seemed they could not. The Dutch and British constituents were highly complementary. The Dutch specialized mainly in edible fats, the British in soap. Geographically, while the Dutch were strong in Continental Europe, the British focussed on the Commonwealth countries and also had a presence in the US.

Unilever's dominant logic is an interesting mixture of traits derived from both sides of the marriage. The Lever legacy was the pursuit of market leadership through product and geographical expansion based on high volumes and low cost[36] – a manufacturing version of Tesco's "pile it high, sell it cheap" approach. Inherited from the Dutch side was an insistence on settling rivalries by pooling profits and equalizing interests – a reflection of the history of near-suicidal competition between the two founding margarine companies. The margarine wars thus indirectly shaped Unilever's dual Anglo-Dutch parent structure (which had been first adopted by the Van den Berghs) and Unilever NV and Unilever Ltd's identically populated boards.[37] Both parents were holding companies supervising the operations of hundreds of manufacturing and trading firms worldwide. The responsibilities of the parent companies were clearly demarcated: Unilever NV would focus on edible fats in Continental Europe, whereas Unilever Ltd would be responsible for soaps, detergents, and personal care products in Britain, the Commonwealth countries, and the US.

Memories of early family rivalry also shaped the decision to bar family members from the chairmanship, the Unilever boards deciding in 1930 to delegate executive authority over the two holding companies to a non-family Special Committee headed by the chairmen of NV and Ltd, and a third member, who was always chairman-in-waiting for either NV or Ltd.[38] Former Unilever NV Chairman Floris Maljers counted the elimination of family infighting "a great blessing ... The fact that the families were removed from the succession process with one stroke of the pen helped enormously."[39] Certainly in the short term, these provisions paid off. Because of its small size, the Special Committee was much better able to balance national interests and act swiftly as an inner cabinet for the organization as a whole, while the elimination of the family for succession purposes allowed the emergence of a generation of professional managers capable of leading the organization through the troubled 1930s.[40]

Transition between old and new world order

Unilever's historical legacy made it not only instantly "global," but also highly decentralized, reflecting a very European belief in the virtues of local initiative and control. After World War II, however, the former front-runner found itself increasingly out of step with quite different governance and innovation logics coming out of the US. These were much less tolerant of geographical and product diversification and much more geared to borderless economies of scale – an obvious reflection of North America's founding experience of a mass home market and an instinctive preference for scientific rationalism.[41] In corporate terms, the North American focus was on efficient corporate control, mass marketing, and R&D-led innovation.

That it would take a decade or more for Unilever to feel the pinch of the changing corporate order was perhaps not surprising. Even in the mid-1960s Unilever was enormous compared with its international rivals, with sales and employment totals dwarfing the figures of US-based Procter & Gamble and Colgate, German Henkel, and Swiss Nestlé put together.[42] The sheer breadth of its geographical, product, and brand range was also huge. Unilever could legitimately claim it was the established party, defending its position against upstarts such as Procter & Gamble.

Up to the mid-1950s rising global demand floated all boats; competition seemed a secondary issue. When margins started shrinking in the ensuing years, however, rivalry sharpened in Europe and North America. True to tradition, Unilever responded by yet more diversification, adding companies in new areas such as food and chemical manufacturing. Meanwhile, Procter & Gamble and Colgate's depredations in the areas of detergents and personal home care products had not gone unnoticed. In 1959 a study group under the chairmanship of the head of research, Dr. E.G. Woodroofe,[43] had sounded the alarm bell, noting that while detergent products and processes had been revolutionized in the 75 years of the industry's existence, Unilever had only timidly taken the changes on board. To Woodroofe it was plain that Unilever had to drastically streamline its operations and strategy to match the strides made by US rivals. In food and toilet preparations too, demand for research from the marketing side was continually increasing.[44]

Unilever's problem was an overreliance on sales and an underinvestment in innovative research feeding directly into new mass-marketing initiatives – the FMCG dynamic. Only in 1965 did Unilever introduce biodegradable detergents into the US, UK, and Germany, so firmly focussed were its 11 research establishments on "protective research" to prop up existing products rather than leading-edge work to create new ones.[45,46] Unilever urgently needed to reorient itself; indeed, with the move to synthetic detergents, the company found itself involved in a new world of chemical technology, far distant from the family of problems associated with the old technology of oils and fats.[47]

Another increasingly difficult problem was the US business, which had become a law unto itself, largely insulated from central priorities and control. According to Michael Angus, who in the late 1970s was charged with bringing it back into line, the North American management believed that the Europeans had nothing to give America and therefore kept the Europeans at arm's length. The reining in of the US came late, however. For decades, Unilever's traditions of decentralization and respect for local autonomy would preclude attempts to break the power of the national barons. This brings us to Unilever's other competitive disadvantage compared with rivals such as Procter & Gamble. Unhindered by a history of multicompany, multinational relationships, these companies had grown up within a single mass continental market. Building on such mass-marketing beginnings, Procter & Gamble had developed an innovative brand management system as early as 1931. Thus, in the 1960s, Procter & Gamble had a double advantage with which to exploit the new European Common Market, or European Economic Community (EEC), and the decline of European imperial preference.

Obviously, the EEC was also an opportunity for Unilever, theoretically enabling it to consolidate operations and concentrate production in lower cost countries. At the same time, the EEC provided the ideal pretext to standardize multinational brands.[48] In a move in that direction, and also to establish a better balance between the corporate center and national management, Unilever introduced in 1959 a mechanism called "coordinations" to impose a measure of uniformity on policies for its international brands.[49] Despite a few modest successes, however, the endeavors of the London-based coordinators encountered much resistance.[50] National managements resented what they saw as attempts to modify the Anglo-Dutch balance or tighten the company's loose-knit character. The US – which went to extraordinary lengths, even including anti-trust claims, to resist central interference – was not even included in the coordination mechanism. With the Special Committee as ever responding to any whiff of conflict with soothing assertions of faith in the status quo, the first round of the corporate battle was lost before it had begun. The real situation was tellingly encapsulated in the famous 1963 description of the group by Unilever Ltd's chairman George Cole as a "fleet of ships … the ships many different sizes, doing all kinds of different things, all over the place."[51,52]

A mutinous "fleet of ships" in need of a captain

Although not without its strengths in a decade when diversification became fashionable again, Unilever's motley fleet – covering operations as varied as fishing and shipping, retailing, packaging and plastics, and products ranging from convenience foods, ice cream, tea and other drinks, personal care products, specialty chemicals, and animal feeds to the original oils, fats, and detergents – badly needed an admiral. The group could no longer afford to focus all its time and effort on managing the relationship between the corporate center and the local business units. Financial performance was already suffering: over the period 1970–74 Unilever had a trading yield inferior to that of almost all its rivals.[53] Could any of Unilever's leaders control the fleet, anticipate the trends, and get the ships sailing in the right direction?

At first, the hope was that things would change after the departure of the George Cole–Frits Tempel duo from the Special Committee. Replacements Harold Hartog, chairman of NV from 1966 to 1971, and Ernest Woodroofe, his Unilever Ltd counterpart between 1970 and 1974, were both modernizers bent on instilling a measure of central strategic direction. Determined to make Unilever add up to the sum of its parts, Woodroofe pushed the cause of coordination and the need for more professional management, particularly financial. Providentially, the pair could count on the support of Cob Stenham, finance director of Ltd since 1970, and the first outsider to be appointed to the Unilever boards. Stenham introduced a management accounting system that imposed a degree of central control over business performance levels. He also took the unprecedented step of talking to the financial community about the business and future plans. Crucially, Stenham mentored the up-and-coming Niall FitzGerald, an Irishman who served as Stenham's personal assistant from 1972 to 1974.[54]

Despite the Special Committee's efforts, however, language relating to the need for strategic redirection remained tentative. For instance, in answer to its own question of "whether any strategic redirection or guidance should be given to the business on the basis of the long-term plan," a 1975 strategy document detailed the evidence of two decades of increasingly unfavorable financial ratios, yet gave no clear-cut answer.[55] The noncommittal language was not only due to the tension surrounding coordination; it also reflected ongoing Anglo-Dutch tensions, as well as the Special Committee's limited overall authority.

All in all, for Unilever the 1970s was a decade of "lost growth and profitability" that would last into the early 1980s. Apart from a few new champions, as we shall see later, each generation of leaders blocked attempts to break at least one log-jam that was holding Unilever back. Thus, coordination took a back seat to Anglo-Dutch equalization of interests. Most damagingly, the "US problem" continued to fester. This was especially difficult for two reasons. Given its position in the most innovative detergents and personal products market, Unilever's US business should have been a source of dynamism and mobility for the corporate center. But it was nothing of the kind. Instead of functioning as a bulwark against Procter & Gamble, Colgate, Henkel, and Nestlé, Unilever in the US suffered a severe attack of financial sclerosis, sending profitability and market shares plummeting in the 1960s and 70s.

The case of Birds Eye in frozen foods demonstrates in microcosm Unilever's underdeveloped ability to keep itself ahead of the game. Unilever had taken a majority stake in Frosted Foods Ltd in 1943 from its then US parent, thereby gaining access to US innovations in marketing, manufacturing, and distributing frozen foods. Frosted Foods was rebranded as Birds Eye when Unilever took full ownership in 1957. With a 60 percent UK market share, innovative mass-marketing techniques, and a direct-to-store-cabinet distribution system over which retailers had little control, Birds Eye soon became a top performer in the Unilever fleet.[56]

By the early 1970s, however, clouds were forming. Birds Eye's sales had been predominantly under its own label, a strategy that worked well enough in a fragmented UK retail market where the company could use a strategy of divide and rule. Yet as retailers grew bigger and the market became increasingly oligopolistic, Birds Eye's competitive position was eroding. To compound the problem, retailers were beginning to develop cheaper own-label brands to differentiate themselves from low-cost newcomers such as Aldi and Netto.

Birds Eye shows graphically how Unilever's steady-as-she-goes business model could be undermined by a failure to act on problems that had become visible years before. Lacking outlets for challenge and positive disagreement both within the company and in relation to suppliers and even competitors, the group scored one own goal after another. One of its most glaring handicaps was the inability to import ideas and innovations from the US, home to the liveliest consumer product markets in the world, as well as the most creative thinking and toughest competition.

A "slow-motion coup," the Unilever way

After its lost decade, external analysts as well as more dynamic Unilever staff were clamouring for change. Fortunately, in the 1980s a new, less conventional breed of leaders such as Kenneth Durham, Floris Maljers, and Michael Angus began to make it through to the Special Committee. In the wings were waiting others such as Morris Tabaksblat, the Dutch personal products coordinator, Michael Perry, chairman of the United

Africa Company (UAC), and Niall FitzGerald. Thanks to these managers, Unilever would during the 1980s and 90s make a slow and belated return to basics.

It would take a Herculean effort on the part of the new leadership to break through the historical inertia and build momentum for change. Revolution being impossible, the new generation's emergence amounted rather to a very slow-moving coup. Unable to draw substantially on external ideas and energy for support, these "unconventionals"[57] would steer Unilever on a change path that was gradualist, even bloodless, rather than confrontational. Durham, Maljers, Angus, and FitzGerald differed from their predecessors in that all were willing and able both to contest the status quo and to put forward more vigorous alternatives. Faced with the previous regime's refusal to rock the boat in the US, third man Durham had stuck to his guns, insisting on the retirement of the North American CEO of Lever Inc. in favor of Angus in 1980. Durham would find a significant ally in Maljers, who as the "longer term thinker" in the trio would become a pivotal actor in Unilever's turn to core competences in the 1980s and 90s. The conventionality of Maljers' career track was matched only by the unconventionality of his character, at least in Unilever terms: he was critical, challenging, and tolerant only of clear strategic objectives. Angus, for his part, was almost the polar opposite of the emollient David Orr, chairman of Ltd/PLC from 1974 to 1982, at least when it came to the thorny US issue. More even than his predecessor George Cole, David Orr had allowed the US division to function as a separate entity.

Initially as a member of the personal products coordination, Angus had developed a keen interest in the US business, which eventually earned him the chance to try to turn it around. By then, in the 1970s, the Lever business in the US was barely making money in a detergents industry it had largely relinquished to Procter & Gamble, making a loss in personal products, and struggling to turn a profit in margarine and edible fats.

After a comprehensive strategic review in 1976,[58,59] the Special Committee finally decided to force a change. In 1978, in the largest ever US acquisition by a foreign company, Unilever bought chemicals company National Starch for a record fee. The acquisition provided a substantial boost to Europe and the corporate center. Over the next 4 years, as chairman of first the new US holding company and then Lever Inc., Angus pushed through extensive investment programs in plant, management, and R&D. Ultimately, Angus' familiarity with the tougher upfront US business culture was instrumental in enabling him to break the Unilever conventions of consensus-seeking and power politics, and to upend the refusal to contemplate the possibility of a hostile takeover – taboo for Unilever's old guard.

Angus' return to London in 1984 as the third man in the Special Committee coincided with a meeting, which would later become famous, to brainstorm corporate strategy. The meeting, held in Marlow, would be a milestone on Unilever's transformation path. Durham and Maljers had been brooding on a strategic reorientation since 1982, when they had ordered a strategic review of, among other things, the longer term prospects for the US and Africa (UAC).[60] According to Maljers, "The Marlow meeting was a seminal moment. For the first time ever, a Special Committee decided to be proactive."[61] To reverse Unilever's fortunes, the Marlow participants decided to attempt to return the group to its core competences with a back-to-basics campaign entitled "Operation Core Business Strategy." No longer was Unilever a "general economic enterprise" that would be "all things to all men;" it was specifically recasting itself as an FMCG company.[62] At the same time, "accountability was now very important … it was no longer a gentlemen's club … we had to be rather tougher with the people who were running the divisions."[63] From now on, the Special Committee would take a harder nosed approach, and the boards of directors were invited to follow suit.

From the start, the trio recognized that the initiative would fail unless corporate and national managers took ownership. Accordingly, they organized sessions with top managers, challenging them to propose solutions to the problems they had diagnosed. Remarkably, most of them came up with very similar answers. As Maljers quipped, it is easier to sell something to people who believe they came up with the idea in the first place.[64] Operation Core Business Strategy gained further momentum with the acquisition of Europe's leading tea company, Brooke Bond – Unilever's first-ever hostile takeover, whose boldness was taken as an indication that the Special Committee meant business. The way in which Brooke Bond was susequently integrated also signaled a new mentality. Before Brooke Bond, the "Unileverization" of acquired companies was slow and minimal, often involving not much more than a standardization of accounting systems. On the other hand, with National Starch as the prototype, a rapid absorption and restructuring of core and noncore elements at Brooke Bond signified the advent of a different type of Unileverization.[65]

Further evidence of progress in building traditions of transformation was the speed and decisiveness with which Unilever undertook the acquisition, also hostile, of Chesebrough-Pond in 1986. Sensing investor frustration, personal products coordinator Tabaksblat and FitzGerald, now finance director, decided to regain the initiative with Unilever's largest purchase yet. The directors in Rotterdam and the Special Committee instantly agreed.[66] The financial community reacted favorably, if with some surprise, to the speed and boldness of the $3.1 billion deal, which gave a substantial global boost to the profitable personal products business. Following this acquisition, Tabaksblat moved to New York to serve as regional director for North America and chairman and CEO of the US holding company.

Another milestone in Operation Core Business Strategy was divestment of United Africa Company International. The story of UAC neatly illustrates the strengths and weaknesses of corporate headquarters' historical laissez-faire attitude to its geographical subsidiaries. From its acquisition by Lever in 1920, UAC had alternated between problem child and cash cow, unhappy and happy accident.[67] Increasingly specializing in wholesale services, manufacturing, and industrial development equipment, the company had experienced a boom period after World War II, when it actively aided the new African nations to cope with the material demands of independence. Despite the best efforts of corporate and UAC management, however, the company ran foul of postcolonial nationalism,[68] and UAC's share in Unilever's total activities dwindled from 27 percent in 1955 to 15 percent in 1965. Apart from African nationalism, one of the main problems was UAC's insistence on pursuing expansion outside Africa, in recognition of which it changed its name in 1973 to UAC International, and in industrial fields that had little in common with Unilever's core consumer goods business.[69]

UAC's headstrong independence was a headache that was tolerated in the 1970s when the Nigerian and Middle Eastern economies, booming on the back of surging oil prices, fueled a dramatic recovery in the company's fortunes. Unfortunately, the revival was short-lived. By the 1980s the company had not just become a problem child again, but a terminal case. Given that UAC was older than Unilever, winding it up was a hard decision to take. The Nigerian economic crisis of the early 1980s provided the final tipping point. The Core Business Strategy launched after the Marlow meeting was an ideal opportunity to reorganize away the UAC into one big overseas entity in 1987 – the Africa Middle East Group – before disposing of it entirely in 1994. When it came to it, once the transformation intentions of corporate headquarters were complemented by significant grassroots support, the disposal of UAC seemed a self-evident step.

As for the consequences of the Core Business Strategy for the endless tug-of-war between British and Dutch interests, the results were less clear-cut. A positive element was that, perhaps for the first time in its history, Unilever's Special Committee was composed of equally strong British and Dutch executives, complemented by a British third man who shared the two chairmen's willingness to act proactively. One of the outcomes of the

Marlow meeting was an agreement that, to make Unilever "more competitive," Dutch and British would have to "override some of their susceptibilities,"[70] playing down turf preserves[71] and stepping into each other's territory. The rise of Tabaksblat, a member of both boards and the first Dutchman to lead the US division, and FitzGerald, an Irishman who became chairman of PLC, was testament to the new mentality.

Clearly, progress was being made: while Unilever's operating margins averaged around 6 percent between 1970 and 1983, much lower than those of its major competitors, by 1988 they had reached almost 9 percent, only 1–2 percent lower than those of Procter & Gamble, Nestlé, and L'Oreal.[72] But Unilever continued to make more acquisitions than divestitures, partly due to the remnants of the Anglo-Dutch equalization culture, and partly to a lingering unwillingness to rock the boat. It was not until 1989, following an unprecedented buying spree culminating in the acquisition of three high-margin perfume and cosmetics companies, that Unilever began downgrading ancilliary businesses along with chemicals and UAC.[73]

Although Unilever's responsiveness to investor concerns was improving, its ability to anticipate longer term developments was clearly limited. It did not help that, even by the late 1980s, resistance to Operation Core Business Strategy had by no means died down. In particular, the decision to assert product coordinations across formerly autonomous regions remained controversial. Although central efforts to expose failure had borne fruit in better financial performance ratios and some successes in personal products and detergents, divisional risk-taking may actually have diminished. Although many people "saw the common sense in what we were doing," the mentality remained opportunistic and quick to say "'I told you so.'"[74] Fundamentally, Operation Core Business Strategy remained a largely top-down affair; top talent still was not flooding in from the regions to the corporate center,[75] and mobility remained an aspiration rather than a habit.

Catching up with mounting external pressure

At the turn of the 1990s Unilever was still suffering from its historical sources of strategic drift. So while Unilever's divestment record was improving,[76] the accent was still on acquisitions. Although the (Dutch) food business badly needed pruning, more than half of Unilever's 100-odd purchases in the 1980s and 90s had been in foods. In particular, the 1999 Bestfoods buy was widely understood as necessary to restore momentum to the foods business.[77]

The other hangover was the national baronies. This issue of the national baronies in Europe and North America was only really tackled in the 1990s. During the 1980s the organization had still been in "learning mode" about how to combine local accountability with regional profit targets.[78] Unilever made various attempts to integrate geographical units and coordinate product gropups and brands over many years, but more forcefully from the mid-1990s on.[79] The creation of a worldwide food executive headed by Tabaksblat was another crucial precedent. Thus by 2007 the national mafias issue seemed to have been nailed in its coffin – albeit after "a slow and lingering death over the last 20 years."[80]

Resolution of the national baronies issue was eased by the growing realization that the growth markets of the future were in Eastern Europe and, above all, Asia and Latin America. Indeed, Unilever's fastest growing market in the early 1990s was Asia, where sales of personal products, detergents, and packaged foods were growing more than twice as fast as in North America and Europe. While this significantly reduced the bargaining power of the European and North American managements, a signal carrying more symbolic weight would be needed to end their ambivalence to worldwide coordinations and the internationalization of R&D and marketing. This signal finally came in the guise of the Special Committee's transformed attitude toward the failure of a coordination project.

In the 1990s detergents coordinator FitzGerald's efforts to launch the international detergent Persil Power was objectively as ineffective as the 1960s attempts to rein in the US business. Yet while the earlier debacle was simply shrugged off, FitzGerald's lack of success was deemed to be an honest "mistake" in pursuit of a risk that had not come off – in short, a positive venture. As such, beyond the issue at hand, FitzGerald served the larger purpose of building capabilities of transformation as the earlier failure did not. In addition, FitzGerald's promotion to chairman of Unilever PLC sent the strongest signal yet of the company's intent to overhaul group traditions – even if support from the financial community for the respected FitzGerald played a part in the decision.

Besides tackling these two historical sources of drift, Unilever, under first Perry and then FitzGerald, was having to adapt to changing international growth and innovation patterns. After a major strategic review[81] in 1995, the company formally decided to prioritize the faster growing economies of Asia and Latin America over the previous heartlands of Europe and North America.[82]

At the same time, in response to growing investor impatience with the group's complex management structure, the venerable Special Committee was scrapped and replaced by a seven-member Executive Council in a bid by FitzGerald "to instill a more entrepreneurial culture."[83] In another concession to investor concern, this time over strategy, FitzGerald announced that the company would henceforth focus resources on seven corporate categories: fabric wash, personal wash, mass skin, prestige products, yellow fats, ice cream, and tea-based beverages.[84] The specialty chemical business would be sold.

Observers were still not satisfied, however: while all this was "evolutionary and positive," it was neither "going to catapult Unilever to the top of the multinational consumer goods league" nor "improve the speed" of strategic decision-making," the *Financial Times* complained.[85] In response, FitzGerald and Tabaksblat came up with stretching financial targets, most notably "to achieve total shareholder return in the top third of its peer group."[86] In the next year, Unilever's top management addressed yet another of the financial community's worries, announcing new efforts to develop and attract young talent.[87] More ambitious targets followed: under the new "Path to Growth" strategy, the group committed to slashing the brand portfolio from 1,600 to 400, and to increasing annual top-line growth and operating margins to 5 percent and 15 percent, respectively.

Unfortunately, Unilever failed to meet its financial targets, mostly failing to rank in the top seven, let alone the top three, of the total shareholder return peer group. Before his retirement in 2004, FitzGerald had to admit that the company had missed its Path to Growth targets too. On taking his place, Frenchman Patrick Cescau decided to further streamline the top management structure, paring it down to one chairman and one CEO. He declared that the successor to Path to Growth, "Vitality" (2005–10), would be less target-oriented, relying more on "underlying assumptions."[88]

Critics would argue that, although many recent developments had been positive, there had remained something forced and incomplete about Unilever's transformation process. The group's abilities to anticipate events, challenge existing and develop alternative strategies, and get the best out of its diverse and highly talented management cadres were too limited for the transformation gene to be become embedded and self-driven. For instance, the new executive council was more cumbersome and less effective at taking decisions than the three-man Special Committee, which also had the advantage, not shared by its successor, of keeping Anglo-Dutch tensions in balance. In the new millennium, the baronies were starting to rear their heads again, and the atmosphere within the group was again intensely political. In short, Unilever was still searching for the traditions that would allow it consistently to add up to more than the sum of its many parts.

At the start of 2009 Unilever appointed its first ever chief executive from outside, Paul Polman, who had risen in its arch rivals Procter & Gamble and Nestlé. His appointment was applauded by the financial markets. He quickly announced a focus on emerging markets and on sustainability. In 2011 he restructured the company to decentralize operations but to have product categories under global heads reporting to him.

SSL INTERNATIONAL

SSL International did not compete directly with Smith & Nephew but did operate in similar healthcare sectors.

The child of its parents

The concept of a dominant logic for SSL International is tenuous, given the combined group's short and turbulent history. It was founded in two successive rounds in 1998 and 1999 by the mergers of, respectively, Seton and Scholl, and then Seton Scholl and the London International Group. It therefore makes more sense to discuss the dominant logics of the founding companies and how these relate to each other within the combined firm. Fortunately, SSL's constituent companies shared a similar dominant principle throughout their history, which was to use a *power brand to command a premium, and to increase the earnings-to-cost ratio by diversifying geographically and in product terms around this core strength.*

The oldest of SSL's founding entities was the Scholl Manufacturing Company (1904), founded in Chicago and named eponymously after William Mathias Scholl. A medical student, Scholl manufactured and marketed foot-care products such as the "Foot-Eazer" and an array of foot plasters and powders; in time, his arch supports would be associated with the global Dr Scholl brand. Scholl did not develop his research interests; besides manufacturing, he focussed on marketing arch supports in Europe to famous clients such as Kaiser Wilhelm II and Olympic champion Paavo Nurmi. Diversifying outward from the premium Scholl brand was William's route to sustainable advantage. His brother Frank opened Dr Scholl's London Foot Comfort Shop in 1913, setting the pattern for ensuing decades, during which the Scholl Manufacturing Co. among other things launched a line of Dr Scholl branded shoes.

The London International Group was born as the London Rubber Company in 1915. The name of the company came about through founder

L.A. Jackson's singular practice of including rubber condoms in his stock of barber sundries. Ultimately, sales of German-manufactured condoms would help Jackson turn his small shop into a world leader in a global industry. Two landmarks stand out in London Rubber's prewar history: the trademarking of Jackson's condoms under the brand name Durex, standing for "Durability, Reliability, and Excellence," and the launch of his own latex condom factory in England in 1932, using a newly invented German process and material. The construction of the UK factory was later to prove a happy accident when London Rubber was cut off from its German suppliers during World War II.

Seton Healthcare was the latest-born of the future SSL family. Founded in 1952 by the charismatic Ivor Stoller, the company sold tubular nonelastic bandage products. Like its SSL stablemates, it soon focussed on a star brand in the shape of Tubigrip elasticized bandages, initially bought in but then manufactured in-house from the 1960s. As with Scholl, Seton was a real family company: Norman Stoller, son of founder Ivor, became managing director in 1962 and retained a firm grip on company strategy until the 1980s.

Throughout their lives, all three constituent companies would pursue variants of a similar dominant logic. To reinforce their premium brand position, they all swiftly attempted to build international economies of scale. And from the outset, each was highly sales-oriented, with a take on medical innovation that was driven not by internal research but by external opportunities to distribute high-margin consumer products.

For a while, it seemed that London Rubber would be most successful with this simple formula. With the aid of steadily improving manufacturing and testing, not only did it hold a virtual monopoly of the British condom market by the 1950s, but it would also soon take a 50 percent share in Western Europe, and successfully expand into the Commonwealth too. Finally, in 1962 London Rubber acquired the US condom manufacturer Schmid Laboratories to provide entry into the North and Latin American markets. Acquiring new routes to market was its single driving idea.

Sell more, not sell better

Like London Rubber, Seton Healthcare pursued international routes to market for its highly profitable Tubigrip product – a brand which, like Durex and Dr Scholl, commanded a premium price. By the late 1970s almost a third of Seton's sales were overseas, using third-party distribution arrangements to expand. Its strategy was simple: to use the profits accruing from the Tubigrip patent to broaden the portfolio of products that could be sold through the same distribution channels. Norman Stoller was motivated chiefly by sales as he was a salesman at heart. But he had no ambition to transform the company qualitatively – in a medical industry gearing up for waves of consolidation, specialization, and internationalization, Stoller was content that the company should be known as a less-than-glamorous "hospital supply company."[89]

Scholl meanwhile was experiencing the calm before the storm. When founder William died in 1968, his heirs decided to incorporate Scholl as a public company. Soon thereafter, the company was split in two parts, each run by a nephew of the founder. Internationally, the deal between William and brother Frank was formalized by making one nephew – Jack – vice-president and general manager of the US operations, and another nephew – William – company president, overseeing markets in Europe, Japan, Latin America, Canada, and New Zealand. In terms of sales, the split between the two spheres of influence was 55:45. These changes notwithstanding, the 1960s and early 1970s were a time of relative stability for Scholl, with sales increasing steadily across the board.

Adherence to tradition – almost despite everything

Although opportunities for development and transformation were not lacking, the three companies did not take them. Despite soaring sales, considering the company to be thinly spread, the Scholl nephews decided to look for a buyer. In 1978 they struck a deal for the non-US operations with the Schering-Plough Corporation, William Scholl becoming president of the international consumer products division. Unfortunately, the acquisition came at the tail-end of the diversification cycle, and in 1987, with William now retired, Schering sold its Scholl operation to European Home Products, a UK manufacturer of household electrical appliances that was itself in search of a makeover. In name terms, the transaction was a reverse takeover, the merged entity taking the name Scholl plc. However, although the survival of the Scholl name gave an appearance of continuity, so much management effort was absorbed in adapting to the changes of ownership and regaining a sense of what the business was all about that there was little left for developing real traditions of transformation.

London Rubber, for its part, faced a steep drop in sales following the approval of the birth control pill in the late 1970s. In a bid to shake up the company, the board appointed an outsider, Alan Woltz, as chief executive in 1981. Unsurprisingly, Woltz decided that the best way to kick-start growth was to diversify. Ventures in such unrelated fields as fine china (Royal Worcester Spode), electrical supplies, photo processing, and paints followed, as well as more related ventures. No longer primarily a condom maker, the company changed its name to London International Group (LIG) in 1986.

Diversification did not mean that Woltz tolerated the presence of champions of alternative directions in LIG. In 1982 the board had appointed Smith & Nephew's former R&D champion Donald Seymour as nonexecutive chairman. London Rubber's product portfolio by the late 1970s included surgical gloves as well as condoms. Aware of the potential of the latter, Seymour attracted some of the top polymer research talent to the company but soon resigned, in 1985. Two other directors joined him in protest at the decision to allow Woltz to combine the posts of chief executive and chairman. Although UK newspapers commended the three resigning directors for their "independent line," the fact is that their departure left the company without the semblance of a tradition of constructive disagreement. To all intents and purposes, LIG had become a one-man band.

For the third of the group, the consolidation of the healthcare industry in the 1980s had left Seton Healthcare feeling small and vulnerable. This realization coincided with the coming in of fresh blood in the 1970s – such as Roger Gould, finance director since 1972 and deputy managing director since 1980 – and 1980s. In the 1970s Tubigrip had changed Seton's emphasis from hospital supplies to over-the-counter (OTC) pharmacy products, with sales arrangements to match. On the back of a modestly expanding product and geographical portfolio, Seton's sales grew from a lowly £0.7 million in 1970 to £7 million 10 years later. But there still remained a major stumbling block to Seton's growth: the failure (in marked contrast to its peers such as Smith & Nephew) to create a distribution network in the US. So, coinciding with an influx of fresh management blood, notably in the person of financial controller Iain Cater, the company in 1982 decided to acquire an established healthcare company in the US to sell and distribute its products. The company it chose was SePro, an outfit selling very basic underpants, diapers, and incontinence products.

Unfortunately, SePro proved not to be the best vehicle for the sales of Seton's bandages and dressings. Less politely, the acquisition was a disaster. For one thing, the differences between SePro and Seton were too great in terms of both the markets they were operating in and their cultures. At any rate, plans to build a US distribution capacity went horribly wrong. With no R&D of its own to fall back on, the company was left conspicuously short of options.

Seton ended up making considerable losses in the US, to the point that by the mid-1980s the group as a whole was under threat. Seton remained profitable in the UK, however, and was doing reasonably well in terms of exporting to distributors in overseas territories. Picking up the pieces after the US failure, management therefore started looking closely at acquisitions in the UK. Its eye fell on Prebbles, a UK producer of infection-control products, and in 1986 Seton bought it outright. Prebbles was not just a sizeable mouthful to bite off: it was also Seton's first move into pharmaceuticals. Would this be the beginning of a new, high added value company?

Management changes wholesale, not incremental

How did LIG (the largest part of the future SSL International) compare with Smith & Nephew at the end of the 1980s? Whereas Smith & Nephew often took the long view, Woltz's own measure of success was short-term dividends and ability to spend. While Woltz's peculiar combination of diversification and a monopoly of authority had paid dividends in the initial period, from the turn of the 1990s it proved increasingly expensive and detrimental to the long-term health of the company. Having endured further woes with the economic crisis of the early 1990s, many group businesses were in the red by the beginning of 1993. When LIG's figures were finally made public, investors severely punished the company and the share price collapsed.

What followed was the wholesale replacement of LIG's management, Michael Moore becoming chairman and Nick Hodges chief executive. To fix up the company, the new management launched a £115 million rescue rights issue. They also promised a return to core competences. Having run LIG's European operations, Hodges had built up a profitable niche in surgical gloves alongside the main condom business. With that in mind, he shed the company's unrelated divisions, and started cutting costs in the company's core manufacturing businesses. The problem was that the profit margin on condom manufacturing was very low. Even with a share of 80 percent in the UK condom market with its Durex brand, and some 45 percent in Western Europe with other brands, some insiders predicted that the company was headed for bankruptcy.

After enduring further losses in 1994, LIG's management tried to piggyback on the global AIDS epidemic by launching Durex as a global brand. This brought some success. The company became the world's largest condom-maker, with some 15 percent of sales going to government agencies such as the US Agency for International Development by the late 1990s. Overall earnings grew 10–15 percent annually from 1996 on worldwide condom sales, increasing at an annual clip of 3 percent. By 1998 the company had a 50 percent market share in Europe and the same again in most of its Asian markets, while in the US the company's various brands took a combined share of 20 percent. Beyond these figures, the consensus of the 1990s was that although LIG was financially on the mend, an overreliance on a relatively low-margin condom market was leaving it a fragile force. Surgical gloves carried a higher margin, particularly in the US, yet LIG's market share was small. For a company in these circumstances, a complementary merger capable of bringing the company some serious economies of scale in both product and geographical terms had obvious attractions.

Meanwhile, after one turbulent decade in the 1980s, Scholl plc experienced more ups and downs in the next, rendering it more of a candidate for a takeover than a merger of equals. Scholl's management had tried to jumpstart its support hosiery business in 1993 by hiring a young celebrity to endorse the line and moving distribution into supermarkets. Although sales jumped 10 percent in 1994, operating profits were eaten away by high promotion and distribution costs. To improve its figures, Scholl in 1995 sold off a French cosmetics business and closed over 20 retail stores. In the same year, frustrated with protracted financial failure, Scholl shareholders Hambro and Active Value Advisers rebelled, arguing that a stand-alone brand made no sense given the considerable distribution costs involved, and demanding that Scholl put itself up for sale. Although the rebellion was defeated, Scholl's defense had cost an equivalent of 0.7 p a share.

In a bid to calm shareholder unrest, the company appointed Stuart Wallis, best known for his time as CEO of Fisons, as its chairman. Unsurprisingly, Wallis introduced a restructuring program and tasked a new chief executive, Colin Brown, with maximizing shareholder value. Despite these changes and a drastically rationalized product portfolio, however, Scholl remained a sitting duck for a takeover.

In the event, Scholl's acquirer in 1998 turned out to be Seton Healthcare. Before coming to this decision, Seton went through some changes itself. In the wake of Iain Cater, other young and able managers had joined Seton during the 1980s. Marketer Dieno George had joined from Unilever in 1986 at the same time as the Prebbles acquisition, while Graham Collier was hired as technical director. As a result, Seton had a good team on board by the late 1980s, embodying a mixture of experience and dynamism, with Stoller, Gould, Cater, and George making up the front row.

By now, Stoller had taken a back seat, at least in terms of the day-to-day management of the business, leaving his protégé Cater at the helm, backed by George as his right-hand man and Gould as deputy chairman. New blood at Seton did not, however, lead to new thinking, at least about alternative paths to growth. To all appearances, Stoller had successfully imbued the newcomers with his own paternal management style and his father's dominant logic. Although Cater "was more hands-on than Norman, there never was conflict between the two," maybe because Iain was "like a son" to Norman.[90]

Flotation and non-family succession notwithstanding, throughout the 1990s Seton Healthcare retained essentially the management style of a family company, even though its competitive position was inevitably changing. Above all, the acquisition of Prebbles had been a strategic move, and a big step for a small firm. Logically, Seton now had to deal with the consequences of having stepped into the market, very different from that of condoms and surgical gloves, of high-margin prescription pharmaceuticals. Yet despite the comprehensive change of leadership and the impulse provided by the Prebbles acquisition, Seton's management never really changed. Instead, it held on to the same old sales-oriented logic of improving earnings-to-cost ratios opportunistically – although, after flotation in the late 1980s, earnings were now replaced by a focus on immediate share price gains.This public listing was the signal for a rapid extension of its brand portfolio in a number of areas including wound care, dressing retention, compression therapy, infection control, orthopedics and OTC medicines. In 1993 Seton bought 15 brands, 10 of them from Boots, and in 1994 it added nine more, including seven from SmithKline Beecham. The change of emphasis is clearly shown in the revenue totals. Whereas in 1990 OTC medicines, at £2.4 million, formed Seton's smallest sales segment, by 1994 they were the largest, at £13.3 million. By contrast, mature sectors such as orthopedics and compression therapy grew only modestly.

Seton's acquisition of small OTC brands proceeded unabated in the following years. By 1996, however, the strategy was beginning to flag, and the chairman was obliged to announce that headline sales would flatten as the company sought to increase efficiencies and improve its stock control. By the mid-1990s Seton could find no more low-hanging fruit to pick, and top managers were beginning to think that a more substantial step was appropriate, in the form of one or more major acquisitions or mergers. This thinking would ultimately lead to the back-to-back mergers with Scholl (1998) and LIG (1999).

From Seton's point of view, the main drivers for the twin mergers were industry consolidation, a retention of senior talent, and the lack of critical mass in research and channels to market. The fundamental driver behind Seton's mergers and acquisitions activity was its desire to create consistent, profitable growth in the context of a consolidating market. Other routes to this end were not considered: Seton had several brands that were global or near global, but it needed the infrastructure to support them. A company of its size, competing against very large players, had to avoid being spread across several nonsynergistic areas. Therefore the strategy was heavily colored by the need to focus the company's resources.

Seton managers had identified Scholl as a potential merger partner during the early 1990s. Synergies were clear, not least because the companies had maintained a trading relationship since 1971. Yet Seton's management held off as Scholl seemed to lose its way a little, waiting until Scholl's performance had recovered somewhat in 1997 to renew its interest. The merger followed in 1998.

LIG too had been on Seton's radar for some time as a potential partner. There was a clear fit, as both were active in hospital and pharmacy distribution channels. When LIG issued a profits warning, it rapidly precipitated a sequence of events that led to the LIG merger in 1999. The new management claimed that the merger would deliver strategic, commercial, and financial synergies, strengthening the international market presence and providing increased scale and opportunities for growth. Most notably, the merger would provide Seton Scholl with a springboard into the US and offer sales and distribution synergies in the UK and Europe.

Disagreements destroy rather than transform

After the double merger, the company with the rather cumbersome name Seton Scholl London International (SSL) promised to be a force to be reckoned with: it was now a multinational operating in 35 countries, with a significant presence in both medical and health and beauty products, and sales approaching £700 million. The scene was set: would the product of the back-to-back mergers be a serious player in the international healthcare markets? Could the combined company transcend the instinctive preference of its constituent parts for low-hanging fruit and instead show proof of wider strategic vision?

Analysts were initially cautiously optimistic.[91] Although some questioned the wisdom of the simultaneous double integration,[92,93] the tone remained modestly upbeat: "While the City complains that the mergers of Seton, Scholl and LIG have created a company which defies comprehension, SSL International remains a safe play," said *The Independent*,[94] while *The Times* opined: "The merger made sound strategic sense … the fit was good and the opportunity to win synergy benefits was ripe."[95]

In the event, however, SSL International quickly unraveled, with factional disputes between the different merger partners preceding a full-blown legal scandal and the resignation of the entire SSL management team. There were more fundamental problems too. Unlike the mergers with Scholl, the LIG "merger" was a knee-jerk return to Seton's congenital opportunism. The deal, following hard on the heels of that with Scholl, was motivated as much by the company's temporary weakness as its strategic complementarities. Two months after LIG's 1999 profits warning, the Office of Fair Trading announced a second investigation into the company's UK trading practices. LIG's share price tumbled by 30 percent, at which price the immediate pay-off potential of its star brands made it look like a bargain, at least on paper. It seems clear that the company had paid less attention to ensuring the necessary post-acquisition integration skills.

With hindsight, it is easy to see that, like many companies before and since, Seton had allowed its dominant logic to become so ingrained that it turned from a strength into a weakness. In the new conditions, continuity – sticking single-mindedly to the business model that had served it in the past – was no longer enough. It needed also to cultivate the underdeveloped habits of anticipating and preparing for change, challenging existing strategies and vigorously building alternatives, and harnessing and developing fresh management talent. Had it done so, it might have moved away from the path of being too sales-driven. A continuous high growth of revenues proved to be a difficult record to maintain, but the delay in changing this strategy ensured a much greater reaction when it did occur. After the merger, SSL entered a period of high share price volatility, punctuated by the discovery of accounting irregularities leading to the prosecution of five directors by the Serious Fraud Office and a 60 percent fall in the share price.

Commentators have attributed this situation to Iain Cater[96] – just as they credit its subsequent turnaround to the single-handed efforts of his successor, Gary Watt.[97] Both diagnoses are misleading in that they overestimate the transformational effects of one set of leaders and underestimate the hidden role played by traditions of transformation, built and passed on over several generations. From that viewpoint, two conclusions are perhaps warranted. Both Cater and Watt possessed undeniable leadership talents. However, Cater was caught in a spiral of inflating expectations that had started under his predecessors and was compounded by his own failure to develop a counterweight to the company's overly dominant logic. Watt, by contrast, felt the weight of investor pressures in his much-anticipated efforts to correct the excesses of the past. He subsequently competently developed a less extravagant version of the company's success formula.

What most analysts have missed in all this is that both Cater and Watt devoted their leadership efforts principally to perfecting and reinventing the company's dominant logic – an unchanging, inflexible, business model – ignoring the other success factors that a company must depend on for the long term, notably the complementary traditions that can only emerge through several generations of effort. These omissions did not occur through oversight or even lack of opportunity. For instance, the merger between Seton Scholl and LIG was originally justified primarily in terms of the two companies' combined strength in high added value medical products – more precisely, marketing, R&D, geographical, and production synergies in international markets for surgical gloves and wound management. Yet in their bid to reduce SSL to a pure-play consumer product business, Watt and his predecessor divested exactly those two healthcare areas that provided the long-term rationale for the merger.

As the fate of SSL's constituent parts shows, companies that live by such single- and simple-minded strategies tend to die by them too. Either the strategy runs out of steam or a predator with grander ambitions and stronger traditions takes them out. This is what happened to SSL, which in its turn was acquired and absorbed into the consumer products group Reckitt Benckiser in 2010. Shareholders got a good price – the deal was worth £2.5 billion, a far cry from the group's beginnings – for this ultimate transformation. A victory of sorts, it was always the likeliest outcome for a company that had, for whatever reasons, never developed lasting traditions of transformation of its own.

Part III

What We Learned

CHAPTER 7

Four Traditions of Transformation

The previous three chapters described the histories of the three pairs of companies. We laid out the stories with a minimum of interpretation; that is the role of this chapter. Here, we use the evidence from the histories of the six companies to explain four "traditions" that we argue provided the context within which our exceptional firms transformed themselves while still successful: traditions of (1) continuity, (2) anticipation, (3) contestation, and (4) mobility. We then explain how these manifested themselves in the period of exceptional performance (1983–2003) we identified in stage 1 of our study.

History is essential to our interpretation. In sum, we found that the foundations of the success of our three successful strategic transformer (SST) companies are to be found in more than 40 years of their history. Starting in the late 1950s and 60s, Tesco, Cadbury Schweppes, and Smith & Nephew, only partly intentionally, began to develop habits, or as we call them traditions, of continuity, anticipation, contestation, and mobility, that became, in effect, dynamic capabilities for change. To repeat, this was not the result of deliberate or coordinated planning but rather a process of historical imprinting, or institutionalization, in each company's organizational blueprint.[1] Together, these traditions formed a platform for the continuous and successful transformation of these companies in the 1980s and 90s without the trigger of financial trauma. Tables 7.1–7.4 below summarise and illustrate the key practices underlying the four traditions.

The historical dimension of performance has by and large been ignored by business academics and commentators. The success of our companies is usually described as the consequence of a "radical break with the past." In fact, in each case they were the logical next steps in a process that had started decades earlier.

A MODEL OF SUCCESSFUL STRATEGIC TRANSFORMATION

Beginning at different times, the four traditions had, by the end of the 1970s, fused into each SST's "organizational DNA," thereby providing a self-generating transformation platform for continuous change. It was self-generating because out of the four traditions developed a tendency for leaders to substitute *devolved improvisational processes* for *central control mechanisms*. As the traditions embedded themselves in the culture of the organizations, the discipline they exerted ensured that improvisational processes would not escalate out of control but would remain anchored in a coherent long game. We will demonstrate how among the three pairs, Tesco, Cadbury Schweppes, and Smith & Nephew incorporated these traditions more strongly than did their comparators, Sainsbury's, Unilever, and SSL International.

Tradition of continuity

The first tradition is the most self-evident, that of continuity (Table 7.1). A company has a tradition of continuity when successive generations of a company's dominant coalition are able to reinvent a timely variation on their company's historical success theme. By dominant coalition we mean a company's established leadership, typically a grouping organized around the CEO, chief executive, chairman, or, in UK companies, sometimes the chief financial officer. Within the tradition of continuity, such leaders have as their primary focus the reinvention of the company's historically distinctive business model in terms befitting contemporary industry conditions.

TABLE 7.1 | Evidence of the tradition of continuity

Tesco	The central thread through Tesco's history can be traced back to founder Jack Cohen's original "pile it high, sell it cheap" formula and his willingness to experiment in the name of customer satisfaction
Smith & Nephew	Smith & Nephew's historical dominant logic is to generate proportionally higher sales revenues from a smaller R&D base than its competitors
Cadbury Schweppes	When Cadbury and Schweppes merged in 1969, it took a decade for the post-merger dominant logic to crystallize: play a long game with brands and geographies – in terms of acquisitions, investment, integration, and divestment – and provide a strong "value for money" proposition in product delivery

As an example, over a century Smith & Nephew's executive teams were chosen based on their ability to reinvent the company's historical business model: generating proportionally higher sales revenues from a smaller R&D base than its competitors. At the beginning of the 20th century, the company achieved its goal by maintaining excellent marketing relations with medical practitioners while cheaply buying in licenses from Germany, then the most advanced healthcare market. In the 1960s the emphasis had switched to being more financially focussed than the competition and leveraging the company's critical mass in textiles. By the end of the 20th century, the company had acquired enough complementary technology and customer relationship assets overseas to market in-house R&D capabilities as a leading strength in the US, now the world's leading healthcare market. At the beginning of the 21st century, Smith & Nephew has shifted the emphasis back to "bolt-on acquisitions," entailing a return to the old days in which the best technologies were acquired and licensed to help grow the business more efficiently than the competition.

Although a much younger company, SSL International also had a dominant logic, derived from the history of its main constituent element, Seton Healthcare. From the earliest stages, Seton's founder, Ivor Stoller, focussed on achieving earnings-to-cost ratios greater than those of its competitors. The dominant logic of Stoller's successors was similar during the 1990s, when the company was listed on the London Stock Exchange, although here it was the earnings-to-share-price ratio that became the focus.

Similarly, the central thread through Tesco's history can be traced back to founder Jack Cohen's original "pile it high, sell it cheap" formula and his willingness to experiment in the name of customer satisfaction. This logic was reinvented first as "lower prices at a good quality" and then "customer value first." Sainsbury's brand name throughout its history has been associated with "quality first," and all of Sainsbury's executive teams since World War II have dutifully reinterpreted this mantra.

Cadbury's historical dominant logic was "enterprising and fair, but conservative," all these qualities reflecting in varying degrees its enduring Quaker roots. Schweppes's historical dominant logic, by contrast, was "financial control" and "expansion through shareholder value creation." When the two companies merged in 1969, it took a decade before the post-merger dominant logic emerged; the result was a corporate model of playing a long game with brands and geographies – in terms of acquisitions, investment, integration, and divestment, while ensuring value for money in the product delivery of confectionary and beverages at the business unit level. Four generations of leaders (re)invented this dominant logic: Adrian Cadbury with his "credits and values" program, Michael Gifford with his "25 percent return on assets" mantra, Dominic Cadbury with his "focus on core" message, and John Sunderland with his "managing for value" program. While a fifth generation led by Todd Stitzer tried the same with their "fuel for growth" program, it was arguably less successful, illustrating the difficulty of reinventing an historical success logic.

Lastly, Unilever provides perhaps the best example of a tradition of continuity, but perhaps too much so. Ever since the founding Anglo-Dutch merger of 1929, the group's dominant logic was one of product and geographical leadership, based on a rationale of making itself too big to fail. As a result, Unilever rapidly grew to become one of the most international companies in the world, with an unprecedented range of products and divisions. Successive executive teams remained true to the idea of Unilever as a globally dispersed and managed "fleet" of brands, pulled together by the center's near-continuous cost-cutting operations. Only in the last few years has Unilever made serious cuts in its portfolio of brands and products.

Clearly, however, a tradition of continuity alone is insufficient for long-term outperformance if the environment changes, which it always does. So our successful transformers developed a complementary second tradition of gearing up for change, or anticipation.

Tradition of anticipation

All successful companies must, to some extent, anticipate the future. Some seek to do this through careful planning, some through intuitive leadership, others by trying to ensure they are close to markets and fleet of foot. Here, a tradition of anticipation means something rather different. *A company has a tradition of anticipation when it institutionalizes a space for alternative leaders to anticipate a timely variation on the old success theme and prepare a "behind the scenes" platform for change.* These alternative leaders form an "alternative dominant coalition" or shadow leadership for change, a loosely connected group of executives who fret that the dominant team is failing to anticipate industry changes and who gradually build a behind-the-scenes platform for transformation (Table 7.2).

For example, at Tesco an alternative family coalition formed as early as the 1960s, based on the view that the "pile it high, sell it cheap" retail model was outdated. Autocrat as he was, Cohen gradually ceded enough space for the upstarts to put in place a corporate model of financial control. This alternative grouping was also able to launch new logistical and location ideas that laid the basis of the transformation of the company in the next decades. During the 1970s the shadow leaders came to include more and more non-family members, such as Ian MacLaurin. These people were ready to take over from the old leadership once the latter's obsolescence had become evident – resulting in the swift launch of "Operation Breakthrough" when Cohen and those around him had stepped down at the end of the 1970s.

TABLE 7.2 | Evidence of the tradition of anticipation

Tesco	*Examples of members of an alternative dominant coalition preparing a behind-the-scenes platform of transformation:* 1950s–60s: E. Collar, H. Kreitman, A. Thrush (financial and logistical discipline) 1970s: I. MacLaurin, L. Porter, D. Behar, C. Goodfellow (prepare non-family influence, logistical overhaul) 1980s: D. Malpas, M. Darnell, J. Gildersleeve (geographical site research, cultural overhaul company, focus on food) 1990s: T. Leahy, T. Mason, D. Reid (21st-century retail store, internationalization, return of non-food)
Smith & Nephew	*Examples of members of an alternative dominant coalition preparing a behind-the-scenes platform of transformation:* 1960s: D. Seymour and a team of chemists (in-house R&D) 1970s: (financial discipline with 20%) 1980s: J.A. Suggett, (shift from chemists to engineering R&D base, greater integration of marketing and R&D) 1990s: C. O'Donnell (shift to emerging markets, focus on high-end healthcare)
Cadbury Schweppes	*Examples of members of an alternative dominant coalition preparing a behind-the-scenes platform of transformation:* Early 1970s: A. Cadbury anticipates "credits and values" program Mid-1970s: M. Gifford anticipates "25% return on assets" mantra Late 1970s – early 1980s : D. Cadbury anticipates "focus on core" Late 1980s: D. Wellings and D. Kappler bring international acquisition expertise Mid-1990s: J. Sunderland anticipates "managing for value" program Early 2000s: T. Stitzer, J. Brock, and B. Stitzer anticipate a new organizational and geographical set-up that facilitates the integration of acquisitions

Smith & Nephew, for its part, bought a research unit in 1951, not because the board believed in research but because it was fashionable. While the dominant coalition in the company continued to reflect its members' background in textiles, from the 1950s onwards chief scientist

Donald Seymour and his supporters doggedly defended the central importance of R&D and a new focus on advanced healthcare against all-comers. Eventually, the efforts of this alternative coalition supplied the company with a new corporate model of in-house R&D and a geographical focus on the North American market for advanced healthcare products. These provided the basis for Smith & Nephew's transformational successes in the 1980s and afterwards, as discussed below.

While blessed with very able management teams with a good feel for industry changes, the constituent companies of SSL never allowed for the emergence of an alternative dominant coalition. Ultimately, this cost them dear, as was evident in the 1980s when Seton tried to follow in the footsteps of Smith & Nephew by acquiring a US subsidiary. Lacking the kind of in-house platform for change that Smith & Nephew's R&D capabilities afforded, Seton's US expansion was a disaster. Similarly, while the purpose of the 1999 merger was to create medical synergies, there was no alternative leadership waiting in the wings to carry it through, leading to the company's retreat to a pure consumer business portfolio in 2002.

Interestingly, at Cadbury Schweppes *all* the leaders who emerged after 1960, from Sir Adrian Cadbury to Todd Stitzer, had at some point been part of a group of "alternative leaders" anticipating a different direction for their company while not yet in the driver's seat themselves. This direction eventually crystallized in a renewed dominant logic, as described above. In contrast, the very nature of Unilever's carefully managed succession process, via the triumvirate of the Special Committee with its third member as successor in waiting, made it much harder for alternative leaders to emerge. Indeed, the appointments in 2007 and 2009 of Michael Treschow and Paul Polman, Unilever's first outside chairman and CEO, respectively, the latter from arch-rival Procter & Gamble, is a striking reflection of the company's failure to identify and nurture its own alternative leaders. By contrast, none of the three SSTs has had to reach outside for top leadership.

The role of "happy accidents"

Why were the SSTs able to make effective use of a tradition of anticipation when the comparators were not? Crucially, we find that the alternative leaders were able to accelerate the pace of transformation, not by forcing the issue but by using "*happy accidents*" to gain a broad platform of support. Happy accidents are serendipitous dynamics or events that sit uncomfortably with the status quo, inducing fast bouts of transformation along the path anticipated by alternative leaders.

Remarkably, over the last four decades, successive alternative coalitions in Cadbury Schweppes, Tesco, and Smith & Nephew each took advantage of four major (but different) happy accidents. As we shall see later, their counterparts at Unilever, Sainsbury, and SSL International, by default of a tradition of anticipation, were unable to convert problems or unforeseen events into happy accidents in the same way. So from what happy accidents did the SSTs benefit?

Cadbury Schweppes' happy accidents

Cadbury Schweppes benefited from four happy accidents: post-merger politics, the hostile bid by General Cinema, attacks by Coca-Cola and Pepsi-Cola, and the challenge of the Adams acquisition.

Before the merger with Schweppes in 1969, Sir Adrian Cadbury and Peter Gregory had already been working on a renewal of Cadbury's competitive base, but only at the slow pace that the Cadbury family would tolerate. By contrast, for Schweppes' Harold Watkinson, who became the powerhouse on the board after the merger, "a week is a long time in politics, and even longer in business." Behind the scenes, however, Watkinson's chairmanship did much to energize and speed up the emergence of a new generation of Cadbury leaders, under the leadership of Sir Adrian. This new generation hung on to the Cadbury "long view" but with the best Schweppes elements rubbing off on it, such as bolder international ambitions and a tighter focus on financial performance. When Adrian became chairman, he was able to build on this. So, in one important sense at least, the post-merger politics were a "blessing in disguise."

Another was the takeover threat triggered in the 1980s by the poor performance of the US confectionery business. When General Cinema made its move in 1987, the situation did not look promising. But ultimately, the whole episode turned out to be a happy accident. In response to the bid, the share price rose, generating money for acquisitions and constituting a poison pill that allowed the Cadburys to further refine their long game. It also spurred Dominic Cadbury to accelerate the pace of transformation, not just by divesting the food and hygiene businesses, but also by giving alternative leaders such as Derek Williams and David Wellings the opportunity to run with exciting new developments.

The third happy accident turned out to be the acquisition of Dr Pepper/7Up in 1995. This was a breakthrough as it gave Cadbury Schweppes its first mainstream soft drinks brand. What was not anticipated was that this would change perceptions of the company in several problematic ways. No longer was Cadbury Schweppes perceived by the Cola giants as "nice" but not very effectual. The giants declared war, putting a distribution squeeze on Cadbury Schweppes' brands in the US, while Coca-Cola's direct attack on 7Up soured relations in the Coca-Cola Schweppes

Beverages joint venture. To compound the problems, rumors surfaced about equity dilution as attention centered on Cadbury Schweppes' apparently proliferating franchising businesses. In responding to these challengers, John Sunderland was able to use the changes of perception as a natural catalyst for change.

The acquisition of gum company Adams, the fourth happy accident, was another major breakthrough. But it threatened to be a "life or death issue" if the target was integrated along past lines. As it happened, Todd Stitzer, John Brock, and others had been thinking for a few years about changing the old model by forming regions and reducing the number of business units. Although they had been reluctant to force the issue, Adams provided a natural catalyst to do this.

Tesco's happy accidents

It would have been quite hard at the time to label the poisonous family relationships that bedevilled the Tesco boardroom in the 1960s as a happy accident. Yet there was an important flipside. Arthur Thrush, the retail director, deliberately distanced himself from the political maneuvering. Apart from being an outstanding retailer, Thrush took on board the job of mentoring new talent through the company at a distance from the family ructions. Beginning with Tesco's first management trainee, Ian MacLaurin, Thrush had by the late 1960s collected what some, with the benefit of hindsight, called an "alternative board": MacLaurin, David Malpas, Mike Darnell, John Gildersleeve, and Colin Goodfellow. This outstanding group was firmly of the view that the founder's original business model had outlived its shelf-life. When Leslie Porter took over as chairman, he chose to further distance company decisions from family politics.

Second, Operation Checkout in 1978 ultimately became an initiative with high strategic impact, but not for the reasons advanced by external analysts. Ironically, while Operation Checkout initially had no more than narrow operational intentions, it laid bare severe logistical and distributional problems that were almost fatal. Under these pressures, resistance to the upcoming leadership team's modernization plans crumbled, and a decisive shift from family control to a process of managerial engagement, improvisation, and change began.

Tesco's third blessing in disguise was the economic downturn in the early 1990s, which hit Tesco, with its less established and younger customer portfolio, harder than Sainsbury's. Puzzled why the business was not maintaining its recent levels of success, Malpas decided to spend a day visiting competitors' stores in the company of the up-and-coming Terry Leahy. Leahy subsequently wrote a report concluding that Tesco had lost sight of its customers and was stuck in a 20th-century rather than 21st-century customer proposition. He followed it up by announcing his intention to go back to Tesco's roots and reinvent them in a modern guise, cutting prices and launching Clubcard, to the derision of Sainsbury's and many industry analysts.

The fourth setback-turned-happy-accident was the French supermarket acquisition, Catteau. By the mid-1990s it had become clear that the venture was a failure, so Tesco cut its losses and got out. Yet the acquisition taught the upcoming leadership team some valuable lessons about foreign ventures and retailing in general, whose influence could be seen in subsequent iterations of Tesco's success model.

Smith & Nephew's happy accidents

Smith & Nephew's happy accidents concerned the acquisition of a healthcare research company, the failed takeover bid by Unilever, the OpSite disaster, and the East Asian currency crisis.

By the 1950s Smith & Nephew had become a conglomerate, not by design but because the company was run largely on the basis of personalities and reputations to be defended. It is in this context that the company's acquisition of a healthcare research company should be understood. Smith & Nephew's then chairman had become enthused by the new pharmaceutical business and was eager to jump on the research bandwagon, even though neither he nor the rest of the board knew much about research. By the 1960s it had become clear that Smith & Nephew had neither the means nor the will to become an important pharmaceutical player. But the one research professional, research director Donald Seymour, took advantage of the spotlight on pharmaceuticals to push Smith & Nephew's research in a far more promising direction. Under his protection, Seymour's research team developed the innovative and highly successful OpSite, a wound dressing for use during surgery. Developed via a process of minor failures and happy accidents, OpSite would lay the basis for Smith & Nephew's later transformation from a confusing conglomerate into a focused high-margin healthcare firm.

The abortive takeover bid by Unilever in the late 1960s unintentionally facilitated another major step in Smith & Nephew's transformation. The emotional contest that ensued with the Smith & Nephew board led to not only a significant closing of the ranks, but also the emergence of Smith & Nephew's financial wizard, Kenneth Kemp. Kemp brought order to Smith & Nephew's conglomerate muddle, not least by imposing demanding growth targets for new investment. Unwedded to the increasingly obsolete textile culture that had dominated the company, Kemp joined forces with

Seymour and marketer Alan Fryer to insist on a simplification of the strategic direction and focus of the company. These interventions were timely and providential, preparing Smith & Nephew for the 1970s, a decade that would bring increasing pressures on margins and volume, and a need to outflank increasing international competition in an industry that was steadily concentrating.

After a decade of research, OpSite was launched in 1978. Unfortunately, the distribution of OpSite was a fiasco, allowing US competitors a breathing space. Ultimately, however, this small disaster would prove a blessing in disguise. If OpSite had been an instant success, there would have been little impetus for Smith & Nephew to kick on from the halfway house it had reached in its transformation path (especially given the fact that then CEO Eric Kinder was the voice of the company's textile industry past). Now, however, he had to speed up the pace of evolution by following the lead of the alternative dominant coalition ranged around John Robinson.

Robinson wanted to move into the high-technology medical devices industry by buying an orthopedics company – an acquisition that would eventually provide Smith & Nephew with the platform to transform itself from "the peddler of bandages" into a global innovator in medical devices. Without this platform, the transformation of Smith & Nephew in the 1990s could not have occurred. This was not just a matter of size or product range, but was instead important because it clarified the focus on higher-margin, high-tech products. It is clear from our interviews that these US acquisitions were not part of a planned transformation of the firm. It was rather the reverse: the acquisitions triggered the eventual transformation.

Even before becoming CEO in 1997, Christopher O'Donnell had been pressing for the articulation of a clearer strategic framework. A fourth major happy accident would help to create a head of steam behind his ideas. To placate disgruntled shareholders, O'Donnell's predecessor, John Robinson, had decided to invest heavily in the fast-growing Asian economies. No sooner had he passed on the job to O'Donnell than the East Asian currency crisis struck in 1997, wiping out 40 percent of Smith & Nephew's profits in the space of 18 months. O'Donnell decided to bite the bullet and brought in consultants to carry out comprehensive reviews of strategy and manufacturing, which triggered the decision to exit smaller businesses and focus on the global medical sectors that are now at the heart of the current Smith & Nephew. Most people who before had resisted now jumped on board, allowing O'Donnell to lay the foundations for the company's successful transformation in subsequent years.

Why are some firms repeatedly lucky?

Have Cadbury Schweppes, Tesco, and Smith & Nephew just been lucky with their happy accidents? We do not believe so. The happy accidents we describe have an element of luck, but more precisely they reflect the principle that "fortune favors the prepared mind," as the saying has it, or those already in motion and awaiting the right moment, that is, those with more dynamic traditions. One of the reasons why Unilever, Sainsbury, and SSL International drifted away from leadership positions in their markets is that without fully fledged traditions of anticipation, they were unable to turn serendipitous turns of events to their advantage. For instance, it was always down to John Sainsbury to provide both continuity and anticipation in the company. The same applied to the leaders of the constituent companies of SSL International.

The comparison between Cadbury Schweppes and Unilever is particularly illuminating. Cadbury Schweppes became much more dynamic and self-driven because it allowed for the emergence of alternative leaders in the confectionery and beverages streams. Unilever had two comparable streams, the Dutch in food and the British in household goods. But rather than permit such developments, the Unilever Special Committee tended to pre-empt initiative on one side or the other, always wanting to keep the two in political balance. The Unilever culture of consensus favored "Buggins's turn" rather than letting one view or business become dominant.

Tradition of contestation

The last comparison between Cadbury Schweppes and Unilever points to a second reason why happy accidents occur more to some companies than others. Companies such as Cadbury Schweppes, Tesco, and Smith & Nephew developed a third tradition, that of contestation (Table 7.3). It is evident from our work that contestation has two dimensions that are mutually dependent. The first may be thought of as a *culture of challenge*: *a management style that places emphasis on internal competition, debate, discussion, and self-critical scrutiny of decisions, performance, and improvement*. Our three SSTs demonstrated such contestation whereas the comparator companies manifested cultures of conservatism, characterized by conformity or obedience to a hierarchy, an emphasis on continuity, resistance to ideas from outside the firm and a "not invented here" mentality, defensiveness around decision-making, and the promotion of people likely to "toe the line" rather than challenge the status quo.

TABLE 7.3 | Evidence of the tradition of contestation

Tesco	By the late 1970s Tesco had developed a very eclectic sense of leadership in which different people and generations had a place. Tesco's success was based on trust in a questioning culture. Everyone had the confidence to try to solve a problem. Yet backdoor politics and wasting time was not appreciated. Once a decision was made, everyone was behind it. The whole organization was built on process, rather than on specific systems or people.
Smith & Nephew	New generations came up, and with every new generation the politics became less. By the 1980s people had developed respect for different strategic viewpoints and listened to each other.
Cadbury Schweppes	The company gradually developed a collegial framework without any of the politics of the past. The successive chairmen left lots of freedom to people running the businesses. They trusted in the new champions who came up through the ranks, even though they sometimes had other ambitions and priorities for the business.

When traditions of contestation are examined it becomes clear that they took effect at different levels in the SST firms over time. Traditions of contestation are also reflected in the coexistence of three relatively self-contained leadership subgroups, focussed, respectively, on short-, medium- and long-term transformation issues. These are typically members of three different generations. The incumbent dominant coalition operates at corporate level, the alternative dominant coalition mediates between the corporate and business levels, and champions of alternative industry logics work at the business level. So in the SSTs, strategic development was not solely the province of top management.

As with other traditions, contestation should not be thought of as the outcome of specific managerial decisions but rather as an emergent phenomenon over time. We found that its origins in the SST firms could typically be traced back several decades and over that period took different forms and had different origins. In our SSTs, contestation appeared to develop as the result of at least one of two historical events: either the merger of two different cultures, or strong personal rivalries. Disagreements here escalate from cognitive into emotional conflict. However, such emotional conflict comes to be associated with a failing dominant coalition, whereas the association with cognitive conflict becomes associated with more successful alternative management coalitions. In a kind of Darwinian process of rewarding success, in time, as these alternative coalitions gain power, a tolerance for cognitive conflict comes to be not only accepted by subsequent generations of leaders, but also, ultimately, associated with success, when it takes on its mature form of *respectful difference*.

Contestation at Cadbury Schweppes and Unilever

Cadbury Schweppes is a good example of contestation emerging from the merger of two cultures. In line with their Quaker heritage, Cadbury's leaders had long been keen to foster a corporate culture and image in which "candour, freedom of speech … a spirit of toleration and liberty … are the dominant notes."[2] While this cultural precursor was certainly valuable, the 1969 merger was a corporate clash of civilizations. After the merger, under archetypical Schweppes man and ex-politician Harold Watkinson, emotions ran high for a time, generating a backlash from an alternative coalition of Cadbury managers who were critical of the short-termism that had come to dominate the company and advocated a return to core competences. While staying in the background, board members such as Adrian Cadbury gave their support to champions of the new logic such as Dominic Cadbury and Mike Gifford, both of whom eventually rose to positions of authority.

By contrast, in Unilever the contestation that might have arisen from the founding merger in 1929 was formalized away in the balancing arrangements that governed relations between the Dutch and British holding companies. As a former board director, Clive Butler, put it, "From the merger in 1929 our strategy has suffered from the need to manage the balance between the Dutch and English sides of the business."[3] This was combined with a legacy of doing almost anything anywhere in the world and a consequent growing disconnect between the corporate and business levels. Contestation and innovation across corporate and business levels were hampered by the corporate imposition of equalization agreements between the Ltd and NV halves and by silo-creating resource allocation decisions – most notably about product and geographical responsibilities, but also with regard to acquisitions. For example, the Bestfoods acquisition as late as 1999 could convincingly be read as a political face-saver for the Dutch foods side. It also gave out mixed signals about the intention of doing away with low-performing brands and investing in more promising categories and geographies.

Starting with Angus' efforts to bring the US division back in line, and the 1984 Marlow meeting, Unilever has attempted to drive a tighter focus and exert more financial control from the corporate center. However, as confirmed by our Unilever interviewees, while Anglo-Dutch balancing operations may have been rendered largely obsolete by the progressive internationalization of the corporate executive and nonexecutive teams, the default tendency to pre-empt conflict and seek early consensus is still present.

Contestation at Smith & Nephew and SSL International

With regards to the second origin of traditions of contestability – emotional conflict stemming from personal rivalry – Smith & Nephew provides a case in point. Insiders described processes of decision-making in Smith & Nephew in the 1960s and 70s as "management by argument." During the transition from an industrial, textile-based company to a very different R&D-led medical instruments firm, different coalitions battled for leadership. The existing dominant coalition led by chief executive Kenneth Bradshaw was wedded to the textile roots and opposed any movement to privilege medical instruments or shift resources to the development of in-house R&D capacities. There was also an alternative dominant coalition led by Don Seymour, which argued the contrary case. This second leadership group managed to push high-potential younger executives through the ranks who understood the importance of research and innovation and the need to shift from textile to advanced healthcare markets. One such was future chief executive John Robinson. The greater promise of in-house R&D compared with industrial manufacturing became clear to almost everyone in the late 1970s. The tipping point was reached in 1978 with the achievement of a critical mass of in-house R&D and the commercial launch of the advanced wound management technology OpSite.

In contrast to developments at Smith & Nephew, decision-making at the constituent companies of SSL International were consistently dominated by the thinking of the founding families, as with the Stollers at Seton and the Scholls at Scholl. At Seton Healthcare, London Rubber, and Scholl alike, that thinking centered above all on perpetuating one blockbuster product, respectively Tubigrip, Durex, and Scholl footwear. The acquisition policy reflected the same single-mindedness: unlike the more difficult, transformational acquisitions carried out by Smith & Nephew, London Rubber and Seton confined themselves to opportunistic purchases that were then absorbed into the traditional dominant (and in some cases distinctly patriarchal) logic. With little or no experience of handling fundamental differences within the companies, it was hardly surprising that their merger into the combined SSL in 1999 proved to be a traumatic affair.

Contestation at Tesco and Sainsbury's

A comparison of Tesco and Sainsbury's provides another telling illustration of the importance of providing space for the playing out of personal rivalries. Jack Cohen, Tesco's founder, had transformed his company from a private local player into a national public one more than two decades before Sainsbury's flotation. Early board and top-team meetings at Tesco, largely composed of family members, were renowned for their forthright exchanges, sometimes going beyond the verbal. Much of this stemmed from the dominant role played by Cohen himself. But despite his autocratic tendencies, Cohen was much less hostile to outside influence than his rivals at Sainsbury. Most notably, he gave outsider Ian MacLaurin, Tesco's first management trainee, the opportunities and headroom to grow into a viable alternative leader. It was MacLaurin who, much against family wishes, engineered Tesco's ground-breaking "Operation Checkout" in the 1970s. Meanwhile, Tesco's alternative coalition, both on the board and at the business level, bided its time and accepted the formal dominance of the family clan around Cohen – until the obsolescence of the old dominant logic and the promise of an alternative logic had become sufficiently clear in the 1970s.

By the early 1980s Tesco had developed a "questioning culture" in which it was expected that people throughout the organization would come up with alternative insights and agendas and bring different perspectives and arguments to significant decisions. For example, when Tesco introduced demographic store profiling, the function was not located in the historically dominant property department, as might have been expected, but in marketing, the implication being that information – and arguments – to do with store siting would benefit from both property and marketing insights, and that the two would not necessarily align.

In contrast to Tesco, Sainsbury continued to be dominated by a "patriarch" and his associated group, much like a family clan. While early differences erupted into the open at Tesco, they were long pre-empted at Sainsbury by allocating responsibilities according to inherited positions in the family tree. This meant, for example, that David Sainsbury, like his father, would remain in a largely non-retailing, financial position, at a distance from John Sainsbury. When he became CEO, he not surprisingly lacked John's retailing instincts and experience. Furthermore, with the exception of Roy Griffiths, contestation from non-family members was unheard of during Sir John's tenure. The result was a lack of challenge to the business model, for example during the economic crisis of the early 1990s, and the drastic underestimation of the potential of Tesco's Clubcard initiative. Sainsbury's "implacable leadership" did not allow for the emergence of alternative perspectives or argument, with damaging consequences for its ability to maintain and reinvent its distinctive historical "quality first" business proposition.

Tradition of mobility

A final reason why Cadbury Schweppes, Tesco, and Smith & Nephew have benefited much more from happy accidents than their comparators is that they developed a fourth tradition, that of mobility (Table 7.4). *A company has a tradition of mobility if it has institutionalized routines of recruitment, promotion and exit that are informal tests of ability rather than formal human resources procedures.* These are distinctive informal rules or norms that not only appeal to the most skilled candidates, but, equally crucially, do not filter out a leavening of "skilled mavericks." They link the promotion and exit of employees to their ability to participate in a continuous process of internally generated or home-grown company transformation. In particular, we found that the three SSTs developed a tradition of mobility with four such informal "tests."

TABLE 7.4 Evidence of the tradition of mobility

Alternative logic *Test for recruitment*	**Tesco** The company always actively attracted mavericks, and senior people always sought to mentor them. Sainsbury's recruitment practices were very different and bureaucratic. **Smith & Nephew** The company was usually able to develop leaders within its ranks. People were always allowed to try things in an entrepreneurial culture. Top managers, rather than human resources, sought to mentor talent. **Cadbury Schweppes** Starting with Adrian Cadbury up to Todd Stitzer, all CEOs came up within the ranks and were executives with original ideas and methods.
Alternative dominant coalition *Test for promotion*	**Tesco** The unwritten rule of promotion in Tesco was to solve problems no one else could and keep solving them. For instance, Terry Leahy's unique capacity to solve problems no one else could in collaboration with senior managers earned him an early promotion to the board. **Smith & Nephew** Despite significant initial opposition, Don Seymour's undoubted talent and determination to promote R&D saw him promoted to the board early in the company's history. Chris O'Donnell had the unique capacity to be onside with everybody during large changes. **Cadbury Schweppes** Peter Gregory was promoted to the board because he was effective and completely independent-minded. The assertive and ruthlessly effective Michael Gifford quickly became very influential on the board.

Dominant coalition *Test for promotion*	**Tesco** Ian MacLaurin, rather than a family member from the founder's line, became chairman because he was considered the best guarantee of the company's survival. **Smith & Nephew** In senior promotions, the company looked for flexibility in thinking and not just achievements to date. **Cadbury Schweppes** One candidate for chairman was rejected because he was viewed as too fixed in his beliefs, while the person appointed was seen as a champion of continuous change.
Test for voluntary exit	**Tesco** After Cohen had stayed on as chairman until the age of 79, and some of the family went on as life presidents, the company moved to a culture of early, voluntary exit. This was exemplified by Terry Leahy's retirement as chief executive at the age of only 55. **Smith & Nephew** The company avoided a blame culture and never exited a senior executive on acrimonious terms. **Cadbury Schweppes** Mike Gifford and John Brock left the company of their own accord when they did not become CEO.

An "alternative logic" test

Skilled people with intrapreneurial potential or a "maverick" reputation are recruited and given the space not only to comply with their formal job specification, but also to experiment with and/or refine their knowledge of alternative industry models. So this pursuit of an alternative logic works in tandem with a tradition of continuity. For instance, Tesco systematically hired mavericks and gave them the latitude to experiment with new industry logics. Those able to "solve problems that no one else has before" were earmarked for possible subsequent promotion. This was a pattern established by Ian MacLaurin. As a senior colleague observed: "He had the ability, not to have a series of clones, but to have people who were different; so the people Ian picked for his team … came at issues from different points of view."

An "alternative dominant coalition" test

Intrapreneurs who were flexible enough both to juggle alternative models and to initiate changes alongside members of the dominant coalition were promoted to the corporate level to form part of the alternative leadership grouping. For instance, again in Tesco, those marked out as potential champions were not automatically promoted to corporate-level responsibilities. They only made it to the top if they allied problem-solving with the ability to do so in cooperation with people at the corporate level who were more embedded in the company's culture.

A "dominant coalition" test

Intrapreneurs who successfully completed at least one of the two prior tests of transformative ability *and* demonstrated sufficient affinity with the historical character of the company were often granted a central role in the new dominant coalition. In effect, this test reflects the principle that the most visible change agents often are not the most appropriate CEOs or chairmen. For instance, at Cadbury, Mike Gifford was considered the principal change agent in the 1970s. Confronted with the choice between Gifford and Dominic Cadbury as his successor, however, then CEO Basil Collins chose the latter, because of the widespread fear that Gifford would push his change logic too far to guarantee the safety of company's historical character. Something similar would happen later with John Brock and Todd Stitzer.

An "exit" test

Individuals who either failed (one of) the two first tests of transformative ability or outlived their usefulness at the dominant coalition level were protected from political ostracism and loss of face. At the same time, they were expected either to substantially let go of ambitions incompatible with the new organizational course or to leave the company amicably as part of the "extended family."

For instance, at Cadbury Schweppes, over the three decades of the 1970s, 80s, and 90s Gifford, Dominic Cadbury and John Sunderland worked hard to exit "barons" who had settled into entrenched ways of doing things at either the corporate or the local business level. Our interviewees suggest that the exit criterion of cold performance ratios was never pursued to an obtrusive extent. Rather, it was used to induce self-regulation of behaviors and motivations among all managers. Indeed, the institutionalization of such a self-regulating spirit from the mid-1990s onwards provided the new CEO John Sunderland and his successor Todd Stitzer with a platform to urge remaining "barons" to voluntarily adjust their aims or move on in the interest of the company. At Tesco, lessons were learned from the example of Jack Cohen, who seemed unable to let go. His successors, led by Ian MacLaurin, vowed never to repeat Cohen's mistake. Upholding that commitment, David Malpas voluntarily relinquished the position of chief executive in 1997; Terry Leahy did the same thing in 2011.

How the traditions enabled strategic change

In this chapter, we have elaborated on how the three successful companies developed their four traditions of transformation. By the late 1980s and early 1990s, all three companies were in a position to use these traditions to make drastic strategic changes that were beyond their comparators. It was not so much that individual traditions enabled particular strategies. Rather, it was the constellation of traditions that together created companies that were strategically flexible in both formulation and implementation. In particular, the three successful companies, in contrast to their comparators, were not bound by historical views of their business models or strategies. Ironically, the organizational traditions enabled the companies to give up strategic traditions when necessary. Below, we draw on material that we already presented in Chapter 4, to summarize the key strategic changes made by the three companies in the later years that we studied.

Cadbury Schweppes

From the 1990s onward Cadbury Schweppes made several courageous strategic moves that depended on the flexibility created by the four traditions.

First, in beverages, the company moved into the big league by upping its stake in Dr Pepper to 25 percent, and in 1995 buying the rest of the company. This move brought Cadbury Schweppes into direct competition with two giants, Coca-Cola and PepsiCo. The company rearranged its bottling operations through sales and acquisitions. Cadbury Schweppes also moved away from a global strategy in soft drinks by selling off businesses outside the US, France, and South Africa. Lastly, by acquiring Snapple, it rebalanced its drinks portfolio to 50:50 carbonated and noncarbonated, just in time to reduce its exposure to the Cola War between Coke and Pepsi.

Second, in confectionery, the company, from the late 1990s, increased its revenues in confectionery via international expansion, thereby rebalancing the company portfolio to a better mix between beverages and confectionery. (In contrast, because of its organizational and political constraints, Unilever found such a rebalancing much harder to do.) This push toward confectionery culminated in the highly ambitious and risky expansion into chewing gum through the acquisition of Adams in 2002.

Third, in 2000 the company separated operational responsibility from strategic development in order to give senior management more emphasis on strategy. This was the culmination of the 1996 independent assessment of the capabilities of the top 200 executives. This separation would have been much harder to implement in a company without the openness to change enabled by the traditions.

Fourth, the 1997 launch of "Managing for Value" in order to maximize shareholder value was well ahead of most other companies in fast-moving consumer goods. At the same time, the traditions meant that Cadbury Schweppes did not blindly pursue shareholder value by abandoning the strategic and organizational roots of its successful formula. This emphasis on shareholder value enabled the 2008 demerger into separate confectionery and beverage companies. Unilever, by contrast, despite over 20 years of investor suggestions, has not been able to split its food and household businesses.

Tesco

From the 1990s Tesco also made some bold strategic and competitive changes.

First, Tesco showed the strategic flexibility of returning to its low price roots by deciding to be able to compete with the new hard discounters, such as Asda, and not just focus on competing with Sainsbury's. This was quite a turnaround as it required reversing a previous strategic change from emphasizing price to emphasizing quality. In addition, Tesco went back to the tradition of Green Shield savings stamps, but in the new format of electronically based Clubcards that yield savings with every purchase. Tesco took the bold move in 1993 of introducing the UK's first supermarket loyalty card, in the face of much skepticism and criticism.

Second, Tesco diversified into retail services such as banking and Internet shopping. In the latter case, it defied the conventional wisdom, followed by Sainsbury's, of having a dedicated warehouse. Instead, Tesco used pickers in its existing stores. Again, this was an example of where the traditions allowed informed and intelligent strategic decisions, but done the Tesco way.

Third, Tesco made bold moves in internationalization, a risky strategy in the supermarket sector that has seldom been successful. First, Tesco challenged French giant Carrefour in its home market. This 5-year foray between 1992 and 1997 ended in divestiture but garnered many lessons. Tesco then successfully entered Eastern European and Asian countries. Lastly, in late 2007 Tesco made a truly bold strategic move of entering the most competitive supermarket country of all, the US, and in its most competitive state, California, with its Fresh & Easy venture. The highly unfortunate timing, coinciding with the great recession that began in 2008, should not detract from Tesco's strategic capabilities.

In summary, the traditions had helped Tesco to develop into a highly competitive company that was confident in its own ability to make unconventional strategic decisions. Furthermore, the traditions developed while Tesco was a challenger to Sainsbury's allowed it to maintain its challenger mentality even after it became the market leader in its home market.

Smith & Nephew

In the 1990s Smith & Nephew's key strategic transformations came from the traditions enabling the company to exploit two happy accidents.

First, in early 1995 Chief Executive John Robinson announced that from then on strategic decisions should be the result of a spontaneously "shared process." Initially, senior managers lacked the confidence to take up this remarkable invitation. The turning point was a low-risk acquisition put forward by Chris O'Donnell. Despite the small and "pretty simple" nature of the deal, O'Donnell found himself compelled to do 28 presentations, including five to the full board, to push it through. After that experience, the decision process became much quicker for other acquisitions and strategic moves.

Second, a major happy accident occurred with the expansion into Asia just in time to hit the Asian financial crisis. O'Donnell used this crisis to push for a complete strategic and manufacturing review, bringing in outside consultants. One conclusion was that Smith & Nephew should exit the small, nonglobal businesses. Second, the company would place much more emphasis on exploiting its excellent technology. Third, the company adopted a new management structure and strategy focussing on only three strategic business units. All other businesses were sold for cash to invest in the core. The exited businesses included its heritage brands.

The traditions allowed Smith & Nephew to change its business model in a dispassionate way that included exits from founding businesses. In contrast, SSL International stuck to its rigid and inflexible business model and kept its heritage brands until the entire company was acquired.

A SUMMARY VIEW OF THE TRADITIONS

Table 7.5 summarizes the key elements of the four traditions. In sum, the four traditions – continuity, anticipation, contestation, and mobility – dovetail to provide a simple, robust transformation platform on which different generations of leaders can improvise. It ensures everyone is working on variations on the same theme, by means of a natural division of labor between the different coalitions, following a process that allows for bouts of fast evolution when happy accidents occur.

TABLE 7.5 | Key elements of the four traditions

Tradition of continuity Dominant coalition	• *Oldest generation focuses on continuity* • *Reinvent the historical success model* – Variations on the same theme – Adapted to contemporary circumstances
Tradition of anticipation Alternative dominant coalition	• *Anticipate new variation on a theme* – Relationship between corporate and business levels • *Wait for a "happy accident"* – Broad platform of support – Can accelerate group-wide transformation
Tradition of contestatation	• *Three leadership subgroups/generations* – Dominant coalition – Alternative dominant coalition – Champions of new industry logics • *Origin in* – Merger of different cultures – Personal rivalry
Tradition of mobility	• *Four tests of "transformative ability"* – "Champions" test – "Alternative leader" test – "Dominant coalition" test – "Exit" test

Because the comparator companies did not fully develop these traditions, they could not rely on this elegant and simple interplay. Rather, they had to fall back on cumbersome planning and control structures that were increasingly dysfunctional in their fast-changing environment. Note that the comparator companies also developed traditions of continuity and to some extent traditions of anticipation, which may explain their relatively good performance over the last 20 years. But the three comparators did not develop an alternative growth platform by an alternative leadership coalition.

Dominant coalitions in Sainsbury's, SSL International, and Unilever certainly provided for continuity. However, a development of alternative leaders is essential to the emergence of a full-fledged tradition of anticipation. Nor could the comparator companies build traditions of contestation and mobility, because they never gave sufficient leeway to an alternative dominant coalition. It is the existence of this alternative dominant coalition, together with the development of the traditions of contestation and mobility, that separates our SST from our non-SST companies. We believe that these traditions increased the odds that the companies could both get better at what they were good at in the short term while also making significant changes to reposition themselves in the longer term.

Contestation and mobility are vital for bringing about a type of transformation that is continuous and nontraumatic. In particular, the tradition of contestation ensures the energy supply for transformation by allowing the three leadership subgroups – the champions of new industry thinking, the alternative dominant coalition, and the dominant coalition – to, as it were, "live together apart." As a result, Tesco, Smith & Nephew, and Cadbury Schweppes all benefited from an internally generated tension between the maintenance of order and the bubbling up of new ideas that helped them constantly to renew their platform for growth and their strategic direction. This echoes complexity theorists' propositions that maintaining a sufficient level of tension between order and chaos is fundamental to achieving continual transformation.[4]

The tradition of mobility for its part provides for the gradual, nontraumatic building of coherence in the transformation process. Tesco, Smith & Nephew, and Cadbury Schweppes systematically hired new champions to experiment with new ideas; the most promising recruits were moved into the alternative dominant coalition, and in turn some were promoted into the dominant coalition. Home-grown transformation was thus refreshed and re-energized by injections of outside influence. Strategy development is both enriched and solidified by continuous feedback between the three generations. In short, the tradition of mobility keeps the tension created by leadership diversity within productive bounds by providing a common organizational platform for all three leadership groups.

THE LEGACY OF THE TRADITIONS

While many of the decisions described in our study were, no doubt, systematically considered and planned, it is evident that this is not the case for the traditions themselves. Their development might better be thought of as a process of evolution or emergence over decades. We should also remember that this was in the context of the three SSTs struggling to establish themselves against much bigger competitors. We have shown that it is in this context that the SSTs changed their strategies, often experimented, sometimes more or less successfully, and built on "happy accidents" to develop the strategies that emerged as more consolidated in the 1980s and 90s. We need to recognize, however, that by the 1990s, our SSTs were very different firms: in particular, they were much more established with clearer strategic trajectories.

In this section, we inquire about the extent to which the traditions we identified in our historical analysis are evident during the 1980s and 90s. In so doing, we do not assume that, as these firms became more established, we would see as evidently the same processes at work as in their histories. Indeed, we might expect to see those processes, in so far as they exist, become more taken for granted, more institutionalized, and this is what we found. For example, when we interviewed managers who had retired, they tended to be more reflective about the management processes they recalled. When we interviewed current managers, we found, perhaps not surprisingly, that their focus was more on current recent decisions. They were not as explicit about the processes by which such decisions were taken. So, as explained in Chapter 2, we needed a more detailed analysis of the interviews in order to discern to what extent different management processes, and especially the traditions we identified, seemed evident in the interviews. In what follows, we explain the findings from this analysis.

The overall finding from this analysis is that, in the 1980s and 90s, there continued to be a marked difference between the management processes at work in the SSTs compared with the comparator firms. However, this primarily takes form in the difference between the extent of contestation in the SSTs compared with an emphasis on the more conservative, consensual approach in the non-SSTs. There are other differences too that can be seen to relate to the traditions we identified above, in particular to contestation and conservatism. In what follows, we will explain these findings in more detail.

The historical analysis flagged up the significant role of "*alternative coalitions*" of managers in anticipating future developments. Such coalitions continued into the 1980s in the SSTs but it is less clear that they continued into the 1990s and the new millennium. This is perhaps not surprising given that, by that time, each of the SSTs had become more established in terms of the strategies they were following in their markets. The alternative coalitions of the 1960s, 70s, and 80s developed as these companies sought to identify just what those strategies should be in the face of more dominant competitors. What we see is the benefit of the existence of these alternative coalitions in creating a context in which the SSTs were able to take advantage of the apparently threatening circumstances they faced (the "happy accidents" described above) and in helping to develop a way of managing that was based more on contestation than consensus.

Although our findings are largely based on historical case studies based on our interviews and archival material, as explained in Chapter 2 we also undertook a separate statistical analysis of the interviews.[5] The purpose here was to see if the emphasis placed by our interviewees on explaining how strategy development occurred in their firms reflected our case study findings. What is clear from this analysis is that the *tradition of contestation* existed in the SSTs in the 1980s and 90s, whereas in the non-SSTs it was largely absent. Table 7.6 shows a comparison in this respect between all the SSTs and all the non-SSTs.

TABLE 7.6 Contestation versus conservatism (SSTs versus non-SSTs)

	All SSTs			All non-SSTs		
	Pre 1980	1980–1989	1990–2006	Pre 1980	1980–1989	1990–2006
Contestation	**36.9**	**49.8**	**53.1**	**2.6**	**3.3**	**7.2**
Debate and discussion	14.8	28.3	28.3	0	1.9	6.2
Internal competition	6.8	11.7	4.8	0	0	0.5
Openness to different views	14.5	10.2	23.6	2.8	1.4	1.1
Conservatism	**3.4**	**0**	**1.5**	**42.1**	**51.3**	**47.5**
Continuity	3.4	0	0.7	9.4	14.0	8.7
Not invented here	0	0	0	0.6	10.2	8.4
Obedience	0	0	0.8	23.6	21.4	23.4
Protectionism	0	0	0	5.1	6.7	9.4
Related factors						
Strategic autonomy	7.1	15.2	12.0	11.8	4.5	5.2
Tight/loose culture	29.6	20.8	19.4	0	2.4	2.6
Different cultures across the firm	23.9	13.7	9.9	0	1.1	1.6
Centralized decision-making	0	0.1	0.4	37.2	30.3	26.7
Strategic dependency	0	0	0	9.5	6.1	6.2

The percentages in Table 7.6 represent the relative amount of text coded (in number of words) as evidence of a concept compared across columns. All columns add up to 100 percent. For example, the percentage in the cell in the bottom right corner (6.2) indicates that of all the text coded to the concept in this table for the non-SST interviews related to time period 1990–2006, 6.2 percent was assigned to "Strategic dependency."

Note: Some of the percentages within the columns on contestation and conservatism do not add up to the aggregate scores for contestation and conservatism because some of the content of the interviews were "double-coded." In other words, some of what the interviewees said could be interpreted as relating to, for example, both "Debate and discussion" and "Openness to different views." Therefore, some of the numbers within the subcategories slightly exceed the overall categories.

Within those overall categories, there is a finer grained explanation. In Tesco and Cadbury Schweppes in particular, both prior to and after 1980, the emphasis was on open discussion and debate together with an openness to different views. This included an openness to the challenging of existing ways of doing things. By the 1990s it seems that this had become the taken for granted way of operating. The cut and thrust of management debate was the normal state of affairs, and managers seem to have gained kudos from being prepared to argue their positions and take a stand on key issues or ideas they advocated. In Smith & Nephew, the contestation seems to have been less the expected norm but nonetheless remained as the product of the decentralized and relatively autonomous business units of the past.

There was also evidence of the existence of internal competition between subunits within the SSTs, often at middle management level. These did not appear to be firms "built for comfort." On the other hand, in the non-SSTs we see almost exactly the reverse – a culture of conservatism. By "obedience" is meant a tendency for managers to accept decisions from higher levels of management without much debate, together with the absence of challenging and questioning. In effect, it is the opposite of "debate and discussion." There is also an emphasis on continuity of existing practices and a wariness of significant changes, together with a skepticism about outside views and external influence – a "not invented here" syndrome.

There are other explanations evident in the interviews of how strategies developed in the firms, which seem to relate to the contestation versus conservatism distinction. These are shown in the bottom section of Table 7.6. "Strategic autonomy" refers to the extent to which middle managers influence or obtain the resources to follow through a particular strategy. Although the differences between the SSTs and non-SSTs is not marked here, there does appear to be more emphasis on it in the post-1980 period in the SSTs.

For other factors, the distinction is more marked. "Tight/loose culture" refers to the extent to which the managers in a firm cohere around a clear mission or set of values but accept that these may be expressed differently in different business units. The antithesis of this is organizations that place an emphasis on uniformity throughout the organization. We see a marked difference between SSTs, which tend to have such tight/loose cultures, and non-SSTs, which do not, although there are perhaps indications in the non-SSTs that this is diminishing as the decades proceed. Non-SSTs also place a markedly higher emphasis on centralized decision-making compared with SSTs, where this is little mentioned. It is similar for "Strategic dependency," by which is meant the limited extent to which middle managers are able to take independent action in resourcing strategies.

We also examined the same data by firm to see if there were any differing patterns between each SST firm and its comparator. Table 7.7 shows the summary data for this, which bear out the overall findings. The interviewees in each of the SST firms placed much more emphasis on contestation throughout each of the periods than did those from the non-SST firms, whose interviewees tend to emphasize much more conservatism and much more emphasis on centralized decision-making in Sainsbury and Unilever.

TABLE 7.7 | Contestation versus conservatism by firm

	Contestation			Conservatism		
	Pre 1980	1980–1989	1990–2006	Pre 1980	1980–1989	1990–2006
Tesco	37.2	25.4	19.3	7.2	0	0
Sainsbury	0	2.9	3.4	45.9	63.8	55.8
Cadbury	41.8	36.6	41.5	3.8	0	2.7
Unilever	4.5	1.6	2.1	43.2	30.1	32.0
Smith & Nephew	16.6	33.0	32.6	0	0	3.1
SSL	0	0.6	1.1	0	6.1	6.4

Note: The percentages in Table 7.7 represent, similarly to Table 7.6, the relative amount of text coded (in number of words) as evidence of a concept compared across columns. All columns add up to 100 percent. For example, the percentage in the cell in the bottom right corner (6.4) indicates that of all the text coded to the concept in this table for the SSL interviews related to time period 1990–2006, 6.4 percent was assigned to "Conservatism." These percentages are subject to a small bias. Organizations at which more interviews were conducted (that is, more interview text was available) are more likely to have higher percentages in each cell (when compared across columns). For the first five organizations, the differences in the amount of interview text are relatively small, and the underlying differences are so substantial that they are unlikely to have been caused by this bias. However, we had considerably fewer interviews for SSL.

When we come to the *tradition of mobility*, the data evident from the more detailed analysis of the transcripts bear out that it is especially evident in the period before 1980. However, this diminishes in its emphasis after 1980, after which there is relatively less distinction between the SSTs and the non-SSTs. This is particularly the case for Cadbury, for example, where before the 1980s the evidence of mobility of management was especially marked compared with Unilever, but this declined significantly after the 1990s.

In sum, we are left with the picture that it is contestation and other aspects of management processes related to contestation that most clearly distinguish the SSTs from the non-SSTs. It is as if the traditions that we identified in the earlier decades create a context within which such contestation arises and flourishes. This both flags up the importance of management's historical legacy and raises uncomfortable questions about "path-dependence, where early events and decisions establish 'policy paths' that have lasting effects on subsequent events and decisions"[6] – a concept introduced in Chapter 1. In light of these considerations, just what can managers realistically and proactively do to foster the ability to achieve the agility or ambidexterity that so many management writers call for, which provides the capabilities to both change and maintain high performance, and which may help to avoid the pitfalls of strategic drift? These are the questions we address in the next and final chapter.

CHAPTER 8

Playing the Long Game: Implications for Managers

We began this book by arguing that a major challenge facing executives is the avoidance of strategic drift. Businesses become so wedded to the distinctive capabilities that brought them success that they are either blinded to changes in their environment, with the result that their capabilities become outmoded and their strategy redundant; or, if they recognize the changes taking place, they dismiss them because they are so wedded to the strategy they are following. The ability of firms *both* to exploit the capabilities on which they have built success and to explore new bases of success seems rare. Our interest has been in such exceptional firms (our successful strategic transformers [SSTs]) that developed capabilities upon which they could make transformational changes while retaining high levels of performance. In this chapter, we turn our attention to the implications of our findings for managers and for management practice.

The previous chapter pointed to four key traditions that underpinned these companies' success in achieving both transformational changes and high levels of performance: traditions of continuity, anticipation, contestation, and mobility. It emphasized that, in the SSTs, these traditions took decades rather than years to develop. Which leads to the obvious question: what can managers do today to build such capabilities? Is the best that they can hope to plant the seeds from which the traditions will grow over time? Or can they take action to, in effect, invent traditions from scratch in order to bring the pay-off forward in time – or at least reduce the gestation period for the development of such traditions?

In truth, our research does not provide direct answers to these questions, but it does suggest a number of priorities for management attention. Other research, discussed in Chapter 1, although ahistorical and sometimes even unempirical, seeks to ask related questions: How can executives develop "dynamic capabilities" to renew bases of competitive advantage? How might "organizational learning" take place? Is it possible to manage organizations efficiently and profitably exploit current capabilities while exploring innovative bases of future advantage? And what might the structure and systems of organizations be like if any of this is to be achieved? Our research is unique in that it examines in detail and historically just how very exceptional businesses have managed to develop the capacity to achieve much of this over a period of decades. We can therefore check the relevance of such research against our own and ask: what lessons can we learn?

There are no studies that have examined the specific issues with which we have been concerned. Indeed, there are very few studies that have addressed related issues. One of the few is published in Jim Collins and Jerry Porras's book *Built to Last.*[1] They too asked why it is that some firms are able to maintain high performance over long periods of time, and an implication of their sample is that these are firms that have also made major changes. They too were concerned to tease out the management processes accounting for success, and to do this, they undertook extensive interviews with executives as well as examining secondary data. They identified the firms they studied in very different ways from us and were not very explicit about whether or to what extent changes were made by those firms, so we cannot be sure if we were studying the same phenomenon. Nonetheless, it is the closest research we know, and it is worth asking if the findings from the two studies complement each other.

Like us, Collins and Porras did not put success down to charismatic visionary leaders, but they did emphasize the role of corporate leaders as architects of strategy. They also pointed out that, typically, these leaders are not parachuted in from outside the organizations: home-grown managers predominate. These are not findings we would dispute. In our study, leaders play a key role and also typically come from within. But what we show is that, in firms that both maintain high performance and make major changes, these executives have typically been part of alternative coalitions of senior managers who have been exploring the next generation of strategies for the firm.

Collins and Porras point to what they refer to as the maintenance of "core values," and they acknowledge that successful strategies evolve over time. They are less clear, however, on how this happens. We show that it is dominant coalitions that preserve a continuity of strategy for the firm while the alternative coalition explores future alternatives. In this aspect, both studies de-emphasize formal planning and emphasize the role people play in promoting experimentation and building on what both studies refer to as "accidents." Collins and Porras further recognize that the firms they studied are not comfortable places in which to work. They are very demanding environments. What they do not identify is the central role of the contestation we see as fundamental to the questioning and experimentation that underpins transformation. Nor do they emphasize the historical roots of such contestation, or indeed the other traditions we have identified.

There are, then, similarities. Our study is not out of line with this prior study. But what we do is provide additional dimensions of explanation that illuminate more precisely the management processes underlying long-term successful strategic transformation and in particular the importance of history.

We believe that managers should act on our findings in three different ways. First is in terms of their mindset, how they make sense of their organizational world. Second is in terms of two key priorities that they need to adopt and institutionalize. And third, we put forward 10 practical proposals for building the skills and capabilities for playing the long game.

A MINDSET FOR THE LONG GAME

The way we act and the decisions we take are a product of the way we see ourselves and the world we live in – our mindset. The mindsets of most managers are, inevitably, strongly influenced by their experience in the organizations in which they have made their career. As we have seen, however, most of those organizations are managed in ways that all too often end up in strategic drift. Our research, then, points to the need for a rather different managerial mindset.

Value of history

Executives are frequently urged to take a longer term view of strategy. They are warned of the dangers of pursuing short-term profits and growth at the expense of longer term security of earnings. But even here, "long term" is seen as the antithesis of short term, where this is a year or so. So long term, although rarely specified, typically means 5 or 10 years at the most. This notion of the long term is replicated in academic studies of businesses. There are very few studies that examine the performance of firms and their value-creating capacity over periods longer than a decade.

Indeed, many academic studies are notable for their reliance on current data even though they claim to be concerned with long-term effects. We concur with the need for a longer rather than shorter term perspective for management. However, we contend that the capacity of businesses to create value needs to be conceived of and measured over decades. In the absence of such a long-term perspective, we believe that executives will struggle to avoid strategic drift and the crisis and consequent value destruction that it entails.

One way of putting this is that managers badly need to value history more than they do. Before they can build on the traditions they have inherited from their predecessors, they need to be aware of and understand the legacy of the past. Explaining how Tesco's tradition of contestation evolved, David Malpas, Terry Leahy's predecessor as CEO, traced its origins to the early days of noisy and confrontational argument between Jack Cohen and other members of what was then a family firm. In an increasingly successful company, these habits softened into a tradition of openness and more respectful challenge. The emphasis changed under Leslie Porter:

> He ... allowed the business just to get on without troubling him with too many decisions. The result was that the board meetings in the mid-1980s were very open and argumentative to the point of confrontation, but like a family arguing rather than a group of enemies arguing.

It is a tradition that Malpas believes is still valued, and has continued to be preserved into the current decade. Managers need to recognize and value such legacies. They cannot readily be invented, but they can be nurtured and developed. Perhaps more worryingly, they can be easily done away with by incoming senior executives unaware of the potential treasure they have in their hands. For example, commentators have raised doubts about the extent to which Kraft, the acquirer of Cadbury, understands and values that company's heritage.

There is another reason for valuing history. Complexity theory teaches that lessons can be learned from small events as they develop over time. It is impossible to predict accurately when or where an earthquake or major economic downturn will hit. But just as large earthquakes are preceded by weak tremors or minor quakes, so great economic changes are preceded by smaller ones.[2] An awareness of how such weak signals build up can help actors to anticipate significant events to come. Building an organization in which managers are sensitive to such weak signals and are therefore prepared for major happenings when they occur requires managers to develop an acute and well-honed sense of history. Such sensitivity also provides management with a further benefit. Managers often wrongly assume that history follows a linear course between past and future, cause and consequence. History is nonlinear in that small yet timely changes can be the basis of transformation and can be a great deal more beneficial than one-off major changes. These latter are often spurred by financial downturns that are the consequence of strategic drift.

Values for generations

There is, however, an additional challenge for managers. This is the need to place what they do in a time frame going forward much longer than is conventional. Reports on the length of tenure of chief executives vary from 4.5 to just over 6 years in the UK,[3] less in the US. In that role, they face increasing pressures for continued short-term performance improvement and increasing shareholder returns. There is a good deal of debate about how healthy – or wise – this is for our economies, but even the most passionate defenders of short-termism assume that good management is concerned about the long-term wellbeing of a business. The problem is that a CEO with an expected tenure of 5 years and an investment community demanding improved results next year is likely to prioritize that time frame over a more indefinite future.

The evidence from our study is that senior executives in all our SSTs, while accepting the need to satisfy short-term performance demands, had very long time horizons. This was not so much in terms of concrete, formal plans, but rather in terms of underlying assumptions and values about what would ensure business success in the long term. Thus, Malpas recalls discussions at Tesco about "what are we about," resulting in the conclusion that putting customers rather than shareholders first would most benefit both shareholders and employees in the long term – a philosophy that has guided successive generations of managers ever since. At Cadbury, the historical legacy was consciously reformulated in the 1960s by Adrian Cadbury in what amounted to a "philosophy of Cadbury," his "Character of the Company," which was still being referred to 50 years later.

These pervasive underlying values were not the property of a particular CEO; they were handed on from one generation of managers to another who, while accepting of them, nonetheless had different ways of delivering against them (see the discussion below on management coalitions). Each senior executive led a generation different from the preceding one but linked by underlying values relating to the long-term wellbeing of the company.

Value diversity

Although there are benefits in enduring values, there is a danger in blanket uniformity. Managers typically extol the need for single-minded pursuit of a coherent strategy, with everyone "pulling in the same direction" and no-one "rocking the boat." Not surprisingly, perhaps, the assumption for most managers is that consensus and agreement are crucial. At heart, this betrays a mechanistic view of management and organizations: the ideal business is seen as akin to a well-oiled and efficient machine. After all, isn't the alternative chaos?

As the complexity theorists point out, however, our world has never been in steady state. There are dangers in total disequilibrium, of course – chaos reigns. The alternative to chaos is not, however, steady state but sufficient stability for a functioning system. Indeed, the lessons of strategic drift, reviewed in Chapter 1, make this point forcefully. Organizations that drift do so because they ossify around a set of assumptions, structures, and routines that make them impervious to change. Something similar applies to physical entities: ships or trees have to have flexibility as well as strength to withstand the seas and the wind. The lesson of complexity theory is that there needs to be sufficient order for stability but sufficient lack of ordering to allow for change and adaptability – what we referred to in Chapter 1 as "ambidexterity."

In the rest of this chapter, we suggest some specific ways this can be achieved. But it has to start with the mindset of the managers. If they privilege uniformity, consensus, and the need to follow an established strategy without deviation, the risk of strategic drift is high. The lessons of complexity theory need to be internalized. Systems, be they organizations or ecosystems, innovate not out of uniformity but diversity. This means that managers have to learn to tolerate such diversity[4] in terms of people's ideas and ways of doing things. This does not mean that they must encourage or embrace chaos. The need is for a balance of order and disorder, organization and "disorganization."[5] This state is sometimes known as the "edge of chaos"[6] or "adaptive tension." It may be less comfortable than singularity and uniformity, but the edge of chaos is where creativity and renewal dwells.

It is no easy matter for managers to set aside the machine metaphor of organizations. They have inherited an organizational world built on the precepts of Taylorism and the virtues of a "scientific" approach to management; they have been to business schools that teach them "rational" approaches to management; they live in a management world dominated by scientific innovation. Yet other metaphors can offer powerful insight.

Wrestling with the lessons of complexity encourages managers to think of their organizations not as machines but as organisms or ecosystems. A colleague of ours has developed the metaphor of a garden. Gardens are planned, but the wise gardener also allows diversity; gardens are cultivated, but there is an independence of growth; newness and surprises can be problematic but can also introduce novelty and inspiration. Gardens evolve with the aid of the gardener.

We are aware that these three "mindset" changes are not levers that managers can pull, but rather ways of seeing the organizational world. They are, however, fundamental to the more specific suggested priorities and proposals for management that we now move on to. None of these are short-term fixes – managers must see them in the context of the relevance of history and the long-term development of their organizations. They are investments for the future. Here we are truly concerned with the management of long-term strategy.

PRIORITIES FOR THE LONG GAME

It should be clear that we are not arguing against conventional good practice in terms of the need to take a careful and considered view of future strategy, to seek to understand the competitive environment and the way it is changing, and to manage operational efficiency. We take all these orthodoxies as necessary but not as sufficient for what we call the "long game." For that, there is a need for parallel priorities. From our study, we conclude that two of these are pre-eminent.

Accept and foster alternative management coalitions[7]

All of our SST firms had clear leadership; but they learned over time the dangers of a dominant autocrat. There is a governance issue here, of course: a key role of nonexecutive directors is to ensure that such autocracy is avoided. But there are also benefits in institutionalizing an informal division of labor that is quite likely between the three management coalitions we typically found as our SSTs developed. In each SST, we found a "dominant coalition," typically within the most senior executive levels, together perhaps with longer standing nonexecutives. These were the guardians of the traditions of the past, the associated company values, and a sense of continuity.

We also found an "alternative dominant coalition," a shadow leadership waiting in the wings, which might include members of the top team but more likely comprising the next generation of board members and other senior executives. This management alliance sees its role as anticipating market and industry changes, together with the adjustments to the business model that they might entail. They in turn take it on themselves to sponsor and nurture a third coalition: the champions of new industry thinking, whose focus is on experimentation. This may be a looser alliance, crossing management levels and boundaries, or comprising individuals and subcoalitions pursuing different ideas. Such a division of labor is effective because it allows for an appropriate pacing of short-, medium- and long-term transformation needs. Ignoring formal structures and hierarchies, as also the boundaries between top, middle, and front-line management, it works across generations of managers to ensure that each has the necessary latitude and confidence to pursue the complementary aims of continuity, anticipation, and experimentation that together both maintain a living connection with the organization's past and encourage it to adjust to the future.

In some cases, these alternative groupings may be in competition, not in the sense of a fight for power or of hierarchical dominance, but rather in terms of competing for ideas about the future of the business. Quite likely, power will shift to one of the coalitions over time, but this will be on the basis of that competition for ideas.

This suggests a rather different perspective on leadership from that so often found in conventional leadership texts. Our SSTs experienced periods of dominant, autocratic leadership. But as the businesses matured and developed the traditions we identified, this was no longer the case. Rather, leadership was to be found in each of the coalitions. In the dominant coalition, this was, typically, the CEO. Here the role was to take a directive lead when necessary (see below), but also to accept the presence and development value of the alternative coalitions. In turn, in those alternative coalitions there were "champions" of change, who might be arguing for and offering different future strategies to the dominant coalition. Leadership, then, should be seen as neither purely hierarchical nor unitary. There is rather a need to learn to live with and benefit from plural leaders.

In our experience – and on the basis of our research – there are few organizations in which the top management have the confidence in themselves, or in their management colleagues, to encourage such an approach to the long-term development of their businesses.

Accept and foster constructive tension and contestation

We argued above that managers need a mindset that not only tolerates diversity, differences and paradox, but also encourages and even celebrates them, uncomfortable as it may seem. This was the most consistent and enduring finding in our study. Contestation was clearly evident in our SSTs even when, in the 1980s and 90s, the other traditions underpinning the success of the SSTs was less in evidence: and it was largely absent from the non-SSTs. So, highly successful for many years, Sainsbury eventually stumbled because it came to rely on the vision and skills of one man: there was virtually no dissent and disagreement. This absence of contestation took a different form in Unilever. As Clive Butler, a former board executive director, explained:

> There were some good brains there, a lot of ideas were kicked around, but you have to say that they did not always end up in a shape [calling for] a dramatic plan of action. There tended to be a defusing of the "sharp bits". So if there was a lesser risk we would take it.[8]

Although it took different forms, disagreement and dissent were common at all levels of the organization in all three SST companies. As a result, they all had people constantly weighing up alternatives. When a "happy accident" occurred, there was always someone strong and confident enough to pick up the idea and run with it.

Managers have to learn to live with paradox and ambiguity rather than do away with it (as Tom Peters once aptly wrote, "To be excellent, you have to be consistent. When you're consistent, you're vulnerable to attack. Yes, it's a paradox. Now deal with it"[9]). We have already highlighted how different management coalitions can play a crucial role here. Researchers into the management of paradox suggest that managers need to learn the value of exploring and critically examining the tensions and anxieties that go with paradox and ambiguity, rather than seeking prematurely to close them down, as well as to experiment around such differences. Doing so calls for "paradoxical leadership" – leaders who are comfortable with paradox and can "guide social reflection"[10] around it.

Another way of thinking about the benefit of contestation is to consider the *role of crises*. Our research confirms that very few firms avoid major crises stemming from strategic drift. In the SSTs, on the other hand, the habit of contestation meant that, in effect, the crises were played out internally. The internal "mini-crises" jolted managers out of complacency.

Three further observations about contestation are important. The first is the need for organizations to *institutionalize dissent*. A propensity for constructive dissent is not something that can be readily imposed or fabricated. If managers are expected to focus on compliance and single-minded implementation of current strategy in their daily routine, it is unrealistic and unreasonable to hope they will overturn their consensual norms in the space of a management awayday, for example. Argument and dissent need to be "baked in" to the organization. The second is the avoidance of *premature closure*: allowing token dissent, but only to the extent that dissenters accept that their protest is for form only and in practice will go nowhere. The third is the need for dissent to be biased toward *the cognitive rather than the emotional* – the lesson we learn from Alan Amason.[11] Dissent needs to be on the basis of arguments around issues supported by evidence rather than biases supported by emotion.

BUILDING FOR THE LONG GAME

Managers cannot invent a history that gets them to the happy state of constructive contestation, but they can try to short cut that process by seeking to build an organization where alternative management groupings and a culture of challenge and contestation are given priority. There is no one answer to such a multifaceted question, but we put forward 10 proposals from our research and related literature.

1. Build on history

We have emphasized the importance of valuing history – so build on it. In the case of Tesco and Smith & Nephew, the contestation we saw was built on conflict, even emotional conflict, decades ago. Over time, consciously or otherwise, this evolved into the respectful contestation of later years. In the case of Cadbury, a tradition rooted in the company's Quaker past was reinforced by the culture clash ensuing from the merger with Schweppes. Building on history requires managers to reflect on the evolution of their own organization and the legacy they can draw on. Which of the traditions we have identified in the previous chapter are present, at least in embryonic form, and which are absent? In the light of the answer, which of the following steps could be or have already been taken?

2. Select and develop a different next generation

All good companies carry out succession- and talent-planning. But too often the emphasis is on developing only those who fit the current mold, that is, on ensuring continuity. If the need for traditions of transformation is taken seriously, succession-planning needs to take on board that each new generation must possess *different* capabilities. Furthermore, upcoming generations of leaders have to be groomed and given headroom to develop alternative coalitions and business models.

This is harder to do than to say. To spell it out, current leaders must nurture replacements who will question, modify, or even to some extent reject the former leaders' heritage. Ian MacLaurin and David Malpas recognized this quality in Terry Leahy. Malpas explained his approach to management talent-spotting thus: "I used to categorize youngsters in two: those who believed the corporation was a corporation and they worked for it; and those who believed it was their business."[12] He valued the former group, but it was to the latter that he looked for the next generation of leaders.

3. Accept and encourage constructive mobility

Associated with the previous step, the constructive mobility of management has to be accepted and encouraged. This does not necessarily mean importing outsiders: on the whole our SSTs conspicuously bred their own generations of managers and leaders. It does, however, mean rigorously ruling out a "Buggins's turn" approach to appointments and, conversely, adopting a deliberate policy of mobilizing and bringing on internal talent. In other words, as well as fostering alternative coalitions, welcoming challenge and encouraging divergent perspectives on the future of the business, managers must be prepared to look to future generations of leaders who, while honoring the past, have developed a distinctively different view of the future.

4. Ensure that decision-making allows for dissent

An exchange between David Malpas and Clive Butler[13] illustrates a crucial distinction. At Tesco, said Malpas:

> You have bright people who have ideas and want to mold the business their way, so an initiative gets to the boss at the next level who embraces it and it becomes his scheme: it gets to the next level and he embraces it and it becomes his scheme. How the hell do you stop it?

In Unilever, on the other hand, Clive Butler "recognized the opposite process which comprised several layers of very bright people all able to propose why a new idea would not work." A decision-making process allowing for dissent and challenge cannot, then, be developed without getting people in post who can live with, and indeed welcome, them.

5. Create enabling structures

Creative tension between opposing views can also be fostered by structural means. When Smith & Nephew bought an R&D facility, and Tesco placed responsibility for demographic profiling in the marketing rather than property department, they practically guaranteed that there would be new and different perspectives on an issue. Of itself, of course, such structural alteration alone does not guarantee that alternative views will be heard and taken seriously. That will also be a matter of the perceived relevance of the views and power of those advancing them. Again, then, the structural approach has to go hand in hand with other mechanisms for ensuring that dissenting views are not only uttered, but also heard and reflected on.

6. Get behind decisions when they are made

While constructive confrontation, contestation, and experimentation are vital, at some point they have to stop. Clear decisions are required from the top, and previously dissenting parties need to get behind the decision and make it work. There was not much evidence of such closing of the ranks in the early years of contestation at Smith & Nephew and Tesco, but it grew as managers came to understand and recognize the need. Cadbury, meanwhile, could call on a long tradition built on the Quaker heritage of mutual respect that encouraged managers both to tolerate dissent and cohere around decisions when taken.

There seems to be a lesson here about what we might call "corporate maturity": having the confidence to respect the value of dissent while accepting the need at some stage to override it for the wider good. Achieving this balance is not an argument for suppressing dissent through autocratic top management. Rather, it is an argument for top management to appreciate the benefit of diversity and contestation but at the same time be capable of bringing to bear authority and respect to intervene where necessary – and to possess the skill to be able to distinguish when one or the other is needed. The dangers apparent from our study are not so much top management failure to make decisions – where they fall down is rather managing the contestation necessary to inform the decisions, either stifling it, snuffing it out prematurely, or failing to build management teams sure enough of themselves to handle these ambiguous conditions.

7. Develop an overarching rationale

Although the executives with whom we discussed our findings were wary of the idea of "creating cultures," they were clear that managers could and should pay attention to building a clear understanding of "what we are about." In the 1990s there was an active debate among Tesco managers on this subject, out of which emerged a strong view that by focussing on customers, the company would best benefit shareholders and employees too. "You come back to the values of the company," said Sir Dominic Cadbury. "These do not happen by chance, and they can't drift either. There has to be some management there." He added that values are brought to life by being lived rather than through words. In other words, values had to be believable and evident in top managers' behavior.

The emphasis on clear rationale underpinned with strong values does of course also have to allow for the diversity of views and ideas that are likewise necessary. There was a very clear rationale and set of values at Sainsbury's; unfortunately, one of them was about the dangers of dissent. Here, then, may be a lesson from complexity theory. The need is for the sort of "order-generating" or "simple rules"[14] that, while providing sufficient clarity for the overall direction, also entail variety and differences of views and ideas. They are likely to be few in number but fundamental to the overall rationale and direction of the business.

8. Beware size and dominance

All three SSTs developed the characteristics that, we argue, led them to success as they struggled to assert themselves in intensely competitive markets against dominant leaders. At such times, the SST firms saw themselves as under threat. This was not the case for Unilever and Sainsbury's, which were themselves dominant. As Dominic Cadbury put it: "Unilever was such a different size that … it would be infinitely more difficult to galvanize [the company] to think of itself as an endangered species." Butler conceded, "Unilever would have to grow smaller to be like that."[15] There is an important question here. As once-threatened firms such as Tesco become dominant in their turn, is their management doomed to lose sight of the benefits their legacy has brought them? Although we would not argue that is inevitable, it is at the very least likely to make more difficult the challenge of preserving that legacy and the priorities we have suggested here.

Butler's comment raises the issue of complexity as well as size. By the 1960s Unilever had become a vast unwieldy giant. On the other hand, each of the SST companies that we examined, while substantial, was not highly complex. Tesco had always been a retail business. Cadbury, although having a number of different businesses, was much less diverse than Unilever. Smith & Nephew was likewise less diversified than SSL. We note the tendency of complex diversified organizations such as Unilever to focus on reducing their complexity and focus on core businesses. However, the rationale for this has essentially been a *portfolio* logic. Our argument suggests a different reason for reducing complexity. It is difficult to see how an organization as complex as Unilever, both in terms of numbers of business units and geographical spread, could adopt the traditions we advocate here. Our research underlines the importance of traditions of anticipation and contestation that, in the SST companies, were forged through the building of alternative coalitions of managers. In Unilever, anticipation, in so far as it existed, came about through its devolution to local businesses. It was not a tradition at the corporate level, and it is hard to imagine how, given such complexity, it could be. It may be that for our traditions of anticipation and contestability to work requires relatively focussed businesses.

9. What managers need to avoid

Managers need to avoid several dysfunctional activities: for example, central planning that is overdirective and controlling, such as attempts to determine operational values and behaviors from the center; autocratic leadership; a reliance on heroic "great man" leadership where strategy is vested in one individual; intolerance of dissent or closing down conflict in the name of consensus and harmony; and following management "cults" that every other business is following.

10. Recognize that you are working with time

The institutionalization of enduring traditions is not something that happens overnight. This brings us full circle. Our proposals are the opposite of short-term management. Building the capabilities to avoid strategic drift is of necessity long term. However, there is one important difference. The exceptional organizations we have studied here developed their skills and traditions over decades, without the benefit of the lessons we have been able to draw from them. Now that we have identified how traditions of transformation are developed and function, managers of today's companies can build on the experience of the pioneers to develop their own traditions more quickly and more surely – albeit in the context of "the long game." In both the short and the long term, the prize is great.

CONCLUSION

We showed in Chapter 1 that typical businesses, especially perhaps successful businesses, display some common characteristics. They develop distinctive capabilities that are the bases of their success, as well as managers who can exploit these. These managers become wedded to such capabilities as the bases of success: the business develops a "dominant logic" that drives the strategy. At the extreme, managers overlook or discount external forces and stimuli that might question the relevance of this dominant logic and its underlying capabilities. The consequence is that periods of success gradually, often imperceptibly, turn to periods of strategic drift and eventually to financial downturn. This is made the worse because managers persist in the application of the dominant logic. Eventually the resulting financial crisis triggers major change that may, but often does not, set the firm on a different path of success.

We have painted a picture of a different sort of business where the capabilities and dominant logic are much less rigid, where the patterns of belief and models of conduct we have called "traditions" allow for more continual incremental changes to have transformational effects over time. These are organizations in which managers are used to, and comfortable with, challenging and questioning each other and the premises upon which success is built; where the expectation is that managers at different levels will take the initiative to experiment and senior management will value that; where threats and misfortunes may not always be anticipated, but where the approach to managing the business can turn them into "happy accidents" upon which new opportunities are created. Such companies emphasize the proactive renewal of strategy across long periods of time such that managers can steer away from organizational crises. These are businesses that are built to cultivate good fortune, as epitomized in Pasteur's dictum that "fortune favors the prepared mind."

Notes

Chapter 1

1 Johnson, G., *Strategic Change and the Management Process*, Oxford: Blackwells, 1987; "Re-thinking incrementalism," *Strategic Management Journal*, 9, 75–91, 1988; "Managing strategic change – strategy, culture and action," *Long Range Planning*, 25(1), 28–36, 1992.

2 Leonard–Barton, D., "Core capabilities and core rigidities: a paradox in managing new product development," *Strategic Management Journal*, 13, 111–25, 1992.

3 Arthur, W.B., "Competing technologies, increasing returns and lock in by historical events," *Economic Journal*, 99, 116–31, 1989.

4 Prahalad, C.K. and Bettis, R., "The dominant logic: a new link between diversity and performance," *Strategic Management Journal*, 6(1), 485–501, 1986; Bettis, R. and Prahalad, C.K., "The dominant logic: retrospective and extension," *Strategic Management Journal*, 16(1), 5–15, 1995.

5 In *The Icarus Paradox* (Miller, D., New York: Harper-Collins, 1990), Danny Miller makes a convincing case that organizations' success leads to a number of potentially pathological tendencies, not least of which are tendencies to inflate the durability of bases of success and to build future strategies relatively uncritically.

6 For a review of these points, see the introduction to Dutton, J., Walton, E. and Abrahamson, E., "Important dimensions of strategic issues: separating the wheat from the chaff," *Journal of Management Studies*, 26(4), 380–95, 1989.

7 See Tversky, A. and Kahnemann, D., "Judgements under uncertainty: heuristics and biases," *Science*, 185, 1124–31, 1975.

8 Finkelstein, S., "Why smart executives fail: four case histories of how people learn the wrong lessons from history," *Business History*, 48(2), 153–70, 2006.

9 See Jarzabkowski, P., Giulietti, M. and Oliveira, B., *Building a Strategy Toolkit: Lessons from Business*, AIM Executive Briefing, 2009.

10 This quote by André Malroux and the story of the BMW museum were provided by Mary Rose.

11 Holbrook, D., Cohen, W., Hounshell, D. and Klepper, S., "The nature, sources and consequences of firm differences in the early history of the semiconductor industry," *Strategic Management Journal*, 21(10–11), 1017–42, 2000.

12 Private correspondence with business historian Mary Rose, who suggests that "it links to Schumpeter and his notion of boundary crossing which may be between sectors, between technologies or informing the development and application of old technology with new knowledge."

13 Klepper, S. and Simons, K.L., "Dominance by birthright: entry of prior radio producers and competitive ramifications in the US television receiver industry," *Strategic Management Journal*, 21(10–11), 987–1016, 2000.

14 For a summary paper on dynamic capabilities,see Wang, C.L. and Ahmed, P.K., "Dynamic capabilities: a review and research agenda," *International Journal of Management Reviews*, 9(1), 31–52, 2007.

15 See D'Aveni, R., *Hypercompetition: Managing the Dynamics of Strategic Manoeuvring*, New York: Free Press, 1995.

16 See, for example, Coopey, J., "The learning organization, power, politics and ideology," *Management Learning*, 26(2), 193–213, 1995.

17 The concept of the organization as a set of social networks is discussed by, for example, Granovetter, M.S., "The strength of weak ties," *American Journal of Sociology*, 78(6), 1360–80, 1973, and Carroll, G.R. and Teo, A.C., "On the social networks of managers," *Academy of Management Journal*, 39(2), 421–40, 1996.

18 J.B. Quinn's research involved the examination of strategic change in companies and was published in *Strategies for Change*, Irwin, 1980. See also Quinn, J.B., "Strategic change: logical incrementalism," in Mintzberg, H., Quinn, J.B. and Ghoshal, S. (eds), *The Strategy Process* (European edition), Prentice Hall, 1995.

19 See Hamel, G. and Valikangas, L., "The quest for resilience," *Harvard Business Review*, September, 52–63, 2003.

20 For fuller explanations of the distinction between charismatic and instrumental and transactional leadership, see Kets de Vries, M.F.R., "The leadership mystique," *Academy of Management Executive*, 8(3), 73–89, 1994.

21 For this evidence, see Waldman, D.A., Ramirez, G.G., House, R.J. and Puranam, P., "Does leadership matter? CEO leadership attributes and profitability under conditions of perceived environmental uncertainty," *Academy of Management Journal*, 44(1), 134–43, 2001.

22 For example, see Kotter, J.P., *A Force for Change: How Leadership Differs from Management*, New York: Free Press, 1990, or Tedlow, R.S., *Giants of Enterprise: Seven Business Innovators and their Empires*, New York: Harper Business, 2001.

23 See Collins, J. and Porras, J., *Built to Last: Successful Habits of Visionary Companies*, New York: Harper Business, 2002.

24 The discussion on different approaches of strategic leaders and evidence for the effectiveness of the adoption of different approaches can be found in Goleman, D., "Leadership that gets results," *Harvard Business Review*, 78(2), 78–90, 2000, and Farkas, C.M. and Wetlaufer, S., "The ways chief executive officers lead," *Harvard Business Review*, 74(3), 110–12, 1996.

25 See Collins, J. and Porras, J., Note 22.

26 For a summary of such research, see Kellermanns, F.W., Walter, J., Lechner, C. and Floyd, S.W., "The lack of consensus about strategic consensus: advancing theory and research," *Journal of Management*, 31(5), 719–37, 2005.

27 Amason, A., "Distinguishing the effects of functional and dysfunctional conflict on strategic decision making: resolving a paradox for top management teams," *Academy of Management Journal*, 39(1), 123–48, 1996.

28 Personal correspondence with Steve Floyd.

29 Burgelman, R. and Grove, A., "Strategic dissonance," *California Management Review*, 38(2), 8–28, 1996.

30 Beckman, C.M., "The influence of founding team company affiliations on firm behavior," *Academy of Management Journal*, 49(4), 741–58, 2006.

31 de Geus, A., *The Living Company*, Cambridge, MA: Harvard Business School Press, 2002.

32 Tushman, M.L., and O'Reilly, C.A., "Ambidextrous organizations: managing evolutionary and revolutionary change," *California Management Review*, 38(4), 8–30, 1996.

33 Duncan, R., "The ambidextrous organization: designing dual structures for innovation," in Killman, R.H., Pondy, L.R., and Sleven, D. (eds), *The Management of Organization*, 1, pp. 167–88, New York: North Holland, 1976.

34 Brown, S.L. and Eisenhardt, K.M., "The art of continuous change: linking complexity theory and time-paced evolution in relentlessly shifting organizations," *Administrative Science Quarterly*, 42(1), 1–34, 1997.

35 See Brown and Eisenhardt, Note 34.

36 See McKelvey, B., "Simple rules for improving corporate IQ: basic lessons from complexity science," in Andriani, P. and Passiante, G. (eds), *Complexity, Theory and the Management of Networks*, Imperial College Press, 2004.

37 See Brown and Eisenhardt, Note 34.

38 See McKelvey, Note 36.

39 See Eisenhardt, K.M. and Sull, D.N., "Strategy as simple rules," *Harvard Business Review*, January, 106–16, 2001.

40 For a summary of our study and findings, see Johnson, G., Yip, G. and Hensmans, M., "Achieving successful strategic transformation," *MIT Sloan Management Review*, 53(3), 25–32, 2012.

Chapter 2

1 See, for example, Rappaport, A., *Creating Shareholder Value: The New Standard for Business Performance*, New York: Free Press, 1986, and Danielson, M.G. and Press, E., "Accounting returns revisited: evidence of their usefulness in estimating economic returns," *Review of Accounting Studies*, 8, 493–530, 2003.

2 For a review of the extensive literature on the differences between the Anglo-Saxon, Continental and Japanese business systems, see Dore, R., *Stock Market Capitalism: Welfare Capitalism. Japan and Germany versus Anglo-Saxons*, New York: Oxford University Press, 2000, and Aoki, M., *Towards a Comparative Institutional Analysis*, Cambridge, MA: MIT Press, 2001.

3 See Bond, S.R. and Cummins, J.G., "The stock market and investment in the new economy: some tangible facts and intangible fictions," *Brookings Papers on Economic Activity*, 1, 61–108, 2000, and Day, G., Fein, A.J. and Ruppersberger, G., "Shakeouts in digital markets: lessons from B2B exchanges," *California Management Review*, 45(2), 131–50, 2003.

4 This statistical analysis using the frontier technique was conducted by Professor Timothy Devinney of the Australian Graduate School of Management with the help of Pierre Richard, PhD candidate at the AGSM. For the conceptual basis of our approach to using frontier analysis to measure financial performance, see Richard, P.J., Devinney, T.M., Yip, G.S. and Johnson, G., "Measuring organizational performance as a dependent variable: towards methodological best practice, *Journal of Management*, 35(3), 718–804, 2009. For details of how we identified the 28 superior performing companies and the eight SSTs, see Devinney, T.M., Yip, G.S. and Johnson, G., "Using frontier analysis to evaluate company performance," *British Journal of Management*, 21(4), 921–38, 2010. For details on all the industries analyzed and more on the British companies researched, see Devinney, T.M., Yip, G.S. and Johnson, G., "Measuring long term superior performance: the UK's long-term superior performers 1984–2003," *Long Range Planning*, 43(3), 390–413, 2009.

5 The point being made here is that, without evidence that one firm outperforms another firm on all of the performance dimensions considered, or on a linear combination of those measures, we state that it defines the frontier.

6 Data for the average of 2001–2003. See Yip, G.S., Rugman, A.M. and Kudina, A., "International success of British companies," *Long Range Planning*, 39(3), 241–64, 2006.

7 The 38 companies included plus 43 excluded = 81, which is slightly below the total number of 89 industries in the Osiris database because of some aggregations we made.

8 Porter, M.E. *Competitive Strategy: Techniques for Analyzing Industries and Competitors*, New York: Free Press, 1980.

9 Barney, J.B., "Firm resources and sustained competitive advantages," *Journal of Management*, 17, 99–120, 1991.

10 Morgan Stanley, *The Competitive Edge*, New York: Morgan Stanley, 1998.

11 Peters and Waterman used 20 years (Peters, T. and Waterman, R., *In Search of Excellence*, New York: Collins, 1982); Kotter and Heskett used 11 years (Kotter, J.P. and Heskett, J.L., *Corporate Culture and Performance*, New York: Free Press, 1982); Collins and Porras used up to 15 years (Collins, J.C. and Porras, J.I., *Built to Last: Successful Habits of Visionary Companies*, New York: Harper Business, 1994); Foster and Kaplan used 15 years (Foster, R. and Kaplan, S., *Creative Destruction: Why Companies that Are Built To Last Underperform the Market – and How To Transform Them*, New York: Currency/Doubleday, 2001); Joyce, Nohria and Roberson used 10 years (Joyce, W., Nohria, N. and Roberson, B., *What Really Works: The 4 + 2 Formula for Sustained Business Success*, New York: Harper Business, 2003); and Stadler used 50 years (Christian Stadler, *Enduring Success – What We Can Learn from the History of Outstanding Corporations*, Stanford University Press, 2011).

See also a review of these studies in Kirby, J., "Toward a theory of high performance," *Harvard Business Review*, July–August, 30–9, 2005.

12 Following the approach of Collins, J., *Good to Great*, New York: Harper Business, 2001.

13 Lawrence, B.S., "Historical perspective: using the past to study the present," *Academy of Management Review*, 9, 307–12, 1984.

14 Putnam, L.L., Phillips, N., and Chapman, P., "Metaphors of communication and organization," in S. Clegg, C. Hardy, and W. Nord (eds), *Handbook of Organization Studies*, London: Sage, 1996.

15 Floyd, S.W. and Lane, P.J., "Strategizing throughout the organization: managing role conflict in strategic renewal," *Academy of Management Review*, 25(1), 154–77, 2000.

16 Fincham, R., "Perspectives on authority: processual, institutional and 'internal' forms of organizational authority," *Journal of Management Studies*, 29, 741–59, 1992; Finkelstein, S. and Hambrick, D., *Strategic Leadership: Top Executives and their Effects on Organizations*, Minneapolis, MN: West, 1996; Pearce, J.A., "A structural analysis of dominant coalitions in small banks," *Journal of Management*, 21, 1075–95, 1995; Pfeffer, J., *Authority in Organizations*, Boston, MA: Pitman, 1981; and Thompson, J.D., *Organizations in Action*, New York: McGraw-Hill, 1967.

17 Yin, R.K., *Case Study Research: Design and Methods*, Applied Social Research Methods Vol. 2, Thousand Oaks, CA: Sage Publications, 1994.

18 Ragin, C., "'Casing' and the process of social inquiry," in Ragin, C. and Becker, H. (eds), *What Is a Case? Exploring the Foundations of Social Inquiry*, pp. 217–26, Cambridge: Cambridge University Press, 2000; Ragin, C., *The Comparative Method*, Berkeley: University of California Press, 1987.

19 Hensmans, M., "Magic bullet discourse and the resolution of coordination and cooperation problems," Advanced Institute of Management Working Paper Series: June 2006, AIM, 2006.

20 As noted by Pettigrew, A.M., *The Awakening Giant. Continuity and Change in Imperial Chemical Industries*, Oxford: Basil Blackwell, 1985.

21 Doz, Y. and Kosonen, M., *Fast Strategy: How Strategic Agility Will Help You Stay Ahead of the Game*. Philadelphia, PA: Wharton School Publishing, 2008.

22 Denzin, N.K. and Lincoln, Y.S., "Introduction: The discipline and practice of qualitative research," in N.K. Denzin and Y.S. Lincoln (eds), *Handbook of Qualitative Research*, pp. 1–28, Thousand Oaks, CA: Sage, 2000; Diesing, P., *Patterns of Discovery in the Social Sciences*, Chicago: Aldine-Atherton, 1971.

23 Hall, D.J. and Saias, M., "Strategy follows structure!," *Strategic Management Journal*, 1, 149–63, 1980.

24 For a fuller explanation of this methodology, contact J. Kroezen at jkroezen@rsm.nl.

25 Peters and Waterman (1982; see Note 11).

26 Charnes, A., Cooper, W.W. and Rhodes, E. , "Measuring the efficiency of decision making units," *European Journal of Operations Research*, 2, 429–44, 1978.

27 Bauer, P., "Recent developments in the econometric estimation of frontiers," *Journal of Econometrics*, 46, 39–56, 1991.

28 Day, D.L., Lewin, A.Y. and Li, H., "Strategic leaders or strategic groups: a longitudinal data envelopment analysis of the U.S. brewing industry," *European Journal of Operations Research*, 80, 619–38, 1995; and Devinney, T.M., Midgley, D.F. and Venaik, S., "The organizational imperative and the optimal performance of the global firm: formalizing and extending the integration–responsiveness framework," *Organization Science*, 11, 674–95, 2000.

29 Teece, D.J., Pisano, G. and Shuen, A., "Dynamic capabilities and strategic management," *Strategic Management Journal*, 18, 509–33, 1997.

Chapter 3

1 Without family roots in Britain, founder Jacob Schweppe as early as 1799 sold 75 percent of his interest in the company to three men from the island of Jersey. In 1834 William Evil and John Kemp-Welch, who decided to keep the Schweppes name, bought the company. Although the descendants of especially Kemp-Welch would remain associated with the company until 1950, the company would be run in an increasingly detached fashion from that point onwards. This evolution culminated in the Kemp-Welch family relinquishing the chairmanship as early as 1919 (although two members remained on the board until the early 1940s).

2 The Cadbury family held the vast majority of shares of Cadbury Brothers Ltd up to the early 1960s, and as much as 37.8 percent shares in 1968 (*Private Archives Sir Adrian Cadbury*, "Cadbury Group Limited: Analysis of Shareholdings," October 1968).

3 Williams, I.A., *The Firm of Cadbury 1831–1931*, London: Constable, 1931; Cadbury Brothers Ltd., *Industrial Record 1919–1939*, Bournville: Cadbury Brothers, 1947; Rowlinson, M. and Hassard, J., "The invention of corporate culture: a history of the histories of Cadbury," *Human Relations*, 46(3), 299–326, 1993.

4 Interview with Sir Adrian Cadbury, June 23, 2006.

5 The quote continues: "one may think like an Anarchist so long as one does one's job like a decent citizen;" from Pearce, W.T., *Fry's works magazine: Bi-centenary no. (1728–1928)*, p. 29, Bristol: Partridge & Love, 1928.

6 "Since we opened our first sore, at the height of the Depression in 1929, we have believed in and vigorously operated a cut-price policy. It is based on the simple concept that there is a greater return for capital invested in quick turnover, large-volume sales at a small margin of profit per unit, than in slow-moving, small-volume sales at a large margin of profit per unit" (Cohen paraphrased in Corina, M., *Pile it High, Sell it Cheap: The Authorised Biography of Sir John Cohen, Founder of Tesco*, p. 192, London: Weidenfeld & Nicolson, 1971).

7 Corina, M., *Pile it High, Sell it Cheap: The Authorised Biography of Sir John Cohen, Founder of Tesco*, p. 192, London: Weidenfeld & Nicolson, 1971; Powell, D., *Counterrevolution. The Tesco Story*, London: Grafton, 1991; Seth, A. and Randall, G., *The Grocers: The Rise and Rise of the Supermarket Chains*, London: Kogan Page, 1999.

8 Interview with Victor Benjamin, June 7, 2006.

9 Under H.N. Smith, the company acquired products from Germany that they were to market with great ingenuity and success: Elastoplast in 1929, Cellona/Gypsona, Nivea, and finally Lil-Lets in 1954. H.N. Smith was a fluent German speaker with close friends and associates in Germany (Foreman-Peck, J., *Smith and Nephew in the Health Care Industry*, Aldershot: Edward Elgar, 1995, p. 72).

10 Interview with Sir Adrian Cadbury, 22 June, 2006.

11 *Private Archives Sir Adrian Cadbury*, "Bournville Organisation," Memo to the Board, May 26, 1960.

12 *Private Archives Sir Adrian Cadbury*, "Bournville Organisation," Memo to the Board, February 14, 1961.

13 The British company L. Rose & Co. was founded in 1865 and became famous for its lime juice, often known simply as "Rose's," not to be confused with Cadbury Roses chocolates launched in 1938. Schweppes acquired Rose's in 1957.

14 Interview with James Forbes, ex-financial director of Schweppes and Cadbury Schweppes, November 7, 2006.

15 Interview with James Forbes, November 7, 2006.

16 Schweppes acquired Typhoo Tea to further diversify Schweppes' product line and strengthen its ties to grocery retailers. As testified by Sir Adrian Cadbury (September 28, 2006), however, although Typhoo Tea at first sight looked like a safe bet, its profitability was based on a soon to be expired business model.

17 Interview with James Forbes, November 7, 2006; Interview with Adrian Cadbury quoted in Smith, C., Child, J. and Rowlinson, M., *Reshaping Work: The Cadbury Experience*, Cambridge Studies in Management No. 16, p. 76, Cambridge: Cambridge University Press.

18 Quoted in Vice, A. , *The Strategy of Takeovers: A Casebook of International Comparisons*, London: McGraw-Hill, 1977.

19 See also the excellent study by Smith et al. (1990; see Note 17) on changes in Cadbury's factory management, as well as the emergence of diversification plans.

20 Interview with Sir Adrian Cadbury, June 23, 2006.

21 Interview with Sir Adrian Cadbury, June 23, 2006.

22 *Private Archives Sir Adrian Cadbury*, Memo from G.A.H. Cadbury to the Board, "Acquisition Policy," October 1968.

23 Interview with Sir Adrian Cadbury, June 23, 2006.

24 In 1950 independents held a 56.9 percent share of total grocery sales in the UK, cooperatives 23.2 percent, and multiples 20 percent. In 1966 these figures were respectively 47 percent, 16.7 percent, and 36.3 percent. By 1971 multiples had a greater market share than independents, 44.3 percent for the former compared with 42.5 percent for the latter (data from the UK Census of Distribution).

25 By the late 1950s one British family in three owned a car, and by the early 1960s almost eight million women were in either full- or part-time employment.

26 For instance, Thomas Freake, assistant managing director of Tesco Stores, was the first to suggest to Cohen to finally drop the technique of auctioning goods from the shop fronts. He argued that customers wanted a more respectable store format – such as the self-service format. In contrast with Freake, Carpenter did not seem to threaten Cohen's hegemony in any meaningful way.

27 Corina (1971, p. 125; see Note 7).

28 Quotes from Powell (1991, pp. 78–9; see Note 7). Another quote from Lauren Don. When Edgar Collar joined the board there was nobody who could read a balance sheet properly, and he was the one who first introduced branch accounts to identify such things as the profitability of each store, stock results and leakage. And it wasn't simply a matter of just reading the books, he knew what retailing was about as well."

29 Hyman Kreitman had married Cohen's eldest daughter, Irene.

30 Kreitman also was one of the first to pressure Cohen to replace his old market shutters with proper shop windows.

31 Tesco had become accustomed to the higher retail prices of the war period, and its reputation as a discounter was suffering as a result.

32 Powell (1991, p. 82; see Note 7).

33 Corina (1971, see Note 7); Powell (1991, p. 86; see Note 7).

34 Porter had married Shirley Cohen, Cohen's younger daughter, in 1949. For several years he resisted his father-in-law's invitations to join Tesco. In 1959, however, he agreed to join the board as a part-time consultant on the company's non-grocery lines.

35 A "boffin" is British slang that is officially used to denominate a scientist operating in a military environment, but is colloquially more often used to denote a "nerd" or "geek," that is, a person with few social and strategic skills, but with a keen interest in somewhat obscure, technical skills.

36 British retail pharmacists in the 18th and 19th centuries integrated backwards to production, often of proprietary foods and medicines, to supply the products required by hospitals and healthcare professionals. Companies such as Allen & Hanbury of London, Southalls of Birmingham, Boots of Nottingham, and T.J. Smith emphasized and derived their competitive edge from marketing. When scientific technology became indispensable – in the first half of the 20th century – they imported the expertise in the form of new products. It was only after 1945 that retail pharmacists started developing indigenous technology (Foreman-Peck, 1995, pp. 50–1 [see Note 9]; Coleman, K., *IG Farben and ICI, 1925–53: Strategies for Growth and Survival*, Basingstoke: Palgrave Macmillan, 2006; Quirke, V., *Collaboration in the Pharmaceutical Industry: Changing Relationships in Britain and France, 1935–1965*, London: Routledge, 2003; Reader, W.J., *Imperial Chemical Industries: A History*, Vol. 2, *The First Quarter-Century, 1926–1952*, London: Oxford University Press, 1975; Robson, M.T., The pharmaceutical industry in Britain and France, 1919–1939, Unpublished thesis, University of London, 1993).

37 For more information on research budgets and ICI's problems, see Reader (1975; see Note 36).

38 SANACO Board Minutes, Tuesday, December 5, 1961, "8. Textile Development," p. 2212.

39 Products consolidated with the 1958 acquisition of Berton and Southalls.

40 The internationalization of industries and the entry of new competitors continued unabated, and the UK appeared worse prepared for the 1970s' world recession than most of its direct competitors.

41 Interview with Sir Dominic Cadbury, April 4, 2006.

42 Interview with Sir Dominic Cadbury, April 4, 2006.

43 Interview with Sir Dominic Cadbury, April 4, 2006

44 Interview with Sir Adrian Cadbury, September 28, 2006.

45 Interview with Sir Dominic Cadbury, April 4, 2006

46 *Private Archives Sir Adrian Cadbury*, Memorandum "Organisation," From Group Chief Executive (Basil Collins) to Chairman (Adrian Cadbury), April 6, 1982.

47 Interview with Victor Benjamin, June 7, 2006.

48 Powell (1991; see Note 7); Corina (1971; see Note 7).

49 Powell (1991, p. 77; see Note 7).

50 As with many retailing innovations, out-of-town shopping emerged in the US, with the Country Club Plaza in Kansas opening in 1932. Although initially slow in taking off, out-of-town shopping became hugely popular in the US by the end of the 1960s. The French company Carrefour was the first to pioneer the concept of hypermarketing, the first out-of-town hypermarket opening near Paris in 1963.

51 As early as 1969 Carrefour, in association with Wheatsheaf Distribution and Trading, had received planning permission for the development of a 100,000 square foot store with parking space for 1,000 cars at Caerphilly.

52 Interview with Jim Pennell, quoted in Powell (1991, p. 123; see Note 7).

53 Interview with David Malpas, June 15, 2006.

54 For instance, on the instigation of both Kreitman and Porter, Cohen agreed to the opening in March 1966 of a 16,000-square-foot store in Brixton. Half of the space in this superstore was devoted to groceries, the other half to a Home 'n' Wear and furnishing department – selling many of Tesco's first real own-label products such as Delamare. At that point, the average selling area of Tesco stores was 4,000 square feet. The average size doubled every 5 years after that, driven by the ongoing investment in non-food lines (Powell, 1991, p. 120; see Note 7).

55 By 1973, Porter's Home 'n' Wear division had 62 separate stores as well as large selling areas in many of the group's supermarkets, bringing in about £75 million in annual profits.

56 The food sector operates on high volumes and low margins, whereas non-food shopping tends to rely on high margins and low volumes.

57 Interview with Victor Benjamin, June 7, 2006.

58 For example, Powell (1991, pp. 130–1; see Note 7).

59 Powell (1991, p. 131; see Note 7).

60 Tesco Wholesale was formed in 1965 to act as the company's main purchasing agent, under the executive control of Daisy Hyams as managing director.

61 Interview with David Malpas, June 15, 2006; Powell (1991, p. 40; see Note 7).

62 Cf. Corina (1971, p. 162; see Note 7).

63 Cf. Corina (1971, p. 161; see Note 7).

64 The name Asda came from Associated Dairies, founded by a group of dairy farmers in Yorkshire in the 1920s. Asda soon expanded in food processing and in 1949 went public. In 1965 it formed a new subsidiary, Asda Stores.

65 Cf. Powell (1991; see Note 7).

66 Interview with Victor Benjamin, June 7, 2006.

67 By the early 1970s Tesco was operating out of 830 stores.

68 Interview with Lord MacLaurin, quoted in Powell (1991, p. 154; see Note 7).

69 Interview with Victor Benjamin, June 7, 2006.

70 Interview with John Robinson, May 10, 2006.

71 Interview with Alan Suggett, September 1, 2006.

72 SANACO (Smith & Nephew Associated Companies) Board Minutes, March 14, 1961, "(iii) Five Year Budgets. After a lengthy discussion the Board accepted the recommendation of S.B.C. that all Divisions prepare five year Development plans," p. 2112.

73 Interview with Alan Fryer, July 4, 2006.

74 SANACO Board Minutes, Tuesday, May 8, 1962, "John J. Tatham Ltd.," pp. 2274–5.

75 Interview with John Robinson, May 10, 2006.

76 Following OpSite, in the 1970s there followed a series of other significant patents: the 1973 Haemocol patent – Smith & Nephew's first intentionally multidisciplinary project, the 1974 contact lens polymer patent, which in effect meant that acrylic hydrogen polymer chemistry was now well established in Smith & Nephew, and the 1976 patent for Chryston, a polyacrylate chemistry for splints. In 1973 the burns dressing Flamazine, manufactured with imported US-technology, was also launched.

77 Interview with Alan Suggett, September 1, 2006.

78 Interview with Alan Fryer, July 4, 2006.

79 Interview with Alan Fryer, July 4, 2006.

80 The new executive met at Bradshaw's discretion. The executive deputy chairman and the chief executive were empowered to authorize capital expenditure up to £0.25 million and acquisitions in cognate product areas of £100,000. The chief executive, with the executive deputy chairman, submitted annual budgets to the SANACO board and reported quarterly on the group's operations (Foreman-Peck, 1995, pp. 220–1; see Note 9).

81 Interview with Alan Fryer, July 4, 2006.

82 The trend had begun with the purchase of Clairol by the US pharma company Bristol-Myers. Spurred on by a belief that the research capabilities of pharmaceutical companies would lead to new product innovations in cosmetics, a succession of prominent cosmetics firms were acquired. This belief soon turned out to be ill-founded, and many once prominent brands withered under their new ownership. A key problem, so it appeared, was that product innovation needed to be embedded in creative marketing and branding strategies, and this was hard to achieve given the gap in the culture, marketing, and branding capabilities required to succeed in both pharmaceuticals and cosmetics (Jones, G. *Renewing Unilever. Transformation and Tradition*. Oxford: Oxford University Press, 2005; see p. 232).

Chapter 4

1 Interview with Victor Benjamin, June 7, 2006.

2 Malpas became manager of retailing operations in 1975, and was appointed a board member in 1979. Jack Cohen died in 1979.

3 Darnell was appointed to the Tesco board in 1975 with responsibility for the Home 'n' Wear business. He became distribution director in 1982.

4 Gildersleeve became managing director of retail operations in 1982, and was appointed to the Tesco PLC board in 1984 as personnel and marketing director, before becoming commercial and trading director in 1992.

5 Interview with Terry Leahy, June 12, 2006.

6 Interview with David Malpas, June 15, 2006.

7 Powell, D., *Counterrevolution. The Tesco Story*, p. 155, London: Grafton, 1991.

8 Interview with Victor Benjamin, June 7, 2006; interview with Mike Darnell in Powell (1991, p. 127; see Note 7).

9 Interview with David Malpas, June 15, 2006.

10 Interview with Victor Benjamin, June 7, 2006.

11 Interview with Terry Leahy, June 12, 2006.

12 Akehurst, G., "Checkout: the analysis of oligopolistic behaviour in the UK grocery retail market," *Service Industries Journal*, 4(2), 189–242, 1984.

13 Interview with Terry Leahy, June 12, 2006.

14 Interviews with Terry Leahy and David Malpas on June 12 and 15, 2006, respectively.

15 At the launch of Checkout in 1977, a minimum of 3 and a maximum of 6 years had to be allowed between obtaining an outline planning consent and opening a new store. With the move to out-of-town retailing at the end of the 1970s, this had become a much shorter period (Powell, 1991; see Note 7).

16 Interview with David Malpas, June 15, 2006.

17 Interview with David Malpas, June 15, 2006.

18 "Peter Williams talks to David Reid," *Accountancy Age*, June 19, 1986.

19 In 1966 Tesco's store portfolio consisted of 81 percent out-of-town stores with a sales area in square feet over under 5,000, and only 6 percent in the range 10,001–25,000. In 1987 the portfolio was 12 percent under 5,000, 22 percent 5,001–10,000, and 34 percent over 25,000 square feet. Between 1977 and 1983 Tesco closed 371 supermarkets averaging 3,700 square feet, and opened 97 new stores averaging 30,000 square feet (Smith, D.L.G. and Sparks, L., "The transformation of physical distribution in retailing: the example of Tesco plc," *International Review of Retail, Distribution and Consumer Research*, 3(1), 35–64, 1993; see pp. 48–9). Given the new focus on hypermarkets, the number of Tesco outlets decreased from 771 to 369 in the period 1974 to 1984, but the floor space actually increased from 4,626,000 to 6,826,500 square feet. Most importantly, Tesco's average sales area tripled from 6,000 square feet to 18,500 square feet in the same period. This was a comparatively high figure, given that the average sales area of multiples' shops in 1984 was no higher than 8,988 square feet (Bamfield, J., "Rationalization and the problems of re-positioning: UK co-operatives caught in the middle," in Johnson, G. (ed.), pp. 153–76, *Business Strategy and Retailing*, Chichester: John Wiley & Sons; see Table 3, p. 164). The market share of multiples going into hypermarkets increased from 38 percent in 1972 to 46 percent in 1977, and 55 percent in 1982. Conversely, the market share of

independents over the same period decreased from 46 percent to 38 percent to 31 percent (Segal-Horn, S., "The retail environment in the UK," in Johnson, G. (ed.), *Business Strategy and Retailing*, pp. 13–34, Chichester: John Wiley & Sons, 1987; see Table 7, p. 20).

20 Tesco accepted credit cards for food purchases much earlier than Sainsbury's, based on its early experiments with credit purchases in Home 'n' Wear: "'We have accepted credit in our Home & Wear stores for several years,' Mr David Reid, Tesco finance director, said, 'but research has shown that people are increasingly willing to use credit cards for ordinary food purchases as well'" (*The Times*, November 30, 1985).

21 "Tesco has launched an own-label range of electrical accessories to be retailed through its Home 'n' Wear departments," *Marketing Week*, June 24, 1983.

22 Tesco handled non-food products via a centralized distribution system for a number of years before doing the same for fresh foods.

23 Before the beginning of the 1980s, Tesco's distribution system had been inefficient for the store operations and unable to cope flexibly with increased volumes and quality. In addition, the system allowed almost no control or standardization of the retail outlets and of store managers (Kirkwood, D.A., "The supermarket challenge," *Focus on PDM*, 3(4), 8–12, 1984a; Kirkwood, D.A., "How Tesco manage the distribution function," *Retail and Distribution Management*, 12(5), 61–5, 1984b; Sparks, L., "The changing structure of distribution in retail companies," *Transactions of the Institute of British Geographers*, 11(2), 147–54, 1986.

24 For example, in 1983/84 Tesco moved from wooden pallets to roll cages, and from a basic to a modern computer warehouse system that provided a computer-controlled allocation of warehouse space and a computer-calculated real-time bonus for productivity. Since 1984 the percentage of sales via central warehouses increased steadily from under 30 percent to over 93 percent by the beginning of the 1990s. In 1991 Tesco distribution handled more than 450 million cases at an average rate of 60,000 cases per hour, through its network of 18 distribution centers (Smith and Sparks, 1993, pp. 52–3; see Note 19).

25 Before 1987 the greatly expanded store footage in Tesco had already led to a series of changes in systems – first with article numbering, then with electronic points of sale; and in terms of service, first with the emphasis on in-house training, and then with the rapid expansion of the graduate recruitment scheme; and also in terms of stock controls (Powell, 1991, pp. 196–9; see Note 7). The average store footage had also increased because of the divestment of smaller store operations such as the Victor Value chain in 1986. The origins of this centralization decision can be dated back to 1980, the year the wholesale–retail divide in the company disappeared. Before this, Tesco's system had by and large been inefficient for store operations and unable to cope flexibly with increased volumes and quality. In addition, the system allowed almost no control or standardization of the retail outlets and of store managers (Kirkwood, 1984a, 1984b; Sparks, 1986; see Note 23). Many developments occurred during the 1980s.

26 Interview with Victor Benjamin, June 7, 2006.

27 Cox, R., "The revolution in grocery retailing – multiple strategies," In West, A. (ed.), *Handbook of Retailing*, pp. 31–43, Aldershot: Gower, 1988.

28 Wrigley, N. and Lowe, M., *Reading Retail: A Geographical Perspective on Retailing and Consumption Spaces*, p. 61, London: Arnold, 2002.

29 Wrigley, N., "Retail concentration and the internationalisation of British grocery retailing," in Bromley, R. and Thomas, C. (eds), *Retail Change: Contemporary Issues*, London: UCL Press, 2003. By the end of the 1980s a group of five companies – Sainsbury, Tesco, Asda, Argyll/Safeway, and Gateway – accounted for more than half of the UK retailing market,

leaving only two strong survivors in the regional multiple category – William Low and Morrison's. The market shares of the five majors further rose to 62 percent in 1992, compared with 13 percent for the independents (Owen, G., *Corporate Strategy in UK Food Retailing, 1980–2002*, Institute of Management Seminar Paper, pp. 10–11, London: LSE, 2003).

30 Interview with Sir John Sunderland, March 7, 2006.

31 Interview with Sir Dominic Cadbury, April 4, 2006.

32 Smith, C., Child, J. and Rowlinson, M., *Reshaping Work, the Cadbury Experience*, p. 89, Cambridge, Cambridge University Press, 1990.

33 A position he held from 1975 to 1978.

34 Sir Dominic Cadbury, who was Group Marketing Director from 1977 to 1980, paraphrases Mike Gifford's value for money model: "He taught us to sweat our assets and aim for a 26 percent return on all operating assets." Sir Dominic in 1983 saw Gifford's value for money as extremely timely: "part of the reason we weren't running our assets over fast enough was the fact that we had too complicated a business. We had such a proliferation and therefore the assets were being asked to do an impossible job, and so was manufacturing management being asked to do an impossible job. You couldn't have got the asset turnover speeded up and the improvement of the asset return had you not clarified your marketing strategy and gone for a statement of priorities in marketing terms and a concentration behind your brands. So I think those things sort of came together quite well at the time" (Interview with N.D. Cadbury, December 5, 1983, quoted in Smith et al. 1990: 89; see Note 32).

35 With his appointment to the corporate board in 1988, Mike Clark, after Jim Schadt in 1987, was one of the first North American Cadbury Schweppes Board members.

36 In 1974 the new labor chancellor, Denis Healey, had boldly said that the UK had entered the year in a worse condition than nearly all her partners in the industrial world.

37 Interview with Sir John Sunderland, March 7, 2006.

38 Drake, W., "Operation Fundamental Change," paper prepared for the Manufacturing Review at the Reading Research Centre, November 25, 1982.

39 *Private Archives Sir Adrian Cadbury*, "Cadbury Schweppes Limited Group Objectives to 1990," B.E.S. Collins (Group Chief Executive to Chairman), October 1, 1980. The "key elements of the strategy are:

- invest capital to improve operating efficiencies and productivity in mature businesses
- invest capital and development funds to grow in our core markets in USA
- grow by geographical extension and the development of new business logically related to our existing product markets
- acquire where appropriate to accelerate the achievement of Group objectives."

40 "Guess who's losing the great cola war; hint: it's not Coke and it's not Pepsi," *Wall Street Journal*, May 8, 1985.

41 "Management: Cadbury seeks a slimming cure," *Financial Times*, February 28, 1986; "Profile – Dominic Cadbury, the chocolate redeemer," *Independent on Sunday*, September 8, 1991.

42 "Management: Cadbury seeks a slimming cure," *Financial Times*, February 28, 1986.

43 Hamel, G. and Prahalad, C.K., "The core competence of the corporation," *Harvard Business Review*, 68(3), 79–91, 1990.

44 To the astonishment of some British Board members, Schadt was appointed to the group board as early as July 1987.

45 Dominic Cadbury was assigned more direct responsibility for the group's world soft drinks business. Terry Organ was appointed head of international confectionery. And Jim Schadt became chief executive of the American division, reporting to Dominic for soft drink products and to Organ for confectionery products ("Cadbury Schweppes has reorganised its management structure," *Financial Times*, December 19, 1984).

46 Interestingly, the Sunkist brand was first licensed by Sunkist Growers to General Cinema Corporation, which was the leading independent bottler of Pepsi-Cola products at the time.

47 Interview with Sir Dominic Cadbury, April 4, 2006.

48 Cadbury Schweppes 1988 Annual Report, pp. 13–14.

49 In 1985 Coca-Cola was Britain's number one soft drink, holding an estimated 60 percent share of the UK market of soft drinks. Pepsi-Cola only held about 20 percent ("Company news; Cadbury-Coke British venture," *New York Times*, December 9, 1986).

50 Interview with Sir Dominic Cadbury, April 4, 2006.

51 John Sunderland was one of the founding directors of CCSB.

52 Interview with John Sunderland, March 7, 2006.

53 Cadbury Schweppes 1988 Annual Report, Chief Executive's Review, Dominic Cadbury, pp. 10–11.

54 Collum had been headhunted in 1981 to join Cadbury Schweppes in the role of deputy finance director. In 1983, after Gifford had announced his departure, Collum was appointed Group Finance Director.

55 "Cadbury Schweppes moving beverage headquarters," Reuters News, March 9, 1989. The entire portfolio included Canada Dry, Sunkist and Schweppes soft drinks, Mott's and Red Cheek apple-based juices and sauces, and Holland House, Rose's, and Mr & Mrs T cocktail mixers.

56 As a corporate lawyer on Wall Street, Clark first got involved with Cadbury Schweppes during the Peter Paul acquisition in 1978. He joined Cadbury Schweppes Inc. in Connecticut in 1980, as its first in-house lawyer.

57 Before Schadt and Clark, the board's international pedigree had been very limited, with one short-lived American presence and some more long-standing Australian presence, a legacy of the company's Commonwealth presence.

58 Both Brock and Stitzer joined Cadbury Schweppes in 1983. Both learnt to make their company punch above its weight – with a new non-cola and bottler strategy – like undersized judo masters do: use the superior weight and the slower pace of your opponent to amplify your more agile or faster moves.

59 From 1983 John Brock held several positions in technical and operations functions and marketing at Cadbury Schweppes Inc. He was executive vice-president of Cadbury Beverages International from September 1987 to September 1990, president of Cadbury Beverages International from September 1990 to June 1992, president of Cadbury Beverages North America and president of Cadbury Beverages Europe from June 1992 to July 1993, president and CEO of Dr Pepper/7Up Inc. from 1995 to 1996, chief operating officer of Cadbury Schweppes PLC from 1999 to 2002, and chairman of the Dr Pepper/7Up Bottling Group from March 2000 to January 2003.

60 Stitzer first served as Cadbury Beverages' assistant general counsel from 1983 to 1988, only to become Cadbury Schweppes vice-president and general counsel, Cadbury Beverages in 1988.

61 Interview with Todd Stitzer, March 20, 2006.

62 Interview with Sir John Sunderland, March 7, 2006.

63 The fact that Adrian Cadbury had appointed several nonexecutive directors to the board – some of them heavyweights in the City of London – also played a role in Dominic Cadbury's election.

64 Frank Swan: "One of the things that Dominic found increasingly difficult to cope with was the fact that he was sitting in London; he had Jim in Stamford looking after the beverages stream; he had me in Australia looking after beverages and confectionery for Australasia and Asia; and he had David Wellings up in Birmingham looking after the confectionery stream. Dominic felt we were becoming a company of disparate parts, scattered all around the world, and he wanted to bring the strategic management of the various business units closer in order to have a day-to-day dialogue. And the place to do that, quite obviously, was London, because this is a UK-based and-owned company (cited in "Swan's song: interview," *Beverage World*, July 1, 1992). See also "Profile – Dominic Cadbury, the chocolate redeemer," *Independent on Sunday*, September 8, 1991.

65 Gunthorpe, M., Morgan, W. and Strak, J., "Further-processed and branded products, and alcoholic drinks," in Strak, J. and Morgan, W. (eds), *The UK Food and Drink Industry. A Sector by Sector Economic and Statistical Analysis*, pp. 283–334, Northborough, Cambs: EuroPA & Associates, 1995; see Tables 9.1 and 9.2, pp. 288–9; Tables 9.4 and 9.5, Figure 9.3, pp. 293–4; and Table 9.13, p. 315.

66 "An uncomfortable animal seeks big game status," *Financial Times*, June 8, 1993.

67 Interview with Alan Fryer, July 4, 2006.

68 Interview with Dr Alan Suggett, September 1, 2006.

69 Interview with Sir Christopher O'Donnell, March 17, 2006.

70 Interview with Sir Christopher O'Donnell, July 1, 2007. "The accidental hipster," *Sunday Times*.

71 Minutes of the Smith & Nephew Management Executive Committee meeting, Tuesday February 21, 1989.

72 "Smith & Nephew's speciality," *Management Today*, April 1986.

73 Interview with Sir Christopher O'Donnell, March 17, 2006.

74 Cf. Foreman-Peck, J., *Smith and Nephew in the Health Care Industry*, Aldershot: Edward Elgar, 1995.

75 Interview with Dr. Alan Suggett, September 1, 2006.

76 Interview with Jim Dick, July 5, 2006.

77 Interview with Sir Christopher O'Donnell, June 16, 2006.

Chapter 5

1 "Management: Cadbury seeks a slimming cure," *Financial Times*, February 28, 1986.

2 "An uncomfortable animal seeks big game status," *Financial Times*, June 8, 1993.

3 Interview with Brian Burwell, May 9, 2006.

4 Interview with David Kappler, May 5, 2006.

5 *Wall Street Journal Europe*, November 29, 1993.

6 Much more than the Cadbury brand, the Schweppes and Canada Dry brands were truly global, but they were niche products with limited mass market appeal. Although third in the world's soft drinks market, they represented 4 percent of the market share behind Coca-Cola and PepsiCo (*Marketing*, June 18, 1992).

7 Combined, Dr Pepper/7Up and Cadbury Schweppes would have a 16.7 percent share of the US market, third only to Coca-Cola's 41 percent and PepsiCo's 31 percent. But a Cadbury–Dr Pepper combination would have had greater power than the statistics suggest as both companies operated in fast growing market segments (*Barron's*, November 8, 1993).

8 Cadbury Schweppes had to use 1,000 independent bottlers to sustain 5.5 percent of the US soft drinks market. In contrast, Coca-Cola and PepsiCo used 120 bottling companies each, either independents or ones they owned directly, to achieve market shares respectively of 32.3 percent and 24.1 percent (*Financial Times*, January 24, 1995).

9 Meeting with Sir John Sunderland, Todd Stitzer, Bob Stack, and Mike Clark, January 25, 2008.

10 For example, the *New York Times* ("Distributor to drop some Dr Pepper/Cadbury sodas," March 29, 1996) reported: "In what analysts called a blow to the company's expansion plans, Dr Pepper/Cadbury North America said yesterday that its United States distributor, Coca-Cola Enterprises Inc., had decided to stop distributing several of its soda brands, including A & W Root Beer, Crush, Sunkist and Welch's. ... The decision by Coca-Cola Enterprises, the largest bottling system in the United States, leaves Dr Pepper/Cadbury, the nation's third-largest maker of carbonated beverages, scrambling for distributors in time for the summer months so crucial to market share ... Coca-Cola Enterprises distributes not only Coke's own brands but also nearly 13 percent of Dr Pepper/Cadbury's United States products in convenience stores, supermarkets, mass merchandisers and gas stations. And up to 30 percent of Dr Pepper/Cadbury's beverages are distributed by the entire Coca-Cola bottling network."

11 Interview with David Kappler, May 5, 2006.

12 As testified by Chairman Dominic Cadbury, June 1993: "Our task is to go on growing the business by incremental steps. We've done it in the past 10 years – why should we not be able to in the next 10?" (*Financial Times*, June 8, 1993).

13 "Omens not good for Cadbury Schweppes' global aspirations," *The Independent*, March 3, 1997.

14 Tom Hutchison acted as nonexecutive director and deputy chairman of Cadbury Schweppes from May 1992, and as a nonexecutive director from January 1986 to May 1992.

15 Cadbury Schweppes had been lured in prematurely, based on statistics that Russia was the third largest confectionery market in "Europe," after Germany and the UK (*Birmingham Post*, May 23, 1995). But the 1998 collapse of the Russian economy led to a sharp reduction in the confectionery stream's trading profit – from 10 percent to 6 percent.

16 "Dominic Cadbury commented, 'We're entirely indifferent about being bottlers. The Group believes greater profits lie in being a brand franchiser selling concentrates to bottlers rather than in bottling itself'" (*Financial Times*, 6 June, 1996). The sale was stalled by the European Commission as it gave Coca-Cola a 15-year hold in Britain on Cadbury's drinks such as Sunkist and Schweppes tonic. This would eventually be resolved in 1999 by amending the scope of Coca-Cola's 15-year agreement within the European Union – the UK being the beachhead to Europe for these drinks.

17 Shares went up as the City welcomed £620 million cash reducing the firm's gearing from 100 percent to 44 percent.

18 The deal gave Coca-Cola ownership of the Schweppes, Dr Pepper, Canada Dry, and Crush brands around the world including the UK.

19 Comment by Sir John Sunderland in *The Times*, December 12, 1998.

20 *Financial Times*, April 29, 1997. Cadbury Schweppes acquired two Midwestern bottlers in a deal worth $700 million (*The Times*, December 27, 1997).

21 In spite of the acquisition of Trebor Bassett's competitor Craven Keiller – a £27 million acquisition targeted at integrating the latter company's private labels within the Trebor Bassett business in order to increase volumes and make efficiency gains.

22 Interview with Sir John Sunderland, March 7, 2006.

23 Interview with Sir John Sunderland, March 7, 2006.

24 Interview with Sir John Sunderland, March 7, 2006.

25 Interview with David Kappler, May 5, 2006.

26 2000 was the end of the first phase of Managing for Value, and objectives were set for the next 4 years with the same financial objectives except for an increase in the free cash flow target to £300 million.

27 Goals were set by John Sunderland and the Executive Committee – with Brock and Stitzer – and cascaded down to the regions. They were aimed at being aspirational and were linked to the group's objective of doubling shareholder value every 4 years.

28 "A quiet man with a talent for rolling out the barrels," *The Times*, October 16, 2005. Apparently, with his energetic resolve and ability never to "run out of steam," "Brock always found a way of getting people to work together" ("Interview: Andrew Davidson: the biggest beer boss in the world," *Sunday Times*, October 16, 2005).

29 In 1999 Cadbury Schweppes acquired Wedel, Poland's leading chocolate business.

30 Interview with Todd Stitzer, March 20, 2006.

31 *Citywire*, June 27, 2002.

32 The Adams acquisition gave Cadbury Schweppes a leading volume share of 10 percent in the global confectionery market. The combined product portfolios of Cadbury Schweppes and Adams created the only global confectionery business able to meet the full range of its customers' confectionery needs – chocolate, sugar, and gum (*Market News Publishing*, 17, 2002).

33 Interview with Todd Stitzer, March 20, 2006.

34 Interview with Todd Stitzer, March 20, 2006

35 Most notably, the separation of supply chains from general management.

36 Interview with Todd Stitzer, March 20, 2006.

37 *Reuters News*, July 16, 2004.

38 Later that year, Cadbury bought Green & Black's, a luxury organic chocolate brand, mirroring a still modest shift in customer preferences from milk to dark chocolate.

39 In December 2006 Cadbury's announced its entrance into the UK chewing gum market with the launch of Trident. And in September 2007 Cadbury's completed the acquisition of Intergum, the leading Turkish gum business. On the beverages side, in July 2007 Cadbury's announced the acquisition of Southeast-Atlantic Beverage Corporation, the second largest independent bottler in the US.

40 The board of directors of Cadbury had agreed on a split that would give existing shareholders shares in two new groups, one focussing on its Dairy Milk chocolate and Trident gum side, and the other on its Dr Pepper drinks business.

41 Whereas Cadbury Schweppes had long anticipated a shift of US consumer preferences to noncarbonated, fruity drinks, Coca-Cola had long relied on the faltering soda business. ("Welcome back, bottler," *Barron's*, November 20, 2006).

42 In 2006 7Up and Dairy Milk were ranked respectively numbers five and six in the list of top US grocery brands ("Coca-Cola remains leading brand in State," *Irish Times*, August 24, 2006,).

43 Connon, H., "Chocolate boss needs to raise the bar," *Observer*, June 24, 2007, p. 9; Ashworth, J., "Sweet dreams are made of this," *The Business*, June 23, 2007.

44 Most notably, there were an accounting scandal in Nigeria and a *Salmonella* recall.

45 Incomes Data Services, 2006, p. 1: "While manufacturing lost many jobs and some parts of private services lost jobs, the two sectors identifiably employing many low-paid people held up fairly well. Both retail distribution and hotels and catering had employment levels that remained fairly stable through the recession."

46 For instance, the *Financial Times* wrote (Lex Column, April 7, 1993), "the risk is that Tesco will have neither the brand image nor the price competitiveness to compete in a mature market." Academically, there was the contribution of Cronshaw, M., Davis, E., and Kay, J.A., *On Being Stuck in the Middle or Good Food Costs Less at Sainsbury's*, London Business School Centre for Business Strategy Working Paper Series No. 83, London: London Business School, 1990.

47 The average site cost for a Tesco superstore increased from £15 million to £22 million in the space of a few years – between 1989 and 1992 (Wrigley, N., "Antitrust regulation and the restructuring of grocery retailing in Britain and the USA," *Environment and Planning A*, 24(5), 727–49, 1992). See also *Tesco Under Terry Leahy*, IFCAI Case Study No. 805-060-1, p. 4, Nagarjuna Hills, Hyderabad: ICRM Centre for Management Research, 2005.

48 Owen, G., *Corporate Strategy in UK Food Retailing, 1980–2002*, Institute of Management Seminar Paper, pp. 10–11, London: LSE, 2003.

49 Wrigley, N., "Retail concentration and the internationalisation of British grocery retailing," in Bromley, R. and Thomas, C. (eds), *Retail Change, Contemporary Issues*, London: UCL Press, 1993.

50 *Financial Times*, December 19, 1992. The acquisition, amounting to £175.6 million, was financed from Tesco's internal resources.

51 The first Tesco Metro was opened in Covent Garden, London, in 1992. Tesco Metros are mostly located in city centers, in inner cities, and on the high streets of small towns. Their typical size is 12,000 square feet.

52 Interview with Ian Clarke, June 7, 2006.

53 Interview with David Malpas, June 15, 2006.

54 Interview with Terry Leahy, June 12, 2006

55 Interview with Terry Leahy, June 12, 2006. Tesco suffered more from the economic crisis and the rise in interest rates because its core customers were younger and more heavily indebted than Sainsbury's.

56 Interview with Terry Leahy, June 12, 2006.

57 Interview with Terry Leahy, June 12, 2006.

58 *Financial Times*, September 22, 1993.

59 Interview with David Malpas, June 15, 2006

60 Interview with Terry Leahy, June 12, 2006.

61 Interview with David Malpas, June 15, 2006.

62 "Rivals take a swipe at Tesco loyalty card," *Financial Times*, February 11, 1995.

63 Interview with Terry Leahy, June 12, 2006.

64 Interview with David Malpas, June 15, 2006.

65 Tim J.R. Mason joined Tesco PLC in 1982 and has been director of Tesco PLC since February 16, 1995. He has been the chief executive of US operations of Tesco PLC since March 2006. He also serves as chairman of Tesco.com and director of Tesco Personal Finance and Tesco Mobile.

66 Seth, A. and Randall, G., *Supermarket Wars. Global Strategies for Food Retailers*, pp. 53–4, New York: Palgrave Macmillan, 2005.

67 Interview with Terry Leahy, June 12, 2006.

68 In 2005 Tesco announced a first trial with its new non-food-only store format: Homeplus.

69 The service, which included phone, fax, and Internet shopping, was tested at the same store delivering the home shopping pilot with Ealing social services as Tesco Direct.

70 Out-of-stock items were replaced with related items based on the individual customer's buying history. Replacement items were placed at the top of delivery boxes for immediate review by the customers at the time (evening) of delivery, thereby reducing the potential returns costs to Tesco's.

71 Interview with Tesco.com CEO John Browett in *BusinessWeek*, October 1, 2001: "[but] we never fell into the group-think mentality. It is in our character to go away and do our calculations very carefully."

72 As the success of Tesco.com became evident, the business expanded. The number of participating stores was increased to 100 by September 1999, with 750,000 customers 12 months later, and £5 million worth of orders were processed weekly. By October 2001 a total of 250 stores were participating; Tesco.com was also offering e-banking and financial services and had extended its reach into Ireland. Crucially for Tesco, 50 percent of its online customers had not shopped in a Tesco store before. (Mukund, A., *Tesco.com: A Rare Profitable Dotcom*, Nagarjuna Hills, Hyderabad: Centre for Management Research, 2003).

73 *Business Day*, September 22, 1999.

74 According to *The Grocer* (February 15, 1997), the British were still small fry in the Europond: "By 1997, only two, Delhaize and Ahold were generating more than 50% of turnover from outside their domestic markets."

75 By 2000 Tesco's international business portfolio was as follows:

Country	Stores	1999 sales
Czech Republic	10	£153 million
Hungary	39	£179 million
Poland	34	£93 million
Republic of Ireland	75	£861 million
Slovakia	8	£87 million
South Korea	2	£130 million
Thailand	17	£334 million
UK	659	£18.33 billion

76 *Super Marketing*, April 7, 2000. The overseas expansion has continued with a pilot of the Tesco.com offer in South Korea that commenced in 2002, as well as the development its online partnership with US supermarket Safeway. In 2003 Tesco acquired a stake in a Turkish supermarket chain, identified as a suitable emerging market, and entered the Japanese market through a £173 million acquisition of the convenience store operator C Two-Network.

77 *Financial Times*, July 8, 2003.

78 *Financial Times*, March 4, 2004. In late 2004 the amount of floor space Tesco operated outside the UK surpassed for the first time the amount it had in its home market, although the UK still accounted for more than 75 percent of group revenue due to the lower sales per unit area outside the UK.

79 The commission expressed concern about local monopolies and made a number of recommendations on relations between retailers and suppliers.

80 Interviews with John Robinson, May 10, 2006.

81 Green, D., "An efficacious formula," *Financial Times*, July 12, 1994, p. 22: "Part of the problem, was that the company was unable to 'shed its association with familiar household goods, such as Elastoplast sticking plaster and Nivea cream, rather than its more recent high tech innovations.'"

82 Interview with Alan Fryer, July 4, 2006.

83 Interview with Dr. Alan Suggett, September 1, 2006.

84 Minutes of the Smith & Nephew Management Executive Committee, Monday and Tuesday, January 30 and 31, 1995.

85 Surgeons were Smith & Nephew 's core customers, but O'Donnell was responsible for the medical, not the orthopedic, business.

86 Interview with Sir Christopher O'Donnell, June 16, 2006.

87 Interview with Sir Christopher O'Donnell, June 16, 2006.

88 Interview with Jim Dick, July 5, 2006.

89 Interview with Sir Christopher O'Donnell, June 16, 2006.

90 Interview with Alan Fryer, July 4, 2006.

91 As part of the "Centres of Excellence" project, Sir Christopher O'Donnell had presented a "Review of Manufacturing Strategy for Wound-healing, Casting and Bandaging" at a group management executive meeting in April 1995. In a foreboding move, he maintained that "the key criterion to site selection" was "increased sales revenue rather than cost advantages, based on product differentiation and customisation" (Minutes of the Smith & Nephew Management Executive Committee, Tuesday and Wednesday, April 18 and 19, 1995).

92 Interview with Sir Christopher O'Donnell, June 16, 2006.

93 Minutes of the Smith & Nephew Group Management Committee, Monday, October 26, 1998.

94 Interview with Dr. Alan Suggett, September 1, 2006.

95 Minutes of the Smith & Nephew Group Executive Committee, Friday, January 2, 1999 and Tuesday, October 19, 1999.

96 The Journey Bi-Cruciate Stabilized Knee System, the first knee replacement system designed to restore natural knee motion, was launched by Smith & Nephew Orthopaedic Reconstruction in April 2006. Both Exogen products and Supartz were acquired rather than developed in-house as Journey had been. In 1999 Smith & Nephew acquired

Exogen, manufacturer of a nonintrusive ultrasound technology to speed the healing of fractures. Exogen was the only company to have received US Food and Drug Administration approval for marketing such noninvasive stimulation technology. Its portfolio complemented that of Smith & Nephew in the areas of preclinical developments, including noninvasive devices for cartilage repair and osteoporosis treatment. In January 2001 Smith & Nephew Orthopaedics announced Food and Drug Administration approval of Supartz, the world's number one joint fluid therapy for the treatment of osteoarthritis.

97 To sharpen the focus of its business portfolio, Smith & Nephew decided in December 1998 to prioritize investment in three business areas with strong global prospects: orthopedics, endoscopy, and wound management. The bracing and support systems business was a predominantly US rather than global business.

98 To facilitate a quid pro quo deal, Smith & Nephew set up a joint venture with its German rival Beiersdorf to swap of parts of their medical devices and consumer product divisions. Beiersdorf transferred its wholesale wound care division into a joint venture with Smith & Nephew. In return, Beiersdorf acquired parts of the Smith & Nephew consumer business. The company later acquired Beiersdorf's higher margin advanced wound care business, which used polymers and enzymes. It also announced its intentions to sell its specialist ear, nose, and throat business by the end of 2000.

99 As with Exogen: see Note 96. The company also acquired 3M Corp's shoulder and hip implant and instrumentation segment as a part of new firm's new focus. The company continued to look for strategic partnerships that fitted into its new plan of adding new products and technology and increasing the market presence.

100 Interview with Dr. Alan Suggett, September 1, 2006.

101 For example, see Davidson, A., "The accidental hipster," *Sunday Times*, July 1, 2007, p. 6; Pan, K.Y., "A knack for revitalisation," *Financial Times*, November 3, 2006. Fortunately, there are exceptions to the trend of not giving Robinson his due credit – see Laurance, B., "Smith & Nephew delighted to be on its knees," *Guardian*, August 13, 1993, p. 13l; Lorenz, A., "Why focus favours Smith & Nephew," *Management Today*, January 1996, p. 32.

102 In retrospect, this pattern can be traced back even further in Smith & Nephew's history. At several points in time, analysts have found themselves excited at "sudden" developments in "dull" Smith & Nephew. This first became clear during the 1960s and 70s, when Seymour sponsored the development of R&D products such as OpSite against much opposition. While Opsite's development had long been common knowledge, it was only after its actual launch in 1978 that investors and commentators became enthused, leading the way to many years of interrupted profit and share price growth – which Kemp received credit for. Smith & Nephew took the market by surprise again with Journey. O'Donnell got most credit for this product. Yet Journey was based on Oxinium, a revolutionary material that had been developed in-house since the Robinson era.

103 Robinson experienced a few years of stagnating financial performance, but no real crisis. In addition, Kinder and Kemp, although officially still heading a "Nivea to Elastoplast group," announced their 14th successive year of profit growth in 1989 ("Smith & Nephew – 14th successive year of profit growth," *The Times*, March 22, 1989).

104 "The Lex Column: Smith & Nephew," *Financial Times*, December 14, 1983; "An efficacious formula," *Financial Times*, July 12, 1994; "S&N remains comparatively dull," *The Independent*, August 13, 1997; "O'Donnell focuses on knees, hips and teeth," *Financial Times*, May 9, 2003.

105 Quote from Dr. Alan Suggett, who was at the retirement party (interview, September 1, 2006).

106 *Sunday Times*, "The accidental hipster," July 1, 2007.

107 Interview with Jim Dick, July 5, 2006.

Chapter 6

1 Promotion often meant moving to another branch. From World War I onwards, high standards of training and service were assured by unannounced visits from a team of "samplers." Posing as ordinary shoppers, this group of ladies was trained to notice how well branch staff did their jobs (Williams, B., *The Best Butter in the World: A History of Sainsbury's*, p. 95, London: Ebury Press, 1994.

2 Visits from senior officials were frequent, and although these had other purposes, such as to discuss local trading partners or staffing needs, they were also intended to keep staff on their toes (Williams, 1994, p. 96; see Note 1).

3 Williams (1994, p. 20; see Note 1).

4 Emerson, G. *Sainsbury's: The Record Years 1950–1992*. London: Haggerston Press, 2006.

5 Emerson (2006, p. 26; see Note 4).

6 Emerson (2006, p. 32; see Note 4).

7 Emerson (2006, p. 31; see Note 4).

8 Williams (1994, p. 138); Morelli, C., "Britain's most dynamic sector? Competitive advantage in multiple food retailing," *Business and Economic History*, 26(2), 1997.

9 The total sales area of the new self-service shops increased from 95,000 square feet in March 1960 to 806,000 square feet in March 1970.

10 Williams (1994, pp. 138, 149–50; see Note 1).

11 In a memo to senior executives dated April 3, 1959, Mr Alan envisaged a "transitional period before the fourth generation become responsible for the day-to-day functioning of the business" (Williams, 1994, pp. 138–9; see Note 1).

12 Mr Alan, together with Malcolm Cooper of Allied Suppliers, formed the Distributive Trades Alliance and launched a vociferous campaign against the stamps (Williams, 1994, p. 151; see Note 1).

13 Emerson (2006, pp. 65–6; see Note 4). Practices of stamp trading originated in late 19th-century US as a means of gaining customer loyalty by encouraging shoppers to save them in exchange for gifts. Trading stamps were adopted widely in England from 1961 onwards.

14 Heller, R., *Management Today*, July 1967.

15 Heller, R., *Management Today*, July 1967.

16 Emerson (2006, pp. 67–8; see Note 4).

17 Emerson (2006, p. 19; see Note 4).

18 Emerson (2006, pp. 103–4; see Note 4).

19 Interview with Lord Sainsbury, November 7, 2006.

20 Piercy, N.F., *Market-Led Strategic Change*, 3rd edn, p. 715, Maidenhead: Chartered Institute of Marketing, 2002.

21 Interview with David Malpas, June 15, 2006.

22 *Financial Times*, May 16, 1991; Owen, G., *Corporate Strategy in UK Food Retailing, 1980–2002*, p. 14, Institute of Management Seminar Paper, London: LSE, 2003.

23 Interview with David Malpas, June 15, 2006.

24 Emerson (2006, p. 221; see Note 4).

25 Interview with Ian Coull, October 18, 2006.

26 Also, in a bid to aid further overseas expansion, Sainsbury had acquired a 25.1 percent stake in Edge, a retail chain in Egypt. This stake was soon increased to 80 percent, and the retail chain was renamed Sainsbury Egypt.

27 Proof of the flawed character of this copy-cat behavior, the Reward Card was in 2002 dropped in favor of a joint loyalty card – Nectar – operated in partnership with Debenhams, British Petroleum, and Barclaycard.

28 "Tesco ahead of J Sainsbury," *Financial Times*, April 21, 1995.

29 Interview with Ian Coull, October 18, 2006.

30 Owen (2003, p. 15; see Note 22).

31 Interview with Ian Coull, October 18, 2006.

32 *Financial Times*, January 17, 2004.

33 Interview with Ian Coull, October 18, 2006.

34 A review focussed on improving depot performance, dealing with supply chain issues and improving stock availability.

35 Unilever's predecessors, Lever Brothers and the Dutch margarine companies, had been among the first multinational firms that, during the second half of the 19th century, had begun to build factories in foreign countries rather than merely export products to them

36 Cf. Wilson, C. *The History of Unilever: A Study in Economic Growth and Social Change*, Vol. 2, p. 38, London: Cassell, 1954b.

37 Following the merger, Unilever retained a corporate structure of two holding companies: Unilever Ltd capitalized in British sterling, and Unilever NV capitalized in Dutch guilders. The two legal entities had different shareholders but identical boards.

38 The Special Committee increasingly became the real repository of final authority; originally a body of eight persons, it gradually became reduced to four.

39 Interview with Floris Maljers, April 5, 2006.

40 Furthermore, with its 1937 acquisition, Thomas J. Lipton Company, US manufacturer of tea, was added to the Dutch portfolio.

41 On different types of imperial logics, see Lieven, D., Empire: *The Russian Empire and its Rivals*, London: John Murray, 2000. On the US "Empire of Liberty," see Tucker, R.W. and Hendrickson, D.C., *Empire of Liberty: The Statecraft of Thomas Jefferson*, New York: Oxford University Press, 1990.

42 Jones, G., *Renewing Unilever. Transformation and Tradition*, p. 14, Oxford: Oxford University Press, 2005.

43 Ernest Woodroofe had joined Unilever in 1935 after a distinguished undergraduate and graduate career in physics. He had reached the board in 1955 as Unilever's first research director, representing a new type of entrepreneurial scientist concerned to build bridges between science and industry. He joined the Special Committee as the third man in 1961, and served as chairman of Unilever Ltd between 1970 and 1974. Woodroofe had a sharp and innovative mind, and was as much interested in the long term as Cole was interested

in the short term. Their relationship was not the closest. Like Hartog, Woodroofe desired a higher degree of managerial professionalism and central direction.

44 Minutes of meeting of the Special Committee held at Unilever House, London, on February 3, 1961, with the research division (Box 86, UNI/SC Research Division, 1953–1966, No. Y76).

45 Tide allegedly had superior cleaning powers and did not form insoluble deposits in plumbing systems in the presence of hard water.

46 Minutes of Directors' Conference held at Unilever House on Friday, January 9, 1959: "Dr Woodroofe estimated that between 5/10% of the effort related to entirely new fields; about 10% to developments in our existing businesses which might enable us to get a larger share of the market or to expand the market; some 55% to the protection of our interests by improvement of quality, greater economy in production etc ...; and the balance to purely service activities such as analysis, material testing and other advisory functions."

47 The new washing machines used in Europe demanded detergent products with immediate and low lathering properties. Africa, Asia, and South America, where housewives washed with cold and often soft water, needed high-lathering formulae. The highly sophisticated markets of the US had more specialized demands (Wilson, C., *The History of Unilever: A Study in Economic Growth and Social Change*, Vol. 3, pp. 81–2, London: Cassell, 1970).

48 Minutes of Directors' Conference held at Unilever House on Friday, March 6, 1959, pp/ 125–7.

49 Wilson (1970, p. 41; see Note 47).

50 Minutes of Directors' Conference held at Unilever House on Wednesday, November 11, 1959, p. 705: "Mr. J.P. Van den Bergh reported that for some time efforts had been made to find international brand names for various food products. Agreement had been reached for most countries on ROYCO for dry and canned soup, and on OLA for ice cream. After a provisional decision had been taken to use IGLO as the international name for quick frozen foods, the German National Management had decided against this name on the basis of a psychologist's report. Views on the value of this report were conflicting and the matter was to be discussed again within the next week."

51 Cited in Wilson (1970; see Note 47); interview in *The Observer*, January 6, 1963, p. 13; Publication 5234, Unilever Archival Reference.

52 Concurrently, the mid-1960s saw the first formal attempts to define the company's identity: "Unilever is an international enterprise of Dutch/British origin which combines the abilities of men and women of many nationalities. It specializes in the production, continuous development and mass marketing of nondurable goods for daily use, taking into account and anticipating the demands of the modern independent household" (Ch. E. van Blommestein, "Unilever's public relations objectives for the Netherlands," KUI 122, UAR November 1966).

53 Box 96 Special Committee Supporting Documents, Nos 6581–6624, 1975; Doc. 6587, Board Conference Background Paper B: Competitors' strategies.

54 Interview with Cob Stenham, 18 March 2002, cited in Jones (2005, p. 52; see Note 42).

55 Box 92 Special Committee Supporting Documents Nos 6329–6419, 1975; Doc. No. 6397 (CD33) Rotterdam, April 18, 1975.

56 Monopolies and Mergers Commission, *Frozen Foodstuffs: A Report on the Supply in the United Kingdom of Frozen Foodstuffs for Human Consumption*, House of Commons, November 9, 1976.

57 Wilson (1970, p. 4; see Note 47).

58 Box 96 Special Committee Supporting Documents, Nos 6581–6624, 1975; Strategic Issues and Opportunities, January 9, 1976.

59 Special Committee Documents, Memorandum to All Directors, February 11, 1976.

60 Unilever Special Committee Documents, November 9, 1982, Concern Strategy, Box 335/335, UNI/S, acc 1993/71.

61 Interview with Floris Maljers, April 5, 2006.

62 Interview with Stephen Williams, May 10, 2006.

63 Interview with Sir Michael Angus, February 22, 2006.

64 Interview with Floris Maljers, April 5, 2006.

65 Jones (2005, pp. 312–13; see Note 42).

66 Conference of Directors, November 27, 1986, cited in Jones (2005, p. 307; see Note 42).

67 The United Africa Company Ltd was formed from a merger between the Royal Niger Company Ltd and its rival the African Eastern Trade Corporation Ltd in 1929.

68 Fieldhouse, D.K., *Merchant Capital and Economic Decolonization: The United Africa Company, 1929–1987*, Oxford: Oxford University Press, 1994.

69 During the 1970s UAC responded to growing political risk by making numerous small and medium-sized acquisitions in Europe in sectors that spanned automobile distribution, medical devices, and even garden centers (Jones, G., and Miskell, P., "Acquisitions and firm growth: creating Unilever's ice cream and tea business," *Business History*, 49(1), 8–28, 2007; see p. 12).

70 Interview with Sir Michael Angus, February 22, 2006.

71 Interview with Sir Michael Perry, June 4, 2006.

72 Jones (2005; see Note 42). Unilever's detergent products posted a 50 percent growth in operating profit during the 1980s, while food products grew at a faster than normal rate.

73 In 1989 Unilever obtained Schering-Plough's perfume business in Europe; the Calvin Klein business from Minnetonka, Inc.; and, by far the largest purchase of the three, Fabergé Inc., the American producer of Chloe, Lagerfeld, and Fendi perfumes, for $1.55 billion. All these companies operated in the upper-end cosmetics industry as high-margin businesses.

74 Interview with Sir Michael Angus, February 22, 2006

75 Interview with Stephen Williams, May 10, 2006.

76 Interview with Clive Butler, May 25, 2006

77 Interview with Clive Butler, May 25, 2006.

78 Interview with Sir Michael Perry, June 4, 2006.

79 Interview with Clive Butler, May 25, 2006.

80 Interview with Stephen Williams, May 10, 2006.

81 1994 Annual Report, Unilever.

82 1995 Annual Report, Unilever.

83 *Financial Times*, June 10, 2000.

84 1996 Annual Report, Unilever.

85 *Financial Times*, September 11, 1996.

86 1997 Annual Report, Unilever.

87 1998 Annual Report, Unilever.

88 *Financial Times*, February 13, 2004.

89 Interview with Roger Gould, October 12, 2006.

90 Interview with Roger Gould, October 12, 2006.

91 Armstrong, P., "A healthy choice," *The Times*, May 25, 1999.

92 Durman, P., "SSL struggles to reverse the fortunes of LIG acquisition," *The Times*, December 8, 1999. *The Times* reported that SSL had struggled more than it had expected to incorporate LIG. The costs and losses incurred in the process had been heavier than anticipated, and the share price had fallen steadily since the merger was announced.

93 Voyle, S., "Seton attracted by LIG's strong brands," *Financial Times*, May 5, 1999, p. 29.

94 "SSL International remains as safe play," *The Independent*, December 8, 1999, p. 21.

95 Cole, R., "SSL still healthy in spite of market indifference," *The Times*, June 7, 2000.

96 Clark, A., Hume, N., and Bowers, S., "Durex directors at war," *Guardian*, February 9, 2001, p. 25.

97 Davidson, A., "A ribbing from the king of condoms," *Sunday Times*, November 19, 2006, p. 10. Garry Watt joined the company in 2001, not as CEO but as group finance officer.

Chapter 7

1 For a discussion of institutionalization and imprinting, see Stinchcombe, A.L., "Social structure and organizations," in March, J.G. (ed.), *Handbook of Organizations*, pp. 142–93, Chicago: Rand McNally, 1965.

2 Pearce, W.T., *Fry's Works Magazine: Bi-centenary Number (1728–1928)*, p. 29, Bristol: Partridge & Love, 1928.

3 Interview with Clive Butler, May 25, 2006.

4 Anderson, R., "Complexity theory and organization science," *Organization Science*, 10(3), 216–32, 1999; Stacey, R.D., "The science of complexity: an alternative perspective for strategic change processes," *Strategic Management Journal*, 16, 477–95, 1995.

5 This analysis was conducted by Jochem Kroezen of Rotterdam School of Management, Erasmus University, Rotterdam, the Netherlands.

6 Arthur, W.B., "Competing technologies, increasing returns and lock in by historical events," *Economic Journal*, 99, 116–31, 1989.

Chapter 8

1 Collins, J.C. and Porras, J.I., *Built to Last*, New York: Harper Business Essentials, 1994.

2 Zanini, M., "Power curves: what natural and economic disasters have in common," *McKinsey Quarterly*, June, 2009.

3 Thorburn MacAlister/University of Southampton. "FTSE 350 Board Review 2012," available from http://ebookbrowse.com/report-ftse-350-board-review-2012-pdf-d344855710 (accessed September 30, 2012).

4 This is a central tenet of complexity theory. See, for example, Stacey, R., "The science of complexity: an alternative perspective for strategic change processes," *Strategic Management Journal*, 16, 477–95, 1995.

5 "Disorganization" is a concept used by Allen, P.M., "Evolving complexity in social science," in Altmann, G. and Koch, W.A., *Systems: New Paradigms for the Human Sciences*, pp. 3–38, New York: Walter de Gruyter, 1998.

6 Again, see Stacey (Note 4). See also Brown, S.L. and Eisenhardt, K.M., *Competing on the Edge*, Cambridge, MA: Harvard Business School Press, 1998.

7 Also noted by Beech, N., Burns, H., de Caestecker, L., MacIntosh, R. and MacLean, D., "Paradox as invitation to act in problematic change situations," *Human Relations*, 57, 1313–32, 2004.

8 Clive Butler in a meeting with the authors, David Malpas and Sir Dominic Cadbury, 2008.

9 Peters, T., *Thriving on Chaos*, New York: Knopf, 1987.

10 See p. 767 in Lewis, M., "Exploring paradox: toward a more comprehensive guide," *Academy of Management Review*, 25, 760–76, 2000.

11 Amason, A.C., "Distinguishing the effects of functional and dysfunctional conflict on strategic decision making: resolving a paradox for top management teams," *Academy of Management Journal*, 39, 123–48, 1996.

12 Meeting with David Malpas, Sir Dominic Cadbury, and Clive Butler, 2008.

13 Meeting with David Malpas, Sir Dominic Cadbury, and Clive Butler, 2008.

14 See Brown and Eisenhardt (Note 6).

15 Meeting with David Malpas, Sir Dominic Cadbury, and Clive Butler, 2008.

Bibliography

GENERAL REFERENCES

Amason, A. "Distinguishing the effects of functional and dysfunctional conflict on strategic decision making: resolving a paradox for top management teams," *Academy of Management Journal*, 39(1), 123–48, 1996.

Anderson, R. "Complexity theory and organization science," *Organization Science*, 10(3), 216–32, 1999.

Aoki, M. *Towards a Comparative Institutional Analysis*, Cambridge, MA: MIT Press, 2001.

Arthur, W.B. "Competing technologies, increasing returns and lock in by historical events," *Economic Journal*, 99, 116–31, 1989.

Barney, J.B. "Firm resources and sustained competitive advantages," *Journal of Management*, 17, 99–120, 1991.

Bauer, P. "Recent developments in the econometric estimation of frontiers," *Journal of Econometrics*, 46, 39–56, 1991.

Beckman, C.M. "The influence of founding team company affiliations on firm behavior," *Academy of Management Journal*, 49(4), 741–58, 2006.

Bettis, R. and Prahalad, C.K. "The dominant logic: retrospective and extension," *Strategic Management Journal*, 16(1), 5–15, 1995.

Bond, S.R. and Cummins, J.G. "The stock market and investment in the new economy: some tangible facts and intangible fictions," *Brookings Papers on Economic Activity*, 1, 61–108, 2000.

Brown, S.L. and Eisenhardt, K.M. "The art of continuous change: linking complexity theory and time-paced evolution in relentlessly shifting organizations," *Administrative Science Quarterly*, 42(1), 1–34, 1997.

Burgelman, R. and Grove, A. "Strategic dissonance," *California Management Review*, 38(2), 8–28, 1996.

Cadbury Brothers Ltd. *Industrial Record 1919–1939*, Bournville: Cadbury Brothers Limited, 1947.

Carroll, G.R and Teo, A.C. "On the social networks of managers," *Academy of Management Journal*, 39(2), 421–40, 1996.

Collins, J. *Good to Great*, New York: Harper Business, 2001.

Collins, J. and Porras, J. *Built to Last: Successful Habits of Visionary Companies*, New York: Harper Business, 1994.

Coopey, J. "The learning organization, power, politics and ideology," *Management Learning*, 26(2), 193–213, 1995.

Danielson, M.G. and Press, E. "Accounting returns revisited: evidence of their usefulness in estimating economic returns," *Review of Accounting Studies*, 8, 493–530, 2003.

D'Aveni, R. *Hypercompetition: Managing the Dynamics of Strategic Manoeuvring*, New York: Free Press, 1995.

Day, D.L., Lewin, A.Y. and Li, H. "Strategic leaders or strategic groups: a longitudinal data envelopment analysis of the US brewing industry," *European Journal of Operations Research*, 80, 619–38, 1995.

Day, G., Fein, A.J. and Ruppersberger, G. "Shakeouts in digital markets: lessons from B2B exchanges," *California Management Review*, 45(2), 131–50, 2003.

Denzin, N.K. and Lincoln, Y.S. "Introduction: The discipline and practice of qualitative research," in Denzin, N.K. and Lincoln, Y.S. (eds), *Handbook of Qualitative Research*, pp. 1–28, Thousand Oaks, CA: Sage, 2000.

Devinney, T.M., Midgley, D.F. and Venaik, S. "The organizational imperative and the optimal performance of the global firm: formalizing and extending the integration–responsiveness framework," *Organization Science*, 11, 674–95, 2000.

Devinney, T.M., Yip, G.S. and Johnson, G. "Using frontier analysis to evaluate company performance," *British Journal of Management*, 21(4), 921–38, 2010.

Diesing, P. *Patterns of Discovery in the Social Sciences*, Chicago: Aldine-Atherton, 1971.

Dore, R. *Stock Market Capitalism: Welfare Capitalism. Japan and Germany versus Anglo-Saxons*, New York: Oxford University Press, 2000.

Doz, Y. and Kosonen, M. *Fast Strategy: How Strategic Agility Will Help You Stay Ahead of the Game*, Philadelphia, PA: Wharton School Publishing, 2008.

Duncan, R. "The ambidextrous organization: designing dual structures for innovation," in Killman, R.H., Pondy L.R. and Sleven, D. (eds), *The Management of Organization*, pp. 167–88, New York: North Holland, 1976.

Dutton, J., Walton, E. and Abrahamson, E. "Important dimensions of strategic issues: separating the wheat from the chaff," *Journal of Management Studies*, 26(4), 380–95.

Eisenhardt, K.M. and Sull, D.N. "Strategy as simple rules," *Harvard Business Review*, January, 106–16, 2001.

Farkas, C.M. and Wetlaufer, S. "The ways chief executive officers lead," *Harvard Business Review*, 74(3), 110–12, 1996.

Fincham, R. "Perspectives on authority: processual, institutional and 'internal' forms of organizational authority," *Journal of Management Studies*, 29, 741–59, 1992.

Finkelstein, S. "Why smart executives fail: four case histories of how people learn the wrong lessons from history," *Business History*, 48(2), 153–70, 2006.

Finkelstein, S. and Hambrick, D. *Strategic Leadership: Top Executives and their Effects on Organizations*, Minneapolis, MN: West, 1996.

Floyd, S.W. and Lane, P.J. "Strategizing throughout the organization: managing role conflict in strategic renewal," *Academy of Management Review*, 25(1), 154–77, 2000.

Foster, R. and Kaplan, S. *Creative Destruction: Why Companies that Are Built To Last Underperform the Market – and How To Transform Them*, New York: Currency/Doubleday, 2001.

de Geus, A. *The Living Company*, Boston: Harvard Business School Press, 2002.

Goleman, D. "Leadership that gets results," *Harvard Business Review*, 78(2), 78–90, 2000.

Granovetter, M.S. "The strength of weak ties," *American Journal of Sociology*, 78(6), 1360–80, 1973.

Hall, D.J. and Saias, M. "Strategy follows structure!", *Strategic Management Journal*, 1, 149–63, 1980.

Hamel, G. and Valikangas, L. "The quest for resilience," *Harvard Business Review*, September, 52–63, 2003.

Hensmans, M. "Magic bullet discourse and the resolution of coordination and cooperation problems," Advanced Institute of Management Working Paper, London: AIM, 2006.

Holbrook, D., Cohen, W., Hounshell, D. and Klepper, S. "The nature, sources and consequences of firm differences in the early history of the semiconductor industry," *Strategic Management Journal*, 21(10–11), 1017–42, 2000.

Jarzabkowski P., Giulietti, M. and Oliveira, B. "Building a strategy toolkit: lessons from business," AIM Executive Briefing, 2009.

Johnson, G. *Strategic Change and the Management Process*, Oxford: Blackwells, 1987.

Johnson, G. "Re-thinking incrementalism," *Strategic Management Journal*, 9, 75–91, 1988.

Johnson, G. "Managing strategic change – strategy, culture and action," *Long Range Planning*, 25(1), 28–36, 1992.

Johnson, G. Yip, G. and Hensmans, M. "Achieving successful strategic transformation," *MIT Sloan Management Review*, Spring, 25–32, 2102.

Joyce, W., Nohria, N. and Roberson, B. *What Really Works: The 4 + 2 Formula for Sustained Business Success*, New York: Harper Business, 2003.

Kellermanns, F.W., Walter, J., Lechner, C. and Floyd, S.W. "The lack of consensus about strategic consensus: advancing theory and research," *Journal of Management*, 31(5), 719–37, 2005.

Kets de Vries, M.F.R "The leadership mystique," *Academy of Management Executive*, 8(3), 73–89, 1994.

Kirby, J. "Toward a theory of high performance," *Harvard Business Review*, July–August, 30–9, 2005.

Klepper, S. and Simons, K.L. "Dominance by birthright: entry of prior radio producers and competitive ramifications in the US television receiver industry," *Strategic Management Journal*, 21(10–11), 987–1016, 2000.

Kotter, J.P. *A Force for Change: How Leadership Differs from Management*, New York: Free Press, 1990.

Kotter, J.P. and Heskett, J.L. *Corporate Culture and Performance*, New York: Free Press, 1982.

Lawrence, B.S. "Historical perspective: using the past to study the present," *Academy of Management Review*, 9, 307–12, 1984.

Leonard-Barton, D. "Core capabilities add core rigidities: a paradox in managing new product development," *Strategic Management Journal*, 13, 111–25, 1992.

McKelvey, B. "Simple rules for improving corporate IQ: basic lessons from complexity science," in Andriani, P. and Passiante, G. (eds), *Complexity, Theory and the Management of Networks*, London: Imperial College Press, 2004.

Miller, D. *The Icarus Paradox*, New York: Harper Collins, 1990.

Morgan Stanley, *The Competitive Edge*, New York: Morgan Stanley, 1998.

Pearce, J.A. "A structural analysis of dominant coalitions in small banks," *Journal of Management*, 21, 1075–95, 1995.

Peters, T. and Waterman, R. *In Search of Excellence*, New York: Collins, 1982.

Pettigrew, A.M. *The Awakening Giant. Continuity and Change in Imperial Chemical Industries*, Oxford: Basil Blackwell, 1985.

Pfeffer, J. *Authority in Organizations*, Boston, MA: Pitman, 1981.

Porter, M.E. *Competitive Strategy: Techniques for Analyzing Industries and Competitors*, New York: Free Press, 1980.

Prahalad, C.K. and Bettis, R. "The dominant logic: a new link between diversity and performance," *Strategic Management Journal*, 6(1), 485–501, 1986.

Putnam, L.L., Phillips, N. and Chapman, P. "Metaphors of communication and organization," in Clegg, S., Hardy, C. and Nord, W. (eds), *Handbook of Organization Studies*, pp. 375–408, London: Sage, 1996.

Quinn, J.B. *Strategies for Change*, Homewood, IL: Irwin, 1980.

Quinn, J.B. "Strategic change: logical incrementalism," in Mintzberg, H., Quinn, J.B. and Ghoshal, S. (eds), *The Strategy Process* (European edn), London: Prentice Hall International, 1995.

Ragin, C. *The Comparative Method*, Berkeley, CA: University of California Press, 1987.

Ragin, C. "'Casing' and the process of social inquiry," in Ragin, C. and Becker, H. (eds), *What is a Case? Exploring the Foundations of Social Inquiry*, pp. 217–26, Cambridge: Cambridge University Press, 2000.

Rappaport, A. *Creating Shareholder Value: The New Standard for Business Performance*, New York: Free Press, 1986.

Richard, P.J., Devinney, T.M., Yip, G.S. and Johnson, G. "Measuring organizational performance as a dependent variable: towards methodological best practice," *Journal of Management*, 35(3), 718–804, 2009.

Rowlinson, M. and Hassard, J. "The invention of corporate culture: a history of the histories of Cadbury," *Human Relations*, 46(3), 299–326, 1993.

Seth, A. and Randall, G. *The Grocers: The Rise and Rise of the Supermarket Chains*, London: Kogan Page, 1999.

Stadler, C. *Enduring Success – What We Can Learn from the History of Outstanding Corporations*, Palo Alto, CA: Stanford University Press, 2011.

Stinchcombe, A.L. "Social structure and organizations," in March, J.G. (ed.), *Handbook of Organizations*, pp. 142–93, Chicago: Rand McNally, 1965.

Tedlow, R.S. *Giants of Enterprise: Seven Business Innovators and their Empires*, New York: Harper Business, 2001.

Teece, D.J., Pisano, G. and Shuen, A. "Dynamic capabilities and strategic management," *Strategic Management Journal*, 18: 509–33, 1997.

Thompson, J.D. *Organizations in Action*, New York: McGraw-Hill, 1967.

Tushman, M.L. and O'Reilly, C.A. "Ambidextrous organizations: managing evolutionary and revolutionary change," *California Management Review*, 38(4), 8–30, 1996.

Tversky, A. and Kahnemann, D. "Judgements under uncertainty: heuristics and biases," *Science*, 185, 1124–31, 1975.

Waldman, D.A., Ramirez, G.G., House, R.J. and Puranam, P. "Does leadership matter? CEO leadership attributes and profitability under conditions of perceived environmental uncertainty," *Academy of Management Journal*, 44(1), 134–43, 2001.

Wang, C.L. and Ahmed, P.K. "Dynamic capabilities: a review and research agenda," *International Journal of Management Reviews*, 9(1), 31–52, 2007.

Williams, I.A. *The Firm of Cadbury 1831–1931*. London: Constable, 1931.

Yin, R.K. *Case Study Research: Design and Methods*, Applied Social Research Methods, Vol. 2, Thousand Oaks, CA: Sage, 1994.

Yip, G.S., Rugman, A.M. and Kudina, A. "International success of British companies," *Long Range Planning*, 39(3), 241–64, 2006.

COMPANY-SPECIFIC REFERENCES

Cadbury Schweppes and Unilever

Burns, J. "A synoptic view of the food industry," in Burns, J. McInery, J. and Swinbank, A. (eds), *The Food Industry*, pp. 1–17, London: Heinemann, 1983.

Cadbury, Sir A. "Conversation: an interview with Sir Adrian Cadbury," *Organizational Dynamics*, Winter, 39–58, 1979.

Cadbury, Sir A. "Cadbury Schweppes: more than chocolate and tonic," *Harvard Business Review*, 61, 134–44, 1983.

Cadbury, E. *Experiments in Industrial Organization*, London: Longman, Green, 1912.

Cadbury, E. "Some principles of industrial organization. The case for and against scientific management", *Sociological Review*, 6, 99–125, 1914.

Cadbury Brothers Ltd. *Industrial Record 1919–1939*, Bournville: Cadbury Brothers Limited, 1947.

Cadbury Brothers Ltd. *Industrial Challenge. The Experience of Cadburys of Bournville in the Post-war Years*, London: Pitman & Sons, 1964.

Cadbury Brothers Ltd. and J.S. Fry & Sons Ltd. *The British Cocoa and Chocolate Company Limited. Policy Making and Control in Business*, Birmingham: Hudson & Son, 1962.

Cadbury Schweppes Annual Reports.

Church, R. and Clark, C. "Purposive strategy or serendipity? Development and diversification in three consumer product companies, 1918–39: J. & J. Colman, Reckitt & Sons, and Lever Bros./Unilever," *Business History*, 45(1), 23–59, 2003.

Fitzgerald, R. *Rowntree and the Marketing Revolution, 1862–1969*, New York: Cambridge University Press, 1994.

Gilmore, T.N. *Making Leadership Change*, San Francisco, CA: Jossey Bass, 1988.

Gunthorpe, M., Morgan, W. and Strak, J. "Further-processed and branded products, and alcoholic drinks," in Strak, J. and Morgan, W. (eds), *The UK Food and Drink Industry. A Sector by Sector Economic and Statistical Analysis*, pp. 283–334, Northborough, Cambs: EuroPA & Associates, 1995.

Hoffmann, W.G. "100 years of the margarine industry," in van Stuyvenberg J.H. (ed.), *Margarine. An Economic, Social and Scientific History 1869–1969*, pp. 9–33, Liverpool: Liverpool University Press, 1969.

Jefferys, J.B. *Retail Trade in Britain 1850–195*, Cambridge: University of Cambridge, 1954.

Jolly, W.P. *Lord Leverhulme. A Biography*. London: Constable, 1976.

Jones, G. *Renewing Unilever. Transformation and Tradition*. Oxford: Oxford University Press, 2005.

Leopold, M. "The transnational food companies and their global strategies," *International Social Science Journal*, 105, 315–29, 1985.

Minkes, A.L. and Nuttall, C.S. *Business Behaviour and Management Structure*, London: Croom Helm, 1985.

Parkes, C. "Food industry," *Financial Times*, April 18, 1989, p. 13.

Pearce, W.T. (ed.). *Fry's Works Magazine: Bi-centenary Number (1728–1928)*, Bristol: Partridge & Love, 1928.

Reader, W.J. *Fifty Years of Unilever, 1930–1980*, London: Heinemann, 1980.

Rowlinson, M. and Hassard, J. "The invention of corporate culture: a history of the histories of Cadbury," *Human Relations*, 46(3), 299–326, 1993.

Sharma, P., Chrisman, J., Pablo, A. and Chua, J. "Determinants of initial satisfaction with the succession process in family firms: a conceptual model," *Entrepreneurship: Theory and Practice*, 24(4), 25, 2001.

Simmons, D.A. *Schweppes: The First 200 Years*, London: Constable, 1983.

Smith, C., Child, J. and Rowlinson, M. *Reshaping Work: The Cadbury Experience*, Cambridge Studies in Management No. 16, Cambridge: Cambridge University Press, 1990.

Stopford, J. and Turner, L. *Britain and the Multinationals*, Chichester: John Wiley & Sons, 1985.

Tousley, R.D. "Marketing," in van Stuyvenberg, J.H. (ed.), *Margarine. An Economic, Social and Scientific History 1869–1969*, pp. 227–79, Liverpool: Liverpool University Press, 1969.

Unilever. *The Organization of Unilever: fourth edition [of] an address by Sir Geoffrey Heyworth to the Institute of Public Administration*, London: Unilever, 1953.

Unilever. *The Anatomy of a Business: Unilever Management in Structure and Operations; (speeches of George Cole ... and F.J. Tempel ... in May 1962)*, London School of Economics Pamphlet HD2/C141, London: Unilever, 1962.

Unilever Annual Reports.

Vice, A. *The Strategy of Takeovers: A Casebook of International Comparisons*, London: McGraw-Hill, 1977.

Wagner, G. *The Chocolate Conscience*, London: Chatto & Windus, 1987.

Williams, I.A. *The Firm of Cadbury 1831–1931*, London: Constable, 1931.

Wilson, C. *The History of Unilever: A Study in Economic Growth and Social Change*, Vol. 1, London: Cassell, 1954a.

Wilson, C. *The History of Unilever: A Study in Economic Growth and Social Change*, Vol. 2, London: Cassell, 1954b.

Wilson, C. *The History of Unilever: A Study in Economic Growth and Social Change*, Vol.3, London: Cassell, 1970.

Tesco and J Sainsbury

Akehurst, G. "Checkout: the analysis of oligopolistic behaviour in the UK grocery retail market," *Service Industries Journal*, 4(2), 189–242, 1984.

Bamfield, J. "Rationalization and the problems of re-positioning: UK co-operatives caught in the middle," in Johnson, G. (ed.), *Business Strategy and Retailing*, pp. 153–76, Chichester: John Wiley & Sons, 1987.

Benson, J. and Ugolini, L. (eds). *A Nation of Shopkeepers. Five Centuries of British Retailing*, London: I.B. Tauris, 2003.

Boswell, J. (ed.). *J.S. 100: The Story of Sainsbury's*, London: J Sainsbury, 1969.

Bradley, K. and Taylor, S. *Business Performance in the Retail Sector. The Experience of the John Lewis Partnership*, Oxford: Clarendon Press, 1992.

Burt, S.L. and Sparks, L. "Performance in food retailing: a cross national consideration and comparison of retail margins," *British Journal of Management*, 8, 113–50, 1997.

Child, P. "Taking Tesco global," *McKinsey Quarterly*, 3: 133–44, 2002.

Competition Commission. *Supermarkets: A Report on the Supply of Groceries from Multiple Stores in the UK*, London: HMSO, 2000.

Corina, M. *Pile it High, Sell it Cheap: The Authorised Biography of Sir John Cohen, Founder of Tesco*, London: Weidenfeld & Nicolson, 1971.

Cox, R. "The revolution in grocery retailing – multiple strategies," in West, A. (ed.), *Handbook of Retailing*, pp. 31–43, Aldershot: Gower, 1988.

Cronshaw, M., Davis, E. and Kay, J.A. *On Being Stuck in the Middle or Good Food Costs Less at Sainsburys*, London Business School Centre for Business Strategy Working Paper No. 83, London: London Business School, 1990.

Dawson, J.A. and Burt, S.L. "European retailing – dynamics, restructuring and development issues," in Pinder, D. (ed.), *The New Europe: Economy, Society and Environment*, pp. 157–76, London: John Wiley & Sons, 1998.

East, R. *The Anatomy of Conquest: Tesco Versus Sainsbury*, Occasional Paper No. 29, Kingston upon Thames: Kingston Business School, 1997.

Emerson, G. *Sainsbury's: The Record Years 1950–1992*. London: Haggerston Press, 2006.

Humby, C. and Hunt, T. *Scoring Points: How Tesco Is Winning Customer Loyalty*, London: Kogan Page, 2004.

Incomes Data Services. *The Impact of Economic Recession on Pay Increases and the Low Paid. A Research Report by Incomes Data Services for the Low Pay Commission*, London: Income Data Services, 2006. Available from: http://www.lowpay.gov.uk/lowpay/research/pdf/t0001EDS.pdf .

Kennedy, C.A. *Business Pioneers: Family, Fortune and Philanthropy: Cadbury, Sainsbury and John Lewis*, London: Random House Business Books, 2000.

Kirkwood, D.A. "The supermarket challenge," *Focus on PDM*, 3(4), 8–12, 1984a.

Kirkwood, D.A. "How Tesco manages the distribution function," *Retail and Distribution Management*, 12(5), 61–5, 1984b.

McClelland, W.G. "The supermarket and society," *Sociological Review*, 10, 133–44, 1962.

McClelland, W.G. *Studies in Retailing*, Oxford: Blackwell, 1963.

MacLaurin, I. *Tiger by the Tail: A Life in Business from Tesco to Test Cricket*, London: Pan, 2000.

Morelli, C. "Britain's most dynamic sector? Competitive advantage in multiple food retailing," *Business and Economic History*, 26(2), 770–81, 1997.

Morelli, C. "Constructing a balance between price and non-price competition in British multiple food retailing, 1954–1964," *Business History*, 40(2), 45–61, 1998.

Owen, G. *Corporate Strategy in UK Food Retailing, 1980–2002*, Institute of Management Seminar Paper, London: London School of Economics, 2003.

Palmer, M.J. *International Restructuring and Divestment: The Experience of Tesco*, Marketing and Retailing Working Paper No. 02/4, Coleraine: University of Ulster, Faculty of Business and Management, 2004.

Powell, D. *Counterrevolution. The Tesco Story*, London: Grafton, 1991.

Quarmby, D.A. "Developments in the retail market and their effect on freight distribution," *Journal of Transport Economics and Policy*, 23(1), 75–87, 1989.

J Sainsbury Annual Reports.

Segal-Horn, S. "The retail environment in the UK," in Johnson, G. (ed.), *Business Strategy and Retailing*, pp. 13–34, Chichester: John Wiley & Sons, 1987.

Seth, A. and Randall, G. *The Grocers: The Rise and Rise of the Supermarket Chains*, London: Kogan Page, 1999.

Seth, A. and Randall, G. *Supermarket Wars. Global Strategies for Food Retailers*, New York: Palgrave Macmillan, 2005.

Smith, D.L.G. and Sparks, L. "The transformation of physical distribution in retailing: the example of Tesco plc," *International Review of Retail, Distribution and Consumer Research*, 3(1), 35–64, 1993.

Sparks, L. "The changing structure of distribution in retail companies," *Transactions of the Institute of British Geographers*, 11(2), 147–54, 1986.

Tesco Annual Reports.

Williams, B. *The Best Butter in the World, A History of Sainsbury's*, London: Ebury Press, 1994.

Wrigley, N. "Antitrust regulation and the restructuring of grocery. Retailing in Britain and the USA," *Environment and Planning A*, 24(5), 727–49, 1992.

Wrigley, N. "Retail concentration and the internationalisation of British grocery retailing," in Bromley, R. and Thomas, C. (eds), *Retail Change: Contemporary Issues*, pp. 41–68, London: UCL Press, 1993.

Wrigley, N. "After the store wars: towards a new era of competition in UK food retailing," *Journal of Retailing and Consumer Services*, 1, 5–20, 1994.

Wrigley, N. "Understanding store development programmes in post-property crisis UK food retailing," *Environment and Planning A*, 30, 15–45, 1998.

Wrigley, N. and Lowe, M. *Reading Retail: A Geographical Perspective on Retailing and Consumption Spaces*, London: Arnold, 2002.

SMITH & NEPHEW AND SSL INTERNATIONAL

Coleman, K. *IG Farben and ICI, 1925–53: Strategies for Growth and Survival*, Basingstoke: Palgrave Macmillan, 2006.

Donnithorne, A.G. *British Rubber Manufacturing: An Economic Study of Innovations*, London: Duckworth, 1958.

Foreman-Peck, J. *Smith and Nephew in the Health Care Industry*, Aldershot: Edward Elgar, 1995.

Great Britain Board of Trade. *Boots and Shoes*. Working Party Reports/Great Britain Board of Trade. London: His Majesty's Stationery Office, 1946.

Howells, J., and Neary, I. *Intervention and Technological Innovation: Government and the Pharmaceutical Industry in the UK and Japan*. Basingstoke: Macmillan, 1995.

London Rubber Company. *Directors' Report and Statement of Accounts*. London: London Rubber Company, 1959–1965.

LRC International. *Report and Accounts*. London: LRC, 1969–1985.

Mass, W., and Lazonick, W. "The British cotton industry and international competitive advantage: the state of the debate," *Business History*, 32, 9–65, 1990.

Quirke, V. *Collaboration in the Pharmaceutical Industry: Changing Relationships in Britain and France, 1935–1965*, London: Routledge, 2003.

Reader, W.J. *Imperial Chemical Industries: A History*, Vol. 2, *The First Quarter-Century, 1926–1952*, London: Oxford University Press, 1975.

Robson, M.T. The pharmaceutical industry in Britain and France, 1919–1939, Unpublished thesis, University of London, 1993.

Scholl, W.M. *The Feet and their Care*, London: Scholl, 1927.

Scholl Manufacturing Co. *Scholl News Bulletin*. London: Scholl, 1967–1970.

Smith & Nephew Annual Reports.

SSL Company Magazine "Be Inspired", Issue One, Winter 1994, available from www.ssl-international.com/copy/downloads/Inspired1.pdf (accessed June 23, 2006).

SSL International Annual Reports (previously Seton, Scholl and London International). www.ssl-international.com/copy/press/archive2003.htm#12mar20031 (accessed June 23, 2006).

SSL Press release 12 March 2004.

Index

Ingram Content Group UK Ltd.
Milton Keynes UK
UKHW020734100723
424852UK00006B/317

9 781349 443444